ANALYSIS OF THE COGNITIVE INTERVIEW IN QUESTIONNAIRE DESIGN

SERIES IN UNDERSTANDING STATISTICS

S. NATASHA BERETVAS   Series Editor

SERIES IN UNDERSTANDING MEASUREMENT

S. NATASHA BERETVAS   Series Editor

SERIES IN UNDERSTANDING QUALITATIVE RESEARCH

PATRICIA LEAVY   Series Editor

Understanding Statistics

Exploratory Factor Analysis
Leandre R. Fabrigar and
Duane T. Wegener

Validity and Validation
Catherine S. Taylor

Understanding Measurement

Item Response Theory
Christine DeMars

Reliability
Patrick Meyer

Understanding Qualitative Research

Oral History
Patricia Leavy

Fundamentals of Qualitative Research
Johnny Saldaña

The Internet
Christine Hine

Duoethnography
Richard D. Sawyer and
Joe Norris

Qualitative Interviewing
Svend Brinkmann

Focus Group Discussions
Monique M. Hennink

Qualitative Disaster Research
Brenda D. Phillips

Autoethnography
Tony E. Adams, Stacy Holman Jones,
and Carolyn Ellis

*Analysis of the Cognitive Interview in
Questionnaire Design*
Gordon B. Willis

GORDON B. WILLIS

ANALYSIS OF THE COGNITIVE INTERVIEW IN QUESTIONNAIRE DESIGN

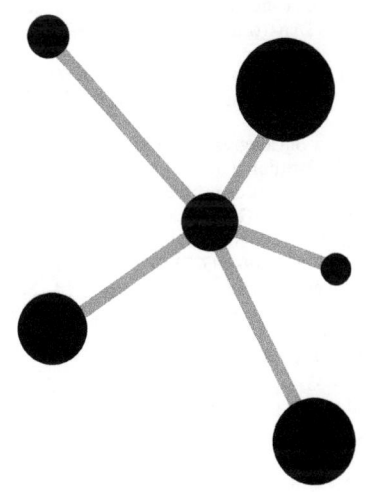

UNIVERSITY PRESS

Oxford University Press is a department of the University of Oxford.
It furthers the University's objective of excellence in research,
scholarship, and education by publishing worldwide.

Oxford   New York
Auckland   Cape Town   Dar es Salaam   Hong Kong   Karachi
Kuala Lumpur   Madrid   Melbourne   Mexico City   Nairobi
New Delhi   Shanghai   Taipei   Toronto

With offices in
Argentina   Austria   Brazil   Chile   Czech Republic   France   Greece
Guatemala   Hungary   Italy   Japan   Poland   Portugal   Singapore
South Korea   Switzerland   Thailand   Turkey   Ukraine   Vietnam

Oxford is a registered trademark of Oxford University Press
in the UK and certain other countries.

Published in the United States of America by
Oxford University Press
198 Madison Avenue, New York, NY 10016

© Oxford University Press 2015

This is a work of the US Government. Foreign copyrights may apply.

All rights reserved. No part of this publication may be reproduced, stored in
a retrieval system, or transmitted, in any form or by any means, without the prior
permission in writing of Oxford University Press, or as expressly permitted by law,
by license, or under terms agreed with the appropriate reproduction rights organization.
Inquiries concerning reproduction outside the scope of the above should be sent to the
Rights Department, Oxford University Press, at the address above.

You must not circulate this work in any other form
and you must impose this same condition on any acquirer.

Library of Congress Cataloging-in-Publication Data
Willis, Gordon B. (Gordon Bruce)
Analysis of the cognitive interview in questionnaire design / Gordon B. Willis.
    pages cm.—(Understanding qualitative research)
Includes bibliographical references.
ISBN 978-0-19-995775-0 (pbk. : alk. paper)   1. Interviewing.   2. Cognition.
3. Questionnaires—Methodology.   4. Social surveys—Methodology.   5. Social
sciences—Research—Methodology.   6. Psychology—Research—Methodology.
I. Title.
H61.28.W548 2014
001.4′33—dc23
2014030423

CONTENTS

Preface vii

CHAPTER 1   INTRODUCTION: THE ROLE OF COGNITIVE INTERVIEWING IN SURVEYS 1

CHAPTER 2   BACKGROUND: THEORY AND DISCIPLINARY ORIENTATION OF THE COGNITIVE INTERVIEW 15

CHAPTER 3   THE PRACTICE OF COGNITIVE INTERVIEWING 35

CHAPTER 4   ANALYSIS STRATEGIES FOR THE COGNITIVE INTERVIEW 55

CHAPTER 5   CRITICAL ISSUES IN ANALYSIS OF COGNITIVE INTERVIEWING RESULTS 125

CHAPTER 6   WRITING THE COGNITIVE INTERVIEWING REPORT 159

CHAPTER 7   CASE STUDIES IN ANALYSIS 169

CHAPTER 8   SUMMARY AND CONCLUSION 235

References 243
Index 253

PREFACE

In 1979, Miles (p. 16) stated that "The most serious and central difficulty in the use of qualitative data is that methods of analysis are not well formulated." It seems clear that cognitive interviewing, which is in basis a form of qualitative research, is currently at the point that Miles described over 30 years ago. Reasonably common methods for the *conduct* of cognitive interviewing have been established and are described in a volume I previously produced (Willis, 2005). However, even though I did devote a chapter to *analysis*, there is an evident need for more attention to this issue, based on an increasing frequency of comments, requests, and observations concerning analysis, from both practitioners and consumers of cognitive interviews.

The increased focus on analysis appears to be due to several factors. First is the recognition that, to borrow a philosophical cliché, multiple observers can look at the same thing and come to very different conclusions. Hence, the same cognitive interviewing data may result in a variety of interpretations, which would seem to violate a major tenet of science—that data speak in a consistent way to those who are listening. Second, the success of cognitive interviewing as a mainstream method for the evaluation of survey questions has led to its increased application to a range of new—and challenging—applications. In particular, the demands of cross-cultural survey research have prompted the conduct of cognitive interviewing across nations, cultures, and languages. This development imposes a rather unforgiving demand that our analysis techniques are consistent and reliable, so that we do not end up documenting differences that reflect only "house effects" or other idiosyncratic sources of variation. Third, as cognitive interview techniques gain adherents who apply the techniques to a wide variety of types of survey questionnaires, it seems as though each new practitioner or laboratory spawns its own variety of analysis techniques. We have not, as yet, stepped back to determine whether there is a core set of analysis practices that are common across these applications, and that should be considered something of a standard toolbox.

I stake no claim regarding the establishment of "best practices" for either the conduct or analysis of cognitive interviews, because we simply do not have enough information to make such claims, and because I am not sure that it is meaningful to specify a one-size-fits-all package. Rather, I seek to wade through the varied approaches that have been taken and to identify where these differ in fundamental ways, but also to determine where different terms and concepts are used to describe similar procedures. Overall, my objective is to steer the reader through a set of critical considerations, such as "What do we mean by analysis?"; "What are the different ways that this can be done?"; and in particular "Which one is the best practice given *my* context with its attendant constraints?" Hopefully I address these questions to such an extent that this book will serve as a valuable resource to the survey methods field and to the individual researcher who struggles with the challenge of deciding "What do my data mean?"

I would like to thank Patricia Leavy, the Series Editor for Understanding Qualitative Research; Abby Gross and Suzanne Walker at Oxford University Press; Saranyaa Moureharry at Newgen Knowledge Works; and Rachel Ballard-Barbash at the National Cancer Institute for allowing me to devote time to this enterprise. Most of all I would like to extend the hope that my wife will forgive me for my failure to abide by my assurance "Don't worry, I won't be writing any more books."

ANALYSIS OF THE COGNITIVE INTERVIEW IN QUESTIONNAIRE DESIGN

INTRODUCTION

THE ROLE OF COGNITIVE INTERVIEWING IN SURVEYS

> *If your result needs a statistician then you should design a better experiment.*
>
> Baron Ernest Rutherford

1.1. Chapter Overview

Although cognitive interviewing originated in the fields of psychology and survey methodology, the method in essence represents a form of *qualitative* inquiry. To open, I discuss the role of this qualitative method as it is applied to the survey methods field, which strongly emphasizes *quantitative* elements. Analysis of cognitive interviews therefore contains elements of both qualitative and quantitative science—that is, both words and numbers—and successfully navigating the tension and interplay between these approaches is fundamental to both conducting the cognitive interview and carrying out a successful analysis.

1.2. The Survey as Qualitative Versus Quantitative

No matter which realm of social science the researcher pursues—political science, public health, demography, and so on—we rely on a common scientific method, developed through several centuries of scientific revolution spurred by Renaissance philosophers such as Galileo and Francis Bacon. Rather than consulting an established text or compendium of knowledge, we seek to answer research questions by collecting empirical information as our primary data. These data are then subjected to critical analysis that in turn leads to generalizable conclusions, which hopefully allow us to better understand the world. Our collected data are often represented by numbers, even for characteristics that cannot easily be quantified or enumerated. For example, the overall happiness of a country's population has been represented in terms of an average number, obtained through questionnaire-based survey self-report in which individual respondents provide numerical ratings using a 10-point scale. As of 2013, according to the World Happiness Report (Helliwell, Layard, & Sachs, 2013), the five most happy countries were Denmark, Norway, Switzerland, The Netherlands, and Sweden. These numbers are "crunched" in various ways, to assess our critical outcome or dependent measure (e.g., self-reported happiness) according to demographic characteristics, including age, sex, income, and geography, and also in association with other interesting measured variables (e.g., self-reported religiosity).

Statisticians are accustomed to dealing with such quantitative, numeric measures. Not all in the world of scientific inquiry is statistical, or quantitative, however. Often our data in original form consist of words—such as by the anthropologist studying a specific culture who takes voluminous field notes and attempts little quantification (Adams, Khan, Raeside, & White, 2007; Miles & Huberman, 1984, 1994). These data—just as numeric data—demand some type of analysis, which results in summarization and reduction to a manageable size, in which the elemental or core information is retained, even at the cost of loss of some detail. Attaining this balance, and in effect separating the proverbial wheat from the chaff, is at the heart of qualitative analysis.

This book is intended to cover a special case of qualitative analysis—the development and testing of survey questionnaires through *cognitive interviewing*—where words are used to guide the collection of data that will ultimately be essentially quantitative in nature. We have all had experience completing various forms and questionnaires, especially those used to collect aggregate statistical data. Each survey question, or questionnaire item, such as "*Do you own a vacation home?*" is expected to produce a response—*Yes, No, I don't know,* or *I refuse to tell you*—that can in turn be assigned a code number (1 = yes, 2 = no, 8 = don't know, 9 = refused to answer). Analysis, in turn, relies on the application of statistics to produce a summary estimate—for example, 5% of the surveyed population reports owning a vacation home.

1.2.1. Where Do Survey Estimates (Really) Come From?

One answer would be the following famous quote (famous, at least, among statisticians):

> The government are very keen on amassing statistics. They collect them, add them, raise them to the n-th power, take the cube root and prepare wonderful diagrams. But you must never forget that every one of these figures comes in the first instance from the village watchman, who just puts down what he damn pleases. (Comment of an English judge on the subject of Indian statistics; quoted in Sir Josiah Stamp in *Some Economic Matters in Modern Life*)

Despite the straightforward, matter-of-fact nature of statements involving survey results, there are several nontrivial steps involved in the sequence that produces the final statistical estimate. The problem we face, and that the practice of cognitive interviewing attempts to address, concerns the fact that this number is not pulled out of the air, nor is it created by our statistical analysis program. Rather, answers are collected from people, one at a time and under conditions of real life, and are filtered through the mind of each individual asked to answer the question. Further, the tool we use to collect this information is conversational speech, or natural language, which is well known to present challenges to information gathering (Grice, 1989). As such, it is of great importance to consider the intricacies of the source: Why does one person say *Yes*, and another *No*, such that they subsequently become represented as either a "1" or a "2," respectively, in our research dataset?

This is the point at which the embellishment of the quantitative by the qualitative comes into play. Put simply, prior to conducting surveys to obtain responses and assign code numbers (yes = 1 and no = 2), we conduct *cognitive interviews* to dig deeper into these responses and to better understand what those responses tell us. To obtain this understanding, researchers literally ask *probe* questions, such as "Why do you say *Yes/No*?" Through such probing, we may find nothing additional to either inform or concern us. When asked whether one owns a vacation home, the individual may reply *Yes*, and when probed further, state that this is because "I own a house in Florida that we use for vacations" or "I don't own any houses—I rent." These types of reactions—words that describe someone's thinking—are essentially what we are looking for, and they serve to reinforce the answer to the evaluated (*target*) item.

More interesting, however, is when the person interviewed instead tells us: "*I said 'Yes' because we have a timeshare arrangement, and we're part owners.*" In this case, a perfectly good explanation reveals a hidden problem: The investigators may decide that they really would have preferred that person to have answered *No*, because the statistics to be gathered depend on unique (as opposed to shared) vacation home ownership. Through cognitive interviewing, the additional information that is obtained from such probing provides context and explanation to the direct answer given to the target question, and further insight into what a 1 or a 2 in the data for this item actually represents. Further, these qualitative data are used as a basis for enacting changes in the question that in turn influence the behavior of our survey respondents. Concerning the wording of the vacation home question, the questionnaire designers may decide to make some change to avoid reports of shared arrangements—for example, adding "Do not include timeshare arrangements."

1.3. Using Cognitive Interviews to Evaluate Survey Questions

The qualitative augmentation of survey responses is the crux of cognitive interviewing, as it is applied to questionnaire design. From a practical point of view, it often makes sense to conduct intensive investigation of the questionnaire early in the development process, prior to unleashing the full survey ("pretesting"), because our findings often lead us to change the survey questions to improve them in some way—that is, to eradicate defects. This investigation is accomplished by administering the questionnaire to a small group of volunteer *participants* (also referred to as *subjects* or as *respondents*), to ferret out difficulties these individuals have with the questionnaire items. Although finding such problems is not the only purpose of cognitive interviewing—and I will get to other major objectives later—*trying out our materials prior to "going into the field"* remains a key purpose, and cognitive interviewing is therefore also often referred to as *cognitive testing*. This product-testing endeavor has become a vital component of surveys, especially large ones conducted by the US federal government. My opening theme—that cognitive interviewing differs in fundamental ways from questionnaire-based data collection—is reflected in Table 1.1, which contains a summary of the major characteristics of the cognitive interview and how these differ from the fielding of a survey questionnaire.

Although is it essential to master a range of activities and processes, such as participant recruitment, the most critical aspects of cognitive interviewing, for most researchers learning to conduct this activity, are (a) interviewing and (b) interpreting the

Table 1.1
Comparison of the cognitive interview and the field survey questionnaire

Critical Feature	Administration of a Survey Questionnaire	Conduct of a Cognitive Interview
Purpose	To collect (usually quantitative) data to be statistically analyzed	To gather information about the functioning of the survey questions—often prior to finalization and field administration
Sample size	As large as possible—to attain adequate **statistical power**	Typically small—may consist of several **rounds** of no more than 10 interviews each

(continued)

Table 1.1 (*continued*)

Critical Feature	Administration of a Survey Questionnaire	Conduct of a Cognitive Interview
Recruitment	**Respondents** are recruited from a sample frame, and they are intended to be a statistically representative sample of the relevant population	**Participants** are obtained through a variety of recruitment strategies, which are intended to produce **variation** in the types of individuals recruited
Interviewers	A group of survey field interviewers is used (for interviewer-administered questionnaires (IAQ) No interviewers are used for self-administered paper or computer-based questionnaires	Generally a small number (1–4) of highly trained **cognitive interviewers** conduct the interviews
Materials presented	A **survey questionnaire** in final form, as the data collection instrument	A **Cognitive Interviewing Guide**, consisting of the survey questionnaire, often in draft form, along with a list of **probe** questions to be asked
Method	Verbatim administration of a **standardized instrument**	**Flexible administration** that relies heavily on **probe** questions to embellish the standardized instrument
Analysis	**Quantitative statistical analysis** of coded responses	**Qualitative analysis** of responses to probe questions, based on interviewer notes or recording of verbatim interviews

results. Procedurally, *verbal probing*—for example, following up a *No* response to the vacation home question by asking "Why did you say no?"—is a key element of cognitive interviewing. The procedures applied in cognitive testing have been described in great detail elsewhere—in particular, within a book I wrote specifically as a guide to the conduct of this activity (Willis, 2005). There are now many articles, book chapters, and examples of the use of cognitive interviewing as survey pretesting, and I encourage readers interested in becoming proficient cognitive interviewers to consult these: Beatty (2004); Beatty and Willis (2007); Collins (2003); Collins, 2015; Conrad and Blair (2004, 2009); DeMaio and Rothgeb (1996); Forsyth and Lessler (1991); and Willis (2005). The emphasis of this book, however, is to extend previous writings on cognitive interviewing and to focus in much more detail on a second major challenge: the conduct of analysis of cognitive interviews—or what one does with the qualitative data obtained. That is, this book is for the analyst.

1.3.1. The Role of the Researcher in Analysis

Analysis of qualitative data—at least in traditional form—may depart fundamentally from that of its quantitative cousin in several ways (Boeije, 2010). Rather than making use of statistical software (like SAS, SPSS, Stata, R, and so on) to produce standard descriptive statistics (mean, variance) and inferential statistical tests (ANOVA, correlation, and regression), we must instead rely on data-reduction techniques that are designed to work with words, whether they are full text summaries, sentence fragments, key terms, or something else that is more word-like than number-like. These analyses involve the filtering of written materials by human researchers, who search for consistent themes and for reliable and useful means for parsing and organizing the data into meaningful categories. A major theme that is often reiterated by qualitative research theorists, in fact, is the central position of the investigator in the data collection and analysis activities, especially in terms of preexisting worldview, assumptions, expectations, and motivations (Chepp & Gray, 2014; Emmel, 2013).

1.3.2. The Cognitive Aspects of Data Analysis

A significant consequence of the complications introduced by the presence of the investigator is that this person necessarily becomes an important component in the analysis chain, an unavoidable fact that demands a consideration of what I will refer to specifically as *the cognitive aspects of data analysis*. I will refer to this principle often, to convey the point that *qualitative analysis is itself a cognitive activity not driven solely by either our data or by any possible algorithmic approach to conducting the analysis.* Parenthetically, I believe that a strong case can be made that this is true of all analysis of research data—including quantitative analysis involving "the hard sciences"—although making that argument is somewhat beyond the scope of this book. For current purposes, I stress that qualitative data analysis demands much that is internally driven (i.e., by thinking about our data in a manner described as *reflexively* by qualitative researchers; Adams Khan, Raeside, & White, 2007) to supplement that which is externally driven (in terms of that which is provided by our raw data sources and analyzed *interpretively*). The necessary intrusion of our own thought processes is a double-edged sword. On the one hand, the active contribution of our cognition helps us to make sense of the small part of the world we are studying. On the other, it risks interjecting biases, prejudices, and beliefs that we may unwittingly (or intentionally) bring to bear. Interestingly, this tension appears to be ubiquitous through multiple realms of scientific inquiry, and it even appears to be wired into the human brain from birth. The developmental psychologist Piaget (1952) distinguished *accommodation*, or altering our existing schema or worldview based on new information, and *assimilation*, or incorporating new information into an existing schema. Analysis of cognitive interviews to assess the function of our evaluated survey questions normally involves elements of both processes, no matter what phraseology one selects to describe them.

1.3.3. Illustration: Analysis of a Small Set of Cognitive Interviews

Consider an example of how the analysis of a set of cognitive interviewing may proceed. Assume that in order to evaluate the survey question *"Are you now covered by health insurance?"* 12 total cognitive interviews have been conducted. This is a small number—although not completely atypical (e.g., see Buers et al., 2013, who reported results of a cognitive test of a patient experience survey with 10 participants). To conduct each interview, we first present the target survey question to be evaluated, such as *"Do you now have health insurance?"* After each participant has answered *Yes* or *No*, we probe further, by asking, *"Why do you say (Yes/No)?"* The interviewer listens to the answer to this probe and writes *interviewer notes* that are either verbatim quotes or represent the interviewer's interpretation of the participant's comments. To then make sense of these data, the analyst reviews the interviewer notes and attempts to categorize the responses into a set of "bins," relating to the observed match between the investigators' intent of the item and the response given (see Table 1.2). Specifically, the investigator determines whether, based on the information gathered through probing, each self-report of Yes (having coverage) or No (not having coverage) is consistent, from the investigator's viewpoint.

A complication is that at this point the cognitive processes of the analyst are invoked to a considerable extent: The analyst must *make use of the totality of information obtained to determine whether each interviewed person, based on his or her verbal report, has provided a response consistent with the item intent, and therefore a successful interpretation of the researcher's objectives.* In our

Table 1.2
Sample cognitive interviewing data: Cross-tabulation comparing survey respondent reports with the investigator's viewpoint, concerning the target question: *Do you now have health insurance?*

Investigator's Viewpoint	Participant Report	
	Has Insurance Coverage	Does Not Have Coverage
Participant has coverage	P1, P2, P5, P7, P10	P4, P6
Participant does not have coverage	P3	P8, P9, P11, P12

hypothetical example, Participants 1 through 12 are represented in our analysis table. Five of them (P1, P2, P5, P7, and P10) indicate that they have health insurance coverage, and their responses to our critical probe suggest that this is in fact the case. Four others (P8, P9, P11, and P12) indicate no coverage and provide explanations that appear perfectly reasonable (e.g., *"I have no job, and therefore no insurance"*; *"I am young and healthy and haven't needed much medical attention, so don't bother with it"*). So far, so good—there are no obvious indications of any issues or problems, or disconnects, between our own conceptualization and those reported by our cognitive interview participants.

There are, however, two remaining cells in our table that are more problematic, yet also informative. Two participants (P4 and P6) indicate that they lack insurance coverage, but it is established based on cognitive probing that the investigators would regard them as covered. The evidence for this conclusion may depend on such statements as *"No, I don't have the coverage—someone else provides it to me"* or *"No, just Medicare, like most older people."* Another potentially interesting case is P3, who answers Yes, but upon probing explains that she is about to start a new job that carries coverage, and so reports that she is covered, thinking to the future. In each of these cases, the respondents provided data (*Yes* or *No*) that are at odds with what the investigators would expect, given the actual circumstances of these individuals' lives. To the extent that the investigators conclude that the respondent is in fact wrong (at least from their own perspective), these findings serve as evidence of survey measurement error—and more precisely, of response error, in which the "true score" and the "reported score" fail to match (see Biemer, 2011, for a review of sources of survey error).

Findings such as those just described cause the questionnaire designers to consider *why* there is a disjunction between what we would like from the people we have interviewed and what we have obtained from them. If we are fortunate, and cognitive probing has been effective in providing rich contextual information to inform us in this regard, the reasons may become apparent. For one, it seems that our asking, *"Do you have health insurance?"* may have been misleading, as it implies that the respondent is the "owner" of the policy—and is in any case not what we really are after. It might occur to the designers that a more appropriate wording would be *"Are you now covered by health insurance?"*

Presumably, asking this variant should solve the problem of inducing people to say *No* only because it is not "their own" insurance but is obtained through a spouse or other family member.

Turning to the person who said *No* because she is covered by Medicare, a different potential problem emerges. In this case, the person may have volunteered during the cognitive interview that she assumed that "health insurance" must consist of a special type of policy beyond the regular coverage provided by Medicare that all people over 65 years are eligible for (e.g., *"You already knew I have Medicare—as you asked my age before and I told you I was 70—so I figured you must mean something else, like Medigap, which I don't have"*).

This is, again, a very reasonable response—and the investigators may again decide that the problem is not with this person but in the question. A potential solution would be to make one further modification to the question and to ask, *"Are you now covered by any form of health insurance, including Medicare or Medicaid?"*—so we clarify that these should be included. Finally, there is the problem of the person who said *Yes* to having coverage—when the investigators would like to hear *No*—due to the fact that she is not literally covered at the moment. They could then consider yet another change and ask, *"As of today, are you covered by any form of health insurance, including Medicare or Medicaid?"*

I have provided a simple example, based on a small number of cognitive interviews. It is likely that additional cognitive interviews would lead to other problems, and other (or better) solutions. Yet this example is typical of what often occurs in cognitive testing and of the disconnect between what respondents understand and what we intend them to understand. The point of our analysis—which again, is the major focus of this book—is to find ways to detect these disconnects and to characterize them in a way that leads us to make decisions, perhaps involving revisions to survey question wording. These decisions ultimately help us to reduce error in the survey data collection process, or they at least help us to understand more about what we are actually getting when we ask a question—even if we are unable to enact changes in order to reduce error. As a bottom line, we must make sure that we are analyzing this qualitative information in a way that is unbiased and ultimately representative of the production survey environment.

1.3.4. Can "Qualitative" and "Quantitative" Analysis Be Separated?

I also stress at this point that although analysis of cognitive interviewing is generally described as a qualitative endeavor, it is also typically quantitative. The qualitative responses represented in Table 1.2 can be quantified simply by tabulating the frequency of each (n = 5, 2, 1, and 4). Therefore, are we in fact dealing again with quantitative rather than strictly qualitative data? This is absolutely the case, and highlights the fact that cognitive interviewing analyses normally involve both quantitative and qualitative data in interplay. There is no need, or even desire, for qualitative analysis to eschew all quantification or use of numbers, and several authors (Boeije, 2010; Chi, 1997) have made the case that the distinction between the purely qualitative and quantitative appears to be receding. In particular, *analysis of cognitive interviews can be conceptualized as a form of mixed-method research and to involve both qualitative and quantitative elements* (Tashakkori & Teddlie, 2003). The case remains, however, that in the initial phases of analysis of cognitive interviews, we almost invariably are faced with qualitative verbal descriptions, and our challenge is to do far more than simply to number-crunch a series of numeric survey responses.

1.4. Is It Clear How to Analyze Cognitive Interviewing Results?

The aforementioned health insurance example—in which qualitative responses are sorted into bins to provide further clarity—is meant to illustrate how to analyze a single target survey question, and it foreshadows some discussion to come. Does this mean that analysis should be done this exact way, for all questions? This is not necessarily the case, and it is unclear what the best approach should be. In fact, several authors have identified analysis as the Achilles heel of cognitive interviewing. Blair and Brick (2010, p. 3739) lament that "there is little consensus on the ways in which the verbal reports should be handled or how the analysis should be conducted" More pointedly, Drennan (2003, p. 62) noted that "analyzing cognitive interview data remains overtly subjective, and this remains the greatest flaw in an otherwise comprehensive method of questionnaire pretesting." Finally, Knafl and colleagues (2007, p. 225) strike a similar theme, noting that typical cognitive interviewing reports, such as by Willis, Royston, and Bercini (1991), "described problems with the relevance, understandability, and ordering of items, but only briefly addressed how interviewers' summary notes were used in team meetings to guide the revision of questionnaire items." Willis and Miller (2008) have represented this gap, as shown in Figure 1.1.

To address this shortcoming, I will address key questions that are intended to close this chasm, concerning the concrete steps taken between collecting data and reporting what we have found. Further, I drill down to a set of more specific considerations:

1. How is data reduction accomplished?
2. Should qualitative data from cognitive interviews be assigned to coding categories?
3. If so, what types of coding scheme should be used?
4. Who does the analysis—the cognitive interviewer or someone else?
5. How many analysts should be involved, and is it ok to only have one?
6. When there are multiple analysts, do they work independently or together?

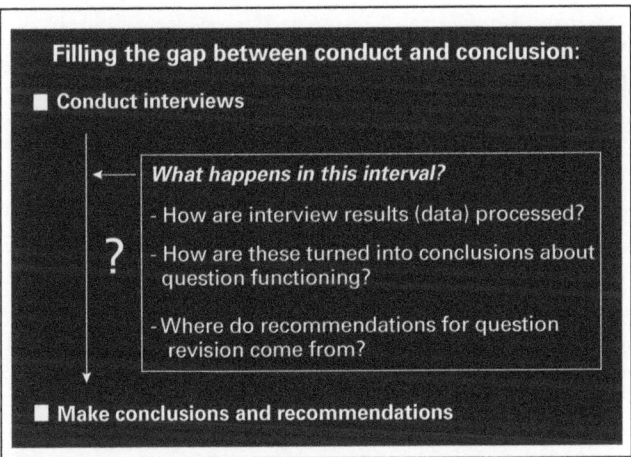

Figure 1.1 The missing link in the conduct of cognitive interviews: Analysis. Source: Willis, G. B., & Miller, K. M. (2008).

7. What types of *data displays* can be used to make sense of reduced data?
8. How are differences in interpretation of results identified, and how are they resolved?
9. How much quantification should be done as part of the analysis of cognitive interviews?

Like the survey questions we evaluate, none of these questions may have a straightforward answer. Later chapters examine these analysis issues in turn, given the current state of the art in cognitive interviewing. Again, because so-called best practices—or even minimal standards—have not been set with respect to these issues, there is no set of established truths to pull from (Buers et al., 2013; Lee, 2014; Miller, 2011; Presser et al., 2004). Rather, I synthesize the existing literature and delve more deeply into issues of analysis than has been attempted to date. First, though, I devote two chapters to necessary background, especially for readers not familiar with the processes and procedures of cognitive interviewing, initially covering its theory and orientation, and then moving to a review of common procedures.

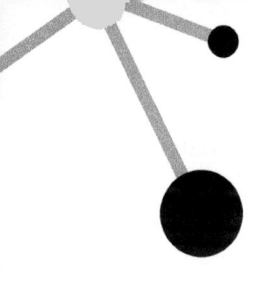

2

BACKGROUND

THEORY AND DISCIPLINARY ORIENTATION OF THE COGNITIVE INTERVIEW

> In theory, there is no difference between theory and practice. But in practice, there is.
>
> Yogi Berra

2.1. Chapter Overview

To fully appreciate the complexities of analysis, it is helpful to have a view of the background of cognitive interviewing as an applied method, especially in terms of its theoretical and disciplinary origins. Divergent views concerning applicable theory may influence the conduct of the interview, and they certainly influence approaches to data reduction, analytic technique, and interpretation. There are several key distinctions of interest:

1. The objectives of cognitive testing: *Reparative* versus *Descriptive* research
2. Theoretical background and disciplinary framework: (a) *cognitive* versus (b) *sociological-anthropological and linguistic*

3. Framework for analysis: the incorporation of analysis procedures from the *qualitative research* tradition

2.2. Defining the Cognitive Interview

To quote Voltaire: "If you want to talk with me, first define your terms." It is especially important to define the *cognitive interview* because, somewhat confusingly, the term refers to two very different procedures—which both involve cognition and interviewing. The cognitive interview described by Fisher and Geiselman (1992) is a procedure used in law enforcement to enhance the reliability of eyewitness testimony. I will not discuss that application (see Willis, 2005, p. 5 for somewhat more detail). Rather, the cognitive interview as practiced in the survey methods field is intended to evaluate, and to improve, self-report survey questions, measurement instruments, research consent forms, and other written materials. As defined by Beatty and Willis (2007, p. 287), the cognitive interview involves: "the administration of draft survey questions while collecting additional verbal information about the survey responses, which is used to evaluate the quality of the response or to help determine whether the question is generating the information that its author intends." Cognitive interviewing can be viewed as either a psychological procedure, or as a special case of qualitative interviewing, as that method is used as a tool for the understanding of psychosocial phenomena (Rubin & Rubin, 2004). However, conceptions of cognitive interviewing have evolved over the past 30 years.

2.2.1. Origins of the Cognitive Interview

As initially conceived, the primary objective of the cognitive interview is to understand the internal mechanisms underlying the survey response process. An equally important aim is contributing to the development of effective practices for writing survey questions that are well understood and that produce low levels of response error. From a more applied perspective, a key objective is the evaluation of a particular set of target items under development by questionnaire designers, to determine means for rewording, reordering, or reconceptualizing these. Hence, as well as providing a broadly based, empirical, psychologically oriented framework for the general study of questionnaire design, cognitive interviewing has been adopted as a production mechanism for the improvement of a wide variety of survey questions, whether factual, behavioral, or attitudinal in nature. Cognitive laboratories devoted to the development, testing, and evaluation of survey questionnaires have been established at several US federal agencies (the National Center for Health Statistics, the US Census Bureau, US Bureau of Labor Statistics); at Statistics Canada; at European statistical agencies (Statistics Sweden, Statistics Netherlands, Statistics Finland); and at several contract research organizations.

In any form, cognitive interviewing relies on the collection of verbal reports, in which individuals who "stand in" for field survey respondents—our participants—answer the survey items but are also asked for additional information about their thoughts regarding each question. This supplementation classically involves either *thinking aloud* (e.g., the participant is asked at the outset to *tell me everything you are thinking as you answer the questions*) or *verbal probes* that endeavor to target particular cognitive processes (e.g., to assess comprehension: *What does the term abdomen mean to you?*). On the basis of the collected *verbal reports*, the investigators make decisions concerning the functioning of the items. For example, it has—unsurprisingly—been found that individuals not trained in anatomy tend to have an inadequate understanding of exactly where their abdomen is (Willis, 2005). Finally, modifications to the items are often made in order to address the problems identified.

2.3. What Is the Purpose of Cognitive Interviewing? Reparative Versus Descriptive Research

The basic objective of cognitive testing may seem clear enough from the earlier definition. However, although a shared aim of researchers is to understand the survey response process, notions of what it is exactly that we are trying to understand, and what we will do with the resultant information, vary widely. Variation in objectives may, in fact, be a major factor responsible for the lack of shared standards and uniformity of procedures. Although it is inevitably risky to propose a clear division to explain a complex world, I nevertheless identify two contrasting objectives: (1) *Reparative* and (2) *Descriptive* cognitive interviewing.

2.3.1. The Reparative Approach

The common, and perhaps default, approach can be most accurately thought of as representing an "inspect-and-repair" model—although I will refer to it, mainly for purposes of brevity, as *Reparative* research. The Reparative focus has dominated the operation of cognitive laboratories that focus on improvements in survey questions and reduction in response error (Miller, 2011; Willis, 2005). Reparative cognitive interviewing was implicitly introduced in Chapter 1, within the example concerning health insurance coverage, as the objective was to inspect the item, to detect flaws, and then to repair it. In my earlier book (Willis, 2005), I introduced the metaphor of inspection of a potentially seaworthy vessel for leaks, and then patching those. Reparative investigations are common—as examples, see Napoles-Springer, Santoyo-Olsson, O'Brien, and Stewart (2006) and Watt and colleagues (2008). Parenthetically, although fully Reparative studies tend to involve both elements of inspection and repair (also referred to simply as *finding and fixing*), I also include in this category studies that truncate the process at the initial point of problem detection, short of enacting the actual repairs.

2.3.2. The Descriptive Approach

An example can be used to highlight an alternative objective: As a measure of psychological functioning, consider the item "*Would you say your health in general is excellent, very good, good, fair, or poor?*" Cognitive interviews would focus on probing participants' thoughts by asking: "*What, to you, is health in general?*" and "*Why do you say (excellent...poor)*"? On the basis of such interviews, it may be found that interpretations of general health vary tremendously, that people vary in terms of the time interval they have in mind when answering the question, and that they fail to agree concerning the interpretation of vague quantifiers such as *very good*. Depending on the research objectives of the investigator, it might be determined that a set of more precise, specific items provide better information—that is, we can "repair the damage" with a new form of the question. The logic of this process is consistent with the Reparative approach described earlier.

Imagine, however, that the researchers take a different view of the cognitive testing results. They may instead conclude that the health status item, in its current form, functions well enough to satisfy the intended purposes of the investigation, and they do not endeavor to make repairs or modifications. Rather, they use the cognitive interviews simply to better understand function—that is, the internal workings—of the item. In this case, cognitive interviews do not uniquely point to a clear improvement; rather, they make clear the implicit issues involved in the use of a particular question formulation. Beatty and Willis (2007) hinted at this viewpoint through a discussion of the inevitable tradeoffs involved in selecting question wording and, in particular, the need to realize that there may not be a single optimal version that applies in all circumstances. Even earlier, Oppenheim (1966) made the prescient observation that a questionnaire-based item may have multiple validities, to the extent that it potentially fulfills multiple measurement objectives.

A more definitive statement of this objective has been made recently by researchers who argue that the focus of cognitive testing should shift from discovering problems and repairing survey questions, toward a more general understanding of how they function as measures of a particular concept. As articulated by Ridolfo and Schoua-Glusberg (2011, p. 422):

> ...analysis has primarily focused on uncovering response errors based on respondents' verbal reports of their cognitive processes when responding to questions (Willis, 2005). Although we learn a lot from cognitive interviews regarding semantic, recall, and computational problems that occur during the response process, often little insight is gained about the type of information the question elicits, particularly when no response errors are found.

I consider the broader approach that Ridolfo and Schoua-Glusberg advocate to be, in concept, *reverse engineering*—due to its emphasis on reduction of the finished product to its elements, in terms of both structure and function. Although the term may bring to mind notions of industrial espionage, I rely on a definition that focuses on reducing complicated things to their component parts, to make them more understandable (Bernard, 1988). For brevity, I will refer to this objective using the term *Descriptive* research—even though I believe that this term fails to fully capture the intent of this viewpoint. In later sections I will consider the ways in which fundamental perspectives concerning the purpose of cognitive interviewing—whether Reparative or Descriptive—in turn can be tied to differentiated analysis strategies.

A few clarifying comments on the Reparative-Descriptive distinction are in order. First, these do not describe a dichotomy, but endpoints of a continuum—many studies contain elements of both, as they are neither mutually exclusive nor contradictory (see Lee, 2014). On the other hand, there is a key conceptual difference between these opposing objectives that is more than a matter of labeling or emphasis, and it recapitulates a key departure in orientation, described by Groves (1989) as delineating two respective camps within the survey methods field: *reducers* versus *measurers*. As the term implies, reducers attempt to minimize error up front, through design modification—as by decreasing survey nonresponse—and so are represented by the Reparative viewpoint. Measurers, on the other hand, endeavor to determine the level of some variety of survey error from the data and are more closely aligned with the Descriptive approach. As such, the distinction between Reparative and Descriptive objectives is not unique to the development and testing of survey items but pervades the survey methods field generally.

A second distinction between Reparative and Descriptive variants of cognitive interviewing is that they may be utilized at different points in the developmental process. The former, inspect-and-repair procedure is typically applied when something exists to be inspected, whether a survey question, a set of survey instructions, an advance letter, or some other tangible product that is under development for inclusion in a planned survey. A Descriptive investigation, on the other hand, may be relevant at several points in the questionnaire development cycle. Sometimes

Descriptive studies are carried out apart from the development of a particular survey instrument, simply to understand how existing survey questions function (e.g., Behr, Braun, Kaczmirek, & Bandilla, 2014; Miller, Willis, Eason, Moses, & Canfield, 2005). Or, at the early end of the development spectrum, one can conduct a Descriptive cognitive study even in the absence of a questionnaire to be tested, as when we are at an initial stage of trying to simply understand how a general concept (e.g., "disability") is likely to be interpreted and processed by survey respondents (Blanden & Rohr, 2009).

2.3.2.1. An Example of Descriptive Cognitive Interviewing: Fruit Versus Vegetable

Thompson, Willis, Thompson, and Yaroch (2011) applied Descriptive cognitive interviewing to address the question: What do people think is a "fruit" versus a "vegetable"? The objective was to explore this concept, as opposed to "finding and fixing a problem" in an existing questionnaire. Near the end of the cognitive interview conducted within a usual, Reparative investigation, participants were presented with a list of foods and asked a probe question concerning whether each was (a) a fruit, (b) a vegetable, or (c) something else. It was illuminating to uncover perceptions of fruit versus vegetable, by both English and Spanish speakers. Analysis was relatively straightforward, and due to the structured nature of the task, quantitative counts were simple to compute. Almost everyone considered corn to be a vegetable. On the other hand, a tomato was felt to be a vegetable by 78%, but a fruit by 20%. A yam was considered a vegetable by 95% of English speakers, but its Spanish equivalent was labeled a vegetable by only 67% of Spanish speakers, who also labeled it a fruit (17%) or something else (8%). Note that the investigators were not primarily interested in fixing survey questions, but rather in understanding the world (of fruits and vegetables, at least). Based on such findings, it is easy to see how questionnaire designers might apply them within a Reparative framework—for example, by supplementing usage of "vegetable" or "fruit" in diet questions with appropriate specific exemplars, as opposed to relying only on the general terms.

2.4. The Role of Theory

It has been argued that any scientific technique ultimately depends on theory, and in order to be accepted as valid, it must demonstrate adherence to some underlying theoretical orientation or model which itself is defensible (Chepp & Gray, 2014). The once commonly accepted practice of bloodletting as therapy for a range of medical conditions was dependent on a model of the human body which supposed that unbalanced "humors" in circulation caused health problems and needed to be removed. Rejection of this technique depended on the development of an alternate conceptualization of how the body works. By analogy, if cognitive testing presupposes an erroneous theory or model, it might be akin to bloodletting—seemingly logical but ultimately anemic in terms of effectiveness.

Hence, it is worth considering whatever theory there is to support the use of the cognitive interview. One view is that theory has been neglected, or at most, attended to in a minimal sense (Willis, 2005); if true, this would seem to present a serious problem to that field. In addressing this issue, it is important again to define terms. A dictionary definition of *theory* is "A system of ideas intended to explain something," and for the purpose of this chapter I interpret this widely and ask: What set of background ideas, assumptions, and scientific disciplines underlie the varied approaches to cognitive interviewing, and especially its analysis?

2.5. Theory of Survey Responding Versus Theory of Cognitive Interviewing

One complication in considering theoretical underpinnings is that two divergent types of theories apply to the cognitive interview. First is the more general theory concerning how individuals respond to survey questions—a theory of the *phenomenon* being studied—here, the survey response process. Second, there may be a theory underlying the use of cognitive interviews as a means to test survey questions—which I refer to as a theory of *method*. Extending a metaphor introduced earlier, a theory concerning the phenomenon of boat flotation may posit that the vessel's hull be free of holes and other structural deformities (e.g., cracks, weak spots, etc.). This theory does not, in itself, however, necessarily speak to how such deformities can be located, analyzed, and patched—that is, the relevant "system of ideas" attempting to explain flotation may not extend to explanations of inspection and repair (presumably involving visual inspection, more sophisticated tests to identify hidden cracks, methods for producing effective welds and patches, and so on). By extension, I believe that discussions of theory applicable to cognitive testing (including Willis, 2005) have become muddled because of a general failure to make clear the critical distinction between phenomenon and method. To rectify this, I dissect this discussion more finely to determine which elements of theory apply to *what* we are studying versus *how* we are studying it.

2.6. Cognitive Theory and the Survey Response Process

Concerning the phenomenon that we purport to study—the survey response process—the cognitive theoretical orientation was given significant life by a movement, born in the 1980s, known as CASM, or the Cognitive Aspects of Survey Methodology (Jabine, Straf, Tanur, & Tourangeau,1984; Jobe & Mingay, 1991). CASM was not developed to apply directly to the cognitive interview itself, but rather to the underlying activities constituting the steps taken by an individual who is presented a survey question—that is, the phenomenon we embark to understand through the use of cognitive testing. The CASM viewpoint is perhaps best espoused by Tourangeau (1984), who introduced the four-stage cognitive model shown in Table 2.1. The model posits a straightforward sequence in which a survey question must first be comprehended by the respondent (e.g., responding to the item "When is the last time you were seen by a doctor or other health professional?" requires comprehension of the key phrase "health professional"). Following this, information necessary to successfully answer the question must be retrieved (here, memory of the last visit). Then, a judgment or estimation step occurs, in which the respondent may evaluate the response retrieved (e.g., "Does that seem right—has it really been a year?"). Finally, a response process—sometimes referred to as response mapping—governs the reporting of an answer (e.g., the respondent must decide whether to say "about a year," "12 months," "I'm not exactly sure," or something else). Somewhat interestingly, the original perspective of CASM, as envisioned by its early proponents such as Loftus (1984) and Blair and Burton (1987), emphasized survey question function, rather than dysfunction—and so represented the Descriptive view rather than the Reparative one. The cognitive model has had impressive staying power, and it is often cited as the dominant source of

---

Table 2.1
Cognitive model of the survey response process (Tourangeau, 1984)

1. Comprehension of the question
  (a) Question intent: What does the respondent believe the question to be asking?
  (b) Meaning of terms: What do specific words and phrases in the question mean to the respondent?

2. Retrieval of relevant information from memory
  (a) Recallability of information: What types of information does the respondent need to recall in order to answer the question?
  (b) Recall strategy: What type of strategy is used to retrieve information? For example, does the respondent tend to count events by recalling each one individually, or does he or she use an alternative strategy?

3. Judgment/estimation processes
  (a) Motivation: Does the respondent devote sufficient mental effort to answering the question accurately and thoughtfully?
  (b) Sensitivity/social desirability: Does the respondent want to tell the truth? Does he or she say something to make him or her look "better"?

4. Response processes
  (a) Mapping the response: Can the respondent match his or her internally generated answer to the response categories given by the survey question?

Source: Reprinted with permission from Willis (2005), p. 36.

theoretical inspiration to those who conduct cognitive interviews (Miller, 2011; Willis, 2005). Despite the historical importance, and continued usefulness, of a purely cognitive model, several authors have worked to augment this model by including the element of motivation, as opposed to just mechanical forms of information processing. An earlier model by Cannell, Miller, and Oksenberg (1981) stressed motivational, as opposed to cognitive, contributors to survey responding to a greater extent than did Tourangeau (although motivation is certainly included within the Decision/Judgment stage). Further, Krosnick (1991) forced a much stronger focus on motivation by applying the notion of *satisficing*, as defined by Simon (1956), within the economic realm to account for situations in which the individual is not sufficiently motivated to contribute full cognitive effort to the task but instead cuts corners. Detailed discussion of cognitive models of the survey response process are contained in Jobe and Herrmann (1996) and Schwarz and Sudman (1996).

2.7. Sociocultural and Linguistic Theory and the Survey Response Process

More recently, conceptions of the survey response process have tended to emphasize elements other than the purely individualistic, psychological perspective promoted by the CASM approach. These newer developments incorporate elements of other disciplines, and in particular *sociology, anthropology, and linguistics*, which emphasize the interaction between individuals in society (generally, for socio-anthropology, and specifically with respect to oral and written communication, for linguistics). Due to these developments, conceptualizations of the survey response process have widened to encompass not only the psychological processes of comprehension, recall, and motivational state but also the sociocultural influences that may impact responses to items (Gerber, 1999; Miller, 2011). For instance, asking for a rating of "your health in general" has been found to elicit varying conceptualizations of general health across cultural and linguistic groups—for example, by English versus Spanish speakers in the United States (Miller et al., 2005).

Especially because I will be focusing mainly on *method*, I will not attempt to promote a particular theory of the survey response *process*. However, as an attempt at reconciliation, I suggest that a unifying theory that will be successful in guiding questionnaire design must ultimately depend on an amalgamation of social, cultural, linguistic, and cognitive factors—and that this theory is yet to be fully developed.

2.8. Cognitive Theory and Cognitive Interviewing

Earlier I discussed the importance of cognition as a feature of the CASM description of the *phenomenon* that we embark to understand: How are survey questions processed by the human mind? I now turn to a discussion of the role of theory associated with the *methodology* consisting of the cognitive interview, based on the belief that ultimately, as expressed by Mitchell and Cody (1993), "all methods are theory driven." Consistent with this viewpoint, cognitive theory has also been enlisted to support the use of cognitive interviewing as a method to study that process. Whether viewed as inspect and repair (Reparative) or as reverse engineering (Descriptive), cognitive interviewing has been advocated for evaluating survey questionnaires because of its fundamental emphasis on cognition. The assumption has tended to be that, if the subject of study involves cognition, then "cognitive" interviewing must, by definition, be a reasonable way to study these cognitions.

It is a potential fallacy, however, to assume that the validity of the Tourangeau model of the survey response process—that is, whether the respondent carries out the four defined processes postulated by that model—directly impacts the issue of whether cognitive interviewing is useful as a method to study these processes. Clearly, the use of the term "cognitive" in conjunction with "interviewing" has served, for several decades, as a convincing feature for practitioners who have developed facilities labeled "cognitive laboratories," and this presumably lends more credibility to the entity than would an alternative moniker, such as "survey checker" (or, even more unappealingly, "survey salon"; O'Muircheartaigh, 1999, p. 57). However, a more convincing argument would depend on an in-depth consideration of the theory underlying the use of participant verbal reports as they are elicited within the cognitive interview. In reviewing the theoretical basis for cognitive interviewing methods, Willis (2005) focused heavily on Ericsson and Simon's (1980, 1984) advocacy of the *think-aloud interview* to externalize the functioning of cognitive processes. In brief, Ericsson and Simon argued that individuals who spontaneously verbalize their thoughts provide a "window into the mind," allowing the researcher to understand the workings of the internal cognitive mechanisms. This theory has not been modified to any measurable degree over the past 30 years, and it stands as the sentinel theoretical basis for the cognitive interview—such that the method is still sometimes referred to as the *think-aloud interview*—even though it increasingly has made use of verbal probing procedures that are *not* dependent on thinking aloud. To a considerable extent, the widespread acceptance of cognitive interviewing as an expression of cognitive theory—whether involving think-aloud or verbal probing—is predicated on a belief in the Ericsson-Simon view that individuals have some access to their underlying cognitive processes and can articulate these as part of a procedure that involves verbal probing activities.

2.8.1. Does Cognitive Theory Support Cognitive Interviewing?

It has never been demonstrated that verbal reports obtained in cognitive interviews are veridical, or that they fulfill the presumed window-into-the mind function. Partly for this reason, just as cognitive interviewers may not necessarily subscribe to the CASM viewpoint concerning the survey response process, there is also no uniformity in acceptance of the Ericsson-Simon (or any other specifically cognitive) view of the utility of verbal reports (Miller, 2011). Such doubts, however, have not impeded practitioners of the activity: Even among those who reject or ignore cognitive theory, there remains wide acceptance of the utility of verbal probing and think-aloud methods, as everyone who conducts such testing apparently does make use of these procedures (and one could hardly do otherwise, given that probes and think aloud constitute the defining elements of the cognitive interview). Further, it is certainly not the case that successful interviewers necessarily have knowledge or training in cognitive theory, and I have not found that an interviewer trained as a PhD in cognitive psychology is better than one with education in any other particular field.

Hence, the fact that a set of fairly common techniques are used, "in the trenches" by even those who have little regard for cognitive theory, suggests that the notion that a strong cognitive theory of method exists may be something of an overstatement. Consistent with this conclusion, several decades ago, a colleague suggested to me that we should refer to the procedure as *intensive interviewing* because "so little of what we do is really cognitive" (P. Royston, personal communication, 1988). Interestingly, such intensive interviewing was first applied well before the cognitive revolution of the 1960s and 1970s (e.g., Cantril & Fried, 1944), and the types of probe questions used in that study were almost identical to those developed for cognitive interviews in the 1980s and beyond (e.g., Belson, 1981). Since that era, cognitive interviewing has increasingly departed from any strict adherence to the CASM viewpoint (O'Muircheartaigh, 1999; Willis, 1999).

Again, I stress the distinction between theoretical explanation of phenomenon versus theory. Even if cognitive interviewing is "cognitive" mainly in name, this observation does not imply that the act of answering survey questions is, in itself, something other than a cognitive activity, or that CASM is misguided as a theory of the survey response process. Rather, the implication would be that the *method* we use to study this process is best understood as not completely dependent on the purely cognitive framework. *The fact that we use the convenient label "cognitive interviewing" may therefore have limited bearing, concerning the nature of any underlying theory supporting the use of this procedure, and by extension, does not necessarily specify the nature of our analysis techniques.* My conclusion is not that cognitive theory is irrelevant—as it may have much to offer. Rather, it may be incomplete or exist as one of several useful perspectives.

2.9. Qualitative Research and Cognitive Interviewing

Once we widen the search for an underlying theory of method beyond the realm of cognitive psychology, it becomes apparent that there are other contenders. In fact, recognizing this possibility helps explain why cognitive interviewing has increasingly been adopted by practitioners other than cognitive scientists. In Chapter 1, I described cognitive interviewing as in essence a qualitative (rather than strictly quantitative) method. Beyond indicating a reliance on words more than numbers, the label *qualitative research* also serves to encompass a particular disciplinary perspective. Especially in recent years, it has been noted by several authors that cognitive interviewing has much in common with the more general field of *qualitative research*, as applied within sociology, anthropology, ethnography, and related fields. In particular, much of the qualitative research literature involves the use of intensive, interview-based methods akin to survey self-report (Denzin & Lincoln, 1994; Miles & Huberman, 1984, Miles, Huberman, & Saldana, 2014). Specifically, the use of the qualitative interview—sometimes called the depth interview—is ubiquitous among those who seek to understand the nature of phenomena that are of interest within the social sciences.

Given these similarities, it is logical to consider the theoretical underpinnings that have been developed as part of the qualitative research tradition (Chepp & Gray, 2014; Miller, 2011). Over the past 20 years, cognitive interviewing has increasingly come to be viewed as a form of qualitative research that can profitably borrow applicable theory from a diverse mix of fields, including ethnography, sociology, anthropology, and linguistics. This development has been furthered by the increased application of cognitive interviewing in the cross-cultural domain, in order to evaluate the functioning of survey questions across racial, ethnic, and linguistic groups, to establish cross-cultural comparability of function (Lee, 2014; Miller et al., 2011; Miller, Mont, Maitland, Altman, & Madans, 2010; Napoles-Springer et al., 2006; Willis & Miller, 2011).

2.9.1. Does Qualitative Research Theory Support Cognitive Interviewing?

In seeking a theory of method to apply to the cognitive interview as an alternative to cognitive theory, we can look to the existing qualitative literature for guidance (e.g., a text on analysis of qualitative data by Boeije, 2010). Reviewing these sources makes clear, however, that there exists no single, generally accepted theoretical orientation that obviously provides a "theory of cognitive testing." Morse (1994) provides a summary table that contrasts the various strands of qualitative research theory, using a single topic—study of human attachment within an airport environment, where the research procedure involves observation of passengers as they leave or are greeted by relatives. She demonstrates how each of several qualitative research strategies would examine the same phenomenon, starting with establishing the research question, determining the sample size, selecting the data collection procedures, and finally, specifying the nature of the data to be analyzed. Condensing her table somewhat, major traditions are shown in Table 2.2.

What is interesting is the degree to which the research questions posed in cognitive interviewing appear to incorporate these approaches:

Grounded Theory: Several authors have advocated the adoption of Grounded Theory by cognitive interviewers (Daveson et al., 2011; Miller, Willson, Chepp, & Padilla, 2014; Ridolfo & Schoua-Glusberg, 2011). Grounded Theory stresses the production of the full range of themes implicit in the data, and the need to exhaustively study the topic until we have achieved saturation and fully explicated the underlying structure of these themes (Charmaz, 2006). This focus seems directly applicable to cognitive interviewing, to the extent that we seek to understand fully how survey questions are understood.

Phenomenology: The phenomenological perspective seeks to determine the meaning of a construct, and strikingly reiterates the theme of ascertaining the comprehension of survey questions by our respondents.

Ethnography: Several authors have advocated an anthropological-ethnographic orientation for cognitive interviews (Gerber, 1999; Gerber & Wellens, 1997). In brief, to administer meaningful survey questions, we must understand the respondent's world (e.g., questions on physical activity need to cover the types of activities carried out by

Table 2.2
Morse's categories of qualitative research that give rise to varied data definition, and analysis strategies

1. *Grounded Theory:* **Develop themes related to the construct—"leaving and arriving"**
   Sample: 30–50 participants
   Method: In-depth interviews, observation
   Data: Description of the socio-psychological processes related to arriving/leaving, and the establishment of a small number of discrete themes associated with the phenomena: e.g., (a) positive affect in reuniting; (b) relief concerning safe arrival

2. *Phenomenology*: **Determining the meaning of a key construct: e.g., "leaving, or arriving home"**
   Sample: Six participants
   Method: In-depth conversation
   Data: Description of the experience (e.g., what it feels like to leave/arrive the airport)

3. *Ethnography:* **Describing the cultural and sociological context: e.g., "What is the arrival gate like when planes arrive or leave?"**
   Sample: 30–50 participants
   Method: Interviews, participant observation, use of airport records
   Data: Description of events at the arrival/departure gates

4. *Ethnoscience*: **What are the different categories of travelers?**
   Sample: 30–50 participants
   Method: Interviews to identify participant subtypes
   Data: Information used to create a taxonomy of types and characteristics of travelers, families

5. *Qualitative ethology:* **What are greeting behaviors of travelers and families**
   Sample: 100–200 participants, with greeting as unit of analysis
   Method: Recordings that are subsequently coded
   Data: Description of patterns of greeting behaviors

Source: Morse, J. (1994).

the respondent population). An ethnographic perspective, mainly obtained through interview, is a necessary component of some types of cognitive interviewing studies, especially those that are multicultural or that involve subcultures (e.g., transgender individuals) that the investigator may not well understand.

Ethnoscience: The focus on a taxonomy of types of individuals is also applicable to cognitive testing, as we endeavor to study a range of respondent type, with respect to the topic the survey questions are being developed for. As an example, surveys of "children" sometimes cover a wide age range (e.g., 8–20 years), and a result of cognitive testing may be to establish that the appropriate approach to content (e.g., sexual behavior) and wording (e.g., use of terms like "kids" or "young people") should differ within this age range (e.g., different wordings for elementary versus high-school students).

Qualitative ethology: Finally, the focus on recording and coding of discrete behaviors described as a feature of ethology is reflected in the use of recording, segmenting of behaviors, and compilation of these segments, which is often featured in cognitive interviewing.

My purpose in pointing out the wide variety of qualitative traditions that share features with cognitive testing is to suggest that there is no single qualitative research tradition that can, or should, serve as a solitary source of theory, or as the natural guide to the conduct of cognitive testing, the data produced, or the necessary analysis strategy. The bad news, perhaps, is that the recognition that cognitive interviewing can be viewed as a qualitative research endeavor does not automatically guide us down a golden path to a clear analysis strategy. The good news is that there are several perspectives at our disposal. Hence, it behooves investigators to consider the entire range of qualitative traditions as providing guidance to both conduct and analysis; in fact, qualitative researchers who have entered the field of cognitive interviewing have encompassed the range of these theoretical perspectives (e.g., Chepp & Gray, 2014; Miller, 2011; O'Brien, Bereket, Swinton, & Solomon, 2013).

2.9.2. The Interpretivist Perspective

Admittedly, however, Grounded Theory is at this point the frontrunner for providing a theory of method applicable to cognitive interviewing. The best developed approach of this type—worthy of special attention—is the *Interpretivist perspective* introduced by Miller (2011) and developed further by Chepp and Gray (2014). The interpretivist approach is characterized by the belief that meaning is constructed socially by the perceiver, within a social environment. It can be distinguished from its opposite—positivism—which holds that a true, concrete world exists and that gives rise to meaning, apart from construction of meanings based on human thought. Most critically, interpetivism is insistent that among the various interpretations of a phenomenon, all are valid, rather than some being either right or wrong.

Based on this viewpoint, the interpretive paradigm heavily emphasizes processes by which survey respondents give meaning to survey questions. This departs in a subtle but important way from the CASM perspective, which views the comprehension of the item as the ability of respondents to understand its core meaning. According to the interpretivist viewpoint, there is no "core meaning." Rather, what is relevant is the meaning produced at the time the question is administered. The interpretivist perspective therefore leads to a tendency to focus on deriving as much information as possible about the respondent's interpretation. As applied to the cognitive interview, this viewpoint can be translated into a set of procedures that focus on the extraction of information concerning interpretive processes, and variation in perceived meaning. Consistent with Grounded Theory, interpretivists emphasize the building up of explanatory themes directly from the qualitative data, as opposed to reliance on a cognitive model.

Because verbal probing is ideal for the study of interpretive process, and for identifying themes in the data, an interpretivist perspective naturally leads to an emphasis on probing within the cognitive interview to ferret out information concerning interpretation—as does the cognitive perspective. However, although cognitive and interpretivist viewpoints both rely on mainstream cognitive interviewing procedures, they tend to diverge markedly with respect to favored approaches for the analysis of those interviews. I will not address these differences within this chapter but reserve that discussion for Chapter 4, which is specifically devoted to analysis models.

Further, before getting to the nuts and bolts of analysis procedures, Chapter 3 will describe in more detail how cognitive testing is accomplished and how it produces the data we are then responsible for analyzing.

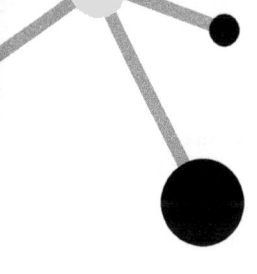

THE PRACTICE OF COGNITIVE INTERVIEWING

Judge a man by his questions rather than by his answers.

Voltaire

3.1. Chapter Overview

A chapter attending to research design and procedures will focus on enabling readers to engage in the full range of cognitive interviewing activities. My prevailing philosophy will be that analysis does not only follow data collection; we do not simply decide after the fact how to analyze what we have collected. Rather, cognitive interviewing is best done according to a proactive view in which we look ahead to our intended analysis strategy, in deciding how to conduct the activity in the first place. Hence, in describing the basic features of the dominant cognitive testing approaches, I also purposely invoke issues directly relevant to the later analysis stage.

3.2. Designing the Verbal Report Method: Think-Aloud and Verbal Probing

As an enterprise in evaluating survey questions, especially for purposes of survey pretesting, cognitive testing has developed over the past decades into a methodology that makes use of a set of targeted procedures. This targeting to some extent depends on the nature of the survey involved: whether it is a survey of *populations* of individuals, or of businesses or other *establishments* (Snijkers, Haraldsen, Jones, & Willimack, 2013); if the respondents are individuals, whether these are members of the general population, versus children, or professionals like physicians; and whether it involves mail, the Internet, or the telephone (see Dillman, 1978, for a guide to *survey administration mode*). With respect to any of these applications, cognitive interviewing designs make use of the two varieties of verbal reporting introduced in Chapter 2: think-aloud and verbal probing. Because think-aloud is generally accomplished simply by requesting that participants "tell me everything you are thinking as you answer the question," the demands on the cognitive interviewer are relatively light. Verbal probing, on the other hand, requires significantly more of the interviewer, given that verbal probes may take a variety of forms. Although there are a number of ways to categorize probe questions (see Willis, 2005), an example of probes that are commonly applied is shown in Table 3.1.

Table 3.2 summarizes the advantages and disadvantages of think-aloud and verbal probing, based on my earlier book (Willis, 2005).

Consider the following example of how cognitive interviewing might look, first based on a participant who is instructed to think aloud (and is good at this), and second on a participant who requires more active probing by the interviewer.

Interviewer (reading target question): In the past 12 months, have you been treated unfairly when out in public because you are [self-reported race: e.g., White, Black, Vietnamese, Asian...]?
Participant (45-year old, male, Caucasian): Let's see—the past 12 months? Well, no, not really, because—you know—I'm White, and I don't tend to be treated badly because of my race—it's not like I'm Black or Hispanic or have to worry about being thought of as a terrorist when I'm really a Sikh but they think I'm Muslim or something. There was one time I was on the bus and... I was getting on... and bumped into a Black guy who had a broken arm or... was injured or something because he said "watch out," and then something I couldn't really hear

Table 3.1
Examples of cognitive probes
1. Meaning-oriented probe: interpretation of specific terms "What, to you, is 'ethnic origin'?"
2. Paraphrase of a question "What is this question asking?"
3. Process-oriented probe "How did you arrive at your answer?"
4. Evaluative probe "Do you feel this question is easy or not easy to answer?"
5. Elaborative probes "Why do you say that?"
6. Hypothetical probe "What would it take for you to say that your health is excellent?"
7. Recall probes "What time period were you thinking about?"
Based on Pan, Wake, Chan, and Willis, 2014.

because it was noisy, but it may have been an ugly type of insult. I don't know if my race had anything to do with it... um, if he did call me a racial thing, I guess that could count as being treated unfairly. But, you know, that would be a stretch, and maybe he was just mad that I hit his arm. So it's not like I got attacked or something 'cause of my race. I guess I'll say no to that one. It just doesn't really fit my... experience or my life history, or whatever.

Consider instead how probing might be done, on the same question as earlier, in the case of a participant who is initially less verbally forthcoming and responds to probes in order to provide the same type of information as the story unfolds:

Interviewer (reading target question): In the past 12 months, have you been treated unfairly when out in public because you are [self-reported race]?
Participant: In the past 12 months? Hmm—not, not really.
Interviewer (probe): What does "treated unfairly when out in a public place" make you think of?

Table 3.2
Features of think-aloud and verbal probing

	Think-Aloud	Verbal Probing
1. Potential for interviewer-imposed bias, and reactivity	Low: The cognitive interviewer just says, "Tell me what you're thinking"	Moderate: The cognitive interviewer asks specific, targeted probes, which can be leading
2. Training requirements	Low: The interviewer doesn't need to learn much other than to keep the participant talking	High: Learning to probe requires practice and proficiency
3. Burden on the participant	High: Constant thinking aloud is difficult for many people	Moderate: Answering probe questions is not much more difficult than answering survey questions but requires some focus and attention
4. Efficiency of conduct	Low: Think alouds tend to require significant time	Moderate: The imposition of probe questions adds time to the interview, but normally less than think aloud
5. Efficiency of analysis	Low: Think-aloud data can require significant time and effort to "wade through"	Moderate: Analysis of written responses to targeted probes can be easier than poring through completely open-ended think-aloud text

Participant: Well, I guess when you're out in the street, in public. Like, I was thinking possibly of the one time that I was on the bus and maybe I was treated unfairly because of my race—I'm not sure.
Interviewer (probe): Can you tell me more about that?
Participant: Uh, let's see now... There was one time I was on the bus and... I was getting on... and bumped into this Black guy who must have had a broken arm or... injured or something

because he said "watch out," and then something I couldn't hear because it was noisy. I don't know if my race had anything to do with it...um, if he did call me a racial thing, I guess that could count as being treated unfairly. But, you know, that would be a stretch, and maybe he was just mad that I hit his arm. So it's not like I got attacked or something 'cause of my race. So I would still need to say no on this one.

Interviewer (probe): Can you remember any other times you might have been treated unfairly in that type of situation—in the past 12 months?

Participant: Well, no, not really, because—you know—I'm White, and I don't tend to be treated badly because of my race—it's not like I'm Black or Hispanic or have to worry about being thought of as a terrorist when I'm really a Sikh but people don't know that and they think I'm Muslim or something.

The example is hypothetical (though based on an amalgam of interviews conducted to evaluate a questionnaire on racial and ethnic discrimination meant for population-wide administration) and only meant to show how the same information might be obtained through either think-aloud or verbal probing. In this case, it would appear that the same basic data had been collected either way. Analysis and interpretation of these results would therefore be similar, such that the issue of think-aloud versus verbal probing would not seem to make much difference, from an analytic perspective. It would be logical to conclude from this that asking about being "treated unfairly" is vague and leaves a lot to the respondent as far as considering what is to be included or excluded. Further, this raises the fundamental problem that even if one were treated unfairly, it may not be clear whether this was due specifically to his or her race or group membership.

Sometimes, however, the use of think-aloud probing can lead to verbalizations that are somewhat more difficult to analyze. Consider the following:

Interviewer (reading target question): In the past 12 months, how many times have you gone to each of the following...A movie theater?

Participant: Oh, I love going to the movies. Today everybody just rents them and brings them home, but there's nothing like seeing it on the big screen. I mean, the screens at home are getting bigger and bigger, so yeah you can call that a big screen, but it's still not like being at the movies. It's not just that the screen is bigger, 'cause you are with a lot of other people, so it's like a big social event. Not that there's anything wrong with being home watching with your family, of course, and it's mostly just strangers and all that, but something about it is different. Of course, at home you don't have stuff like sticky floors and gum on the arms when you sit down, or you sit down and someone seven feet tall sits down in front of you and you can't see and there's nothing you can really say. What are you going to do, tell them to shrink? So you have to get up and find another seat, and maybe by then the theater is full and all that's left is the seats way up front, and then the screen really is too big, you know? So, OK, being home is better in some ways, but I still like going out to the movies.

Now consider the analysis implications of the accumulation of such verbalizations, consisting of multiple data of this type, for a number of questions, and for multiple tested individuals. Qualitative analysis of these data will surely require a lot of reading, reducing, and searching for key indicators that may be something of a needle in a haystack. This is, of course, to be expected, as it is the participant who is in the driver's seat and is deciding (by design, without much self-editing or forethought) what to say. As such, the burden on the analyst will be to separate the limited amount that is truly revealing from everything else. Although the movie theater example is something of an exaggeration, such open-ended streams of thought are fairly common and can create a challenge to both conduct and analysis of the interview.

Probing, because it is more directed by the investigator, and constrained by its hypothesis-driven nature, tends to produce not only less total verbiage to process but also a more limited and easily analyzable set of verbal utterances. Further, the data to be analyzed tend to be very different—rather than a stream of verbatim think aloud from the participant (sometimes called the "cognitive protocol"), we often rely on notes taken by the interviewer describing the participant's reactions. Because these notes depend on an element of interpretation by the interviewer, they have already transformed the original data source by one level of filtering and processing, therefore constituting the initial step in the analysis process.

Looking again at Table 3.2, though, it is because neither procedure is superior in every regard that think aloud and probing both continue to have a place in most cognitive interviewing projects (e.g., Buers et al., 2013). Keep in mind that the analysis requirements do differ between these. I will delve more into what we actually produce, as cognitive interview "data," in Chapter 4.

3.3. Procedures of Verbal Probing

3.3.1. Concurrent Versus Retrospective Probing

We apply probes either as the questions to be tested are administered, or afterward, respectively. The former is labeled *concurrent probing*, the latter *retrospective probing* (or debriefing). Often the choice of procedure will be determined by survey mode. For questionnaires that are read out loud by an interviewer (interviewer-administered questionnaire, or IAQ), it is common to conduct the cognitive interview in the same fashion—aloud— and to interject probes as one is reading the survey questions. For example:

Interviewer (reading target question): The next questions ask about work you may have done last week, either at a job or business. How many hours did you work?
Participant: Uh, about…32, I'd say.
Interviewer (probe): How did you come up with 32 hours?
Participant: Well, I normally work 40 hours in a week, but I remember that last Monday was a holiday, so I worked four days, for 8 hours a day. So, 32.
Interviewer (probe): The question asked about hours you worked. What does that mean, to you?
Participant: I think that…what you want to know is how many hours I was paid for working. Rather than, like, how many hours I was actually sitting at the computer, or…in the office. So it's not like I'm going to say, "Oh, I spent 15 minutes talking with my friend here and 10 minutes in the bathroom there"…and then trying to NOT count those things. That's not going to happen, even if you want it (laughs).

In this case, the interviewer is able to ask probe questions that simply follow up the survey question being evaluated. Many cognitive interviews proceed like this—and it normally seems natural to the participant to simply expound further on what he or she has been telling us already, as prompted by the probe questions. I have often made the case that all that is often necessary to obtain good information is for the interviewer to engage in such *elaborative* or *expansive* probing: "Tell me more about that" (Willis, 2005).

An alternative procedure is to conduct probing retrospectively, after the main interview has been completed—that is, subsequent to the administration of all the target questions. This is also commonly labeled *debriefing*, which has a well-established history in qualitative research (e.g., Leech & Onwuegbuzie, 2008, describe six types of debriefing). The exchange between cognitive interviewer and participant would differ from that shown earlier, in that, by the time of the debriefing, a number of other survey questions would have intervened prior to the probes being asked. Thus, probing would need to take one of two forms:

Variant A (Unreminded)
Interviewer: I also asked you the question [re-read working question]. Do you remember how you answered that one?
Participant: Uh, sure—I said 32 hours.
Interviewer: How did you come up with that?

Variant B (Reminded)
Interviewer: I also asked you the question [re-read working question]. You said 32 hours. Do you remember how you came up with that?

The interview could presumably proceed just as for the concurrently-probed example shown. Note that the major departure concerns the need, in the retrospective interview, for the interviewer to engage in some reconstruction of the prior exchange. It is necessary to "rewind" to that question—and then to induce the participant to recreate the initial response to that question—and finally, to probe as if conducting a concurrent interview, but expecting to have put the individual back into the mental state that existed at the time he or she first answered. Somewhat parenthetically, I have described both *unreminded* and *reminded* forms of retrospective probing, even though there is little uniformity in practice in this regard, scarce evidence concerning the effects of this variation, and virtually no discussion of this variation in the literature on cognitive techniques. However, for current purposes—again focusing on analysis, this can make a difference because the unreminded approach affords an additional potential source of information, relative to the reminded: To what extent could the participant even recall his or her previous answer? Again, I note this to illustrate how modifications in procedure must necessarily be reflected in variation in analysis procedures, once we get to the details concerning those practices.

Returning to the comparison of concurrent versus retrospective probing, note the additional demands on memory that the retrospective approach makes—we are expecting interviewed individuals to not only know how they answered the question but also to remember what they were thinking at that time. What if the participant has forgotten either of these, in the intervening period, due to the passage of time or due to interference from other question-answering behaviors? Again, we can easily address the first problem, by providing a reminder (although if he or she cannot remember, one may wonder about the usefulness of asking, further, how he or she arrived at that answer!). What we are not allowed to do, however, is to provide any hints or reminders concerning how to answer our probe questions—as this information is, after all, what we are seeking from the participant.

So, if the participant cannot remember when asked, "How did you come up with the answer to Question X?"), then she can tell us so ("I have no idea"), which would be disappointing but perfectly understandable. Worse, however, is if she does not remember what she was thinking but still decides to tell us something that seems reasonable and potentially helpful. Unfortunately, though, what we end up with is a fabrication, as opposed to a veridical recounting of the thought processes associated with answering the survey question. Most distressing, there is *no clear way that we can tell this through any analysis technique that can be applied.* I make this point to again tie the process of procedure to that of analysis and to suggest that analysis cannot fix that which was flawed from the start. The common mantra of "garbage in, garbage out" is something to always keep in mind when choosing and applying any analytic procedure. Again, there is nothing about this observation that is unique to cognitive interviewing or to qualitative research generally. If a quantitative measure is incorrect (e.g., a "5" when the correct value is "20"), there is, of course, no way that a statistical program could reveal this, either.

3.3.1.1. Retrospective Probing in Self-Administered Questionnaires

A major reason for conducting retrospective interviews is that this seems especially well suited for self-administered questionnaires, where the respondent will ultimately be interacting only with the survey instrument (by reading questions and then answering them). In such cases, one can legitimately ask whether it is appropriate for the cognitive interviewer to interrupt the participant with probe questions during self-administration. Rather, it may be better to leave the participant alone and to probe by going back through the questionnaire. The available empirical evidence suggests that interjecting probe questions can have at least one undesirable effect: Bates and DeMaio (1989) found that doing so interfered with the ability of participants with low educational level to follow sequencing instructions (skip patterns). Partly for this reason, I find it very useful to conduct retrospectively probed interviews when the mode of instrument administration is self-completion; or, to rely on a hybrid approach, in which retrospective probing is done after each section of a multi-part questionnaire.

3.3.1.2. Reactivity Effects

A further reason for selecting retrospective debriefing is a supposed drawback of concurrent probing—the production of *reactivity effects*. Reactivity refers to the reaction of the participant being probed—and how probing may serve to alter that person's behavior later within the cognitive interview. If someone comes to find that he is being probed after every question, this could certainly have some influence on the care he puts into answering, relative to the completely unprobed (i.e., field) interview. Retrospective probing does avoid this potential drawback. Ultimately, however, neither technique is perfect; thus, the cognitive interviewer must make compromises when selecting his or her preferred procedure and weigh the relative dangers of fabrication, reactivity, or other problematic outcomes. I discuss these procedures, with their relative merits and drawbacks, in much detail elsewhere (Willis, 2005), and I will only summarize these here (Table 3.3).

Table 3.3
Advantages and disadvantages of concurrent versus retrospective probing

	Concurrent	**Retrospective**
1. Degree of adherence to normal conditions of answering survey questions	Low: Interjecting probes during the interview significantly alters the flow of asking and answering the survey questions, relative to a "regular" unprobed interview	High: Because probing is only done after the interview, there is no disruption of the normal flow of ask and answer
2. "Freshness" of relevant thoughts, at the time that probes are asked	High: Because the probe is asked immediately after the participant has answered the question, the relevant cognitions should still be available	Low: Probes are asked at the end of the interview—it is unclear that the participant will still remember the cognitive processes that were operating as each evaluated question was answered
3. Ease of administration of the probes	High: Asking the probe is a natural follow-up to obtaining the answer to the evaluated question (i.e., "Why did you say that?")	Medium: Revisiting questions asked earlier generally requires more reconstruction of context and more words: e.g., When I asked this question, you said X. Why did you say that?
4. Ease of focusing on the questionnaire as a whole	Low: Concurrent debriefing lends itself to specific attention to the individual question level	High: Debriefing lends itself to a global review of the questionnaire, rather than attention to the individual questions

3.4. Critical Issues in the Conduct of Cognitive Interviewing

Besides covering the major procedural variants—think-aloud versus verbal probing and concurrent versus retrospective probing—it is also necessary to defer coverage of analysis procedures, per se, to consider several other issues concerning the conduct of cognitive interviewing that (a) vary considerably in practice, (b) are contentious, and (c) have major implications for analysis. These are as follows:

> Issue 1: How standardized versus free-form probes should be
> Issue 2: The number of cognitive interviews to be conducted
> Issue 3: Whether the interviews should be conducted in one block or as iterative rounds

Again, I will consider these in turn and propose some implications for analysis.

3.4.1. Issue 1: How Standardized Should Probes Be?

One view is that probes should be scripted, and standardized, just like survey questions. This serves to reduce interviewer variation and to allow maximum control by the investigator. The alternative view is that probing should be free, flexible, and unscripted, to allow the interviewer latitude in adapting probes to the situation at hand. For a variety of reasons I prefer a hybrid approach that provides scripted ("anticipated") probes initially but that allows (trained) interviewers to deviate from the script (see Napoles-Springer et al., 2006, as an example). For current purposes, what is essential to consider is that the analysis of probes that depart from a strict standardized approach can create some difficulty. If the probe questions differ, both across participants and interviewers, how can the responses be analyzed as a coherent set? I think the brief answer is that the nature of qualitative research makes analysis possible, as the objective is not to produce cookie-cutter responses to standard stimuli but to enable our participants to provide rich elaborated information in the form of thoughts, comments, explanations, and reflections. Our intent is not to constrain the data we obtain from our participants, by constraining the probes we ask them. Rather, our challenge consists of effectively controlling this purposive variation in our data, in terms of how they can be reduced and what they tell us.

3.4.1.1. Embedded Probing and Web Probing

There is one special case in which cognitive probes are of necessity structured: where *embedded probes* (Converse & Presser, 1986) or *random probes* (Schuman, 1966) are placed within a fielded questionnaire, such that probes are administered by a production survey interviewer as opposed to a trained cognitive interviewer. For example, Schuman (1966) included the probe "Can you tell me a little bit more about what you mean?" and instructed interviewers to enter open-ended responses. A more recent development of this concept involves the use of *Web (or Internet) probing* (Behr, Braun, Kaczmirek, & Bandilla, 2013, 2014), where the embedded probes are self-completed by respondents who type in their open-ended answers. Due to the self-administered nature of the task, there is no interviewer involved at all, let alone a cognitive interviewer. For example, Behr et al. (2014) included a Web probe to assess item comprehension ("What ideas do you associate with the phrase *civil disobedience*? Please give examples"), accompanied by an open text box into which the survey respondent could enter his or her ideas.

Although this procedure is cost effective and many responses can be quickly gathered, Behr et al. (2014) note limitations: (a) only a few target items can normally be included (it is not feasible to test an entire questionnaire); (b) standardization of the probes presents the problems I noted earlier, and respondents do not always directly answer the probe presented; and (c) there is no opportunity for follow-up probing, beyond the initial embedded probe. However, as a supplement to more traditional cognitive testing, initial investigations by Behr and her colleagues, and by Murphy, Edgar, and Keating (2014), have found Web probing to be promising in some situations.

3.4.2. Issue 2: How Many Interviews Should We Conduct?

No matter how they are done, another vital—and unsettled—issue concerns the number of cognitive interviews, or sample size. This issue is germane to both conducting the cognitive interview and in analyzing our data, so I will address the former activity now and the latter in Chapter 5. Determining the number of interviews to complete can be a more difficult question than in the case of purely quantitative research, where statistical power analysis can be conducted based on an assessment of effect size. Within qualitative research there are few metrics that directly govern "how many is enough." There are several approaches to answering this question:

(a) *Do what you can.* This is the practical option and is reflective of what Emmel (2013) labels the *realist* approach to qualitative testing generally. The notion is that *any* testing is better than *no* testing, so we simply conduct as many interviews as our resources allow and discover what we can. So there are cases in which just a few interviews are able to be done, and for various reasons related to US federal regulations, many investigations have been conducted with exactly nine individuals.

(b) *The classical qualitative approach: saturation.* The notion of *saturation* is key to qualitative research: Rather than setting an initial sample requirement, sample size becomes an empirical matter, such that we continue to test until no additional meaningful results are obtained (Emmel, 2013). A modification was provided by Sudman (1976), who proposed that saturation exists when additional interviews are no longer cost effective—rather than bereft of *any* benefit. In either case, this approach departs markedly from the practice of simply conducting however many interviews we can, given available resources. A vital question to cognitive interviewers is, of course: How many interviews do we need to do in order to achieve saturation? If this number is small—and especially if in the realm of the 20–30 interviews that are sometimes recommended (Willis, 2005), then this would present no particular obstacle. If, on the other hand, saturation is not achieved until literally hundreds of interviews have been conducted, then the requirement that we saturate would be truly daunting.

In fact, empirical demonstrations vary markedly: In a study conducted with the aim of studying sample sizes in cognitive interviewing, Blair and Conrad (2011) chronicled the emergence of question flaws as more interviews were conducted and found that problem production followed an increasing trend that did not abate even after 90 interviews had been completed. On the other hand, O'Brien, Bereket, Swinton, and Solomon (2013), relying on established methods from qualitative research, reported achieving saturation after 22 interviews, when evaluating an HIV Disability questionnaire; and Guest, Bunce, and Johnson (2006) concluded that 12 interviews was sufficient for saturating results, in an in-depth qualitative investigation involving women in West Africa.

It is likely that there is no specific number of interviews that provides saturation but that this likely depends heavily on several factors, including the following:

1. The nature of the questionnaire tested (an omnibus survey containing disparate topics may require substantially more interviews to saturate than one on a single, well-defined topic)
2. The variety of participants involved in the evaluation (a homogenous group would likely reach saturation more quickly than a very heterogeneous one)
3. The precise definition of "saturation" used, and procedure for establishing that saturation has been achieved (in particular, the number of instances of additional interviews that produce no new substantive findings need be completed, before we "stop the presses").

(c) *The quantitative-statistical approach.* The final means by which to establish sample size is to conduct a relatively large number of interviews, as for a quantitative study, based on some established method such as statistical power analysis (or even "rule of thumb"). Researchers may have learned rules such as "30 subjects per condition" for an experimental comparison and consider this to be a rough index that can be used—for example, by including 30 in each of several demographic groups to be contrasted for a cognitive testing study. Further, Blair (2011) describes an approach to cognitive testing that involves the explicit use of experimental versions of target items—that is, where probing is applied to assess the functioning of question variants, in parallel. The use of multiple question versions necessarily increases the sample needed in order to make meaningful comparisons between versions, as it would in the case of a purely quantitative experimental design.

Which approach is better? A reasonable response may simply be that "more is better"—and that, of course, we will learn more from doing more interviews. But this is often unrealistic because we may not have enough money, interviewers, or time to do extensive testing. Further, a large project involving many interviews may seem preferable, but not if it ends up being underanalyzed, such that the apparent superiority of conducting more interviews is negated by the failure to conduct an appropriately intensive analysis. Given a set level of resources, it would in most cases be better to conduct 20 interviews that are analyzed fully than 50 that receive only a cursory review (the appropriate term, based on a concept developed by Simon [1956] would be *analysis satisficing*—or doing just enough to fulfill nominal task requirements). Remember that unlike quantitative analysis, we cannot just quickly aggregate the data points—qualitative analysis requires intensive work, and we need to take this into account in deciding what we can accomplish.

What are we attempting to achieve? Reparative versus Descriptive objectives. As a final thought on this topic, I argue that the determination of sample size depends fundamentally on our objectives and, in particular, whether the investigation is intended to be Reparative or Descriptive. If the objective is mainly to iron out severe problems prior to fielding, it might be valuable to conduct even a small number of interviews in an attempt to identify major defects. There is evidence that an empirical experience with a single individual can lead to insights or discoveries that lead to target question revision (Willis, 2005). As one personal example, I once evaluated a questionnaire for breast cancer survivors using perhaps the most minimalistic approach possible—locating three survivors from among staff epidemiologists and quickly evaluating the items. The most salient discovery was that an item asking whether "you are afraid the cancer will return" is inappropriate until after the initial course of treatment has been successfully completed, as evidenced by one woman's animated response that "*I don't even know if the (expletive deleted) cancer is gone, and you're asking me about it returning later!?*"

Findings such as this seem definitive enough that they demand action, and serve as strong apparent justification for having conducted the few interviews that were possible—even when analysis consists mainly of making on-the-spot decisions. On the other hand, it would be extremely difficult to argue that such a process resulted in a comprehensive evaluation of the target items. For an investigation focused on the goal of complete description of what the items conceptually measure, especially across multiple demographic or cultural groups, a completely different approach relying on larger samples would be called for, sufficient for testing until saturation of findings had been achieved within each group.

3.4.3. Issue 3: Should Interviewing Be Done in Iterative Rounds?

A final issue concerning conduct of cognitive interviews is whether the investigation is to incorporate iterative testing. Consistent with the *iterative* nature of qualitative research—which is often described as a core feature of that discipline (Boeije, 2010)—cognitive interviewing is often conducted as a series of interview *rounds*. A frequent approach, within a Reparative investigation, has been to (a) conduct between 8 and 12 interviews, (b) stop to assess results and conduct preliminary analysis, (c) make modifications to the target questions, and (d) continue with an additional round of testing, assessment, and revision (Figure 3.1). Note that at some point the researcher must break out of this cycle, by deciding that enough testing has been accomplished.

Consistent with well-established practices of qualitative interviewing, it may also be advisable to conduct Descriptive research as an iterative procedure. In this case, iterative rounds do not vary in terms of the materials tested, as the survey questions are not generally modified between rounds. Rather, iteration may be done with respect to probing procedures, and perhaps even in such a way that participant recruitment criteria are altered prior to the subsequent round (referred to as *theoretical sampling*; Emmel, 2013; Glaser & Strauss, 1967).

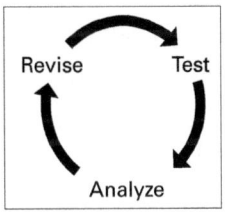

Figure 3.1. Iterative sequence consisting of testing, analyzing, revising, and then testing once again.

Because cognitive interviewing has largely been iterative in nature, it is worthwhile to consider the validity of this cyclical process, especially given that it departs from the procedure that researchers are often taught: to collect the largest amount of data possible, and only then submitting it to statistical analysis. The overall point to iteration is that something is changing through the course of the investigation—a heretical notion in the realm of much purely quantitative, experimental research (where the only variation throughout the entire study should be with respect to the value of the independent variable being studied).

I argue that iteration is not unique to cognitive testing, but it has had a critical role throughout the history of science. Further, I propose that the major difference between so-called quantitative and qualitative research approaches largely rests on this distinction. Contrary to common definition, the major difference between these approaches is not that numbers are used in one and words in the other. Rather, the salient departure between quantitative and qualitative research can largely be viewed in terms of the distinction between *frequentist* and *Bayesian* approaches to data collection and analysis. The frequentist approach advocates the collection of a large amount of data prior to analysis, whereas the Bayesian approach relies on the modification of our viewpoint through successive waves of data collection, with analysis at each collection point (Carlin & Louis, 2009). In essence, cognitive interviewing is consistent with Bayesian logic, whereas standard statistical approaches are frequentist in nature. The Bayesian approach seems consistent with the way that learning occurs in naturalistic circumstances (as Piaget discovered), where we are constantly taking in information and attempting to learn from it, and changing our conclusions as new thinking supersedes the old (i.e., accommodating). Further, as I will elaborate upon later, this description is entirely consistent with the *constant comparison method (CCM)* developed by qualitative researchers (Boeije, 2002; Emmel, 2013; Glaser & Strauss, 1967).

3.4.3.1. Iteration and Analysis

I have labored to defend the use of the iterative approach, mainly because this does need to be defensible, given the trouble and complications it introduces into our analysis. In essence, we must deal with a moving target—if the evaluated survey item is changing throughout the course of the investigation, analysis of the results will need to incorporate that fact. Further, *data collection and analysis are no longer cleanly separated* but are confounded: When items are modified between testing rounds, this is not the result (we hope) of some random process but of the consideration of what the just-completed round has told us, in terms of what we have found (inspection) and what we should then do (repair). In other words, analysis has already been conducted between each round.

Hence, iterative testing of the questions imposes the requirement that our best efforts toward analysis be focused not only at the end of the investigation—when we are back in the office and may have time to conduct analysis—but throughout the entire course of cognitive testing. Miles and Huberman (1984, p. 15) describe an approach to qualitative research that sometimes applies to anthropological studies, in which we are first "in the field" collecting data, and following this step, "It may take from many months to several years to complete a thoughtful analysis." A cognitive interviewer in full Reparative, production mode, who is given a month to test and develop a questionnaire, and who must then provide recommendations for a final version in another week, does not have those months or years. Iterative testing therefore puts severe demands on analysis—such that whatever procedure is used must necessarily be implementable in a short time frame and involve limited staff and the implementation of fairly simple procedures as data are still being collected.

Descriptive research, on the other hand, might take a frequentist approach, as it affords the opportunity to first collect all the data, and then to take one's time to fully and painstaking analyze every interview, in its full qualitative glory. So, although the choice of whether and how to conduct iterative rounds may be dependent on multiple factors, I emphasize elements relevant to the testing objective and the associated time and resources required. If one is pressed for time, it is generally not advisable to incorporate an analytically intensive strategy that requires ceasing data collection for a lengthy period, especially within an iterative testing process.

3.5. Interviewing Logistics: Cognitive *Interviewing* Versus Cognitive *Testing*

Although the terms *cognitive interviewing* and *cognitive testing* are often used synonymously, they differ in one important respect. The former concerns the mechanics of conducting the interviewing process, via think-aloud and verbal probing techniques, and constitutes the bulk of what I covered earlier in this chapter. The latter term pertains to the testing process more generally, and includes the full gamut of activities necessary to conduct a cognitive interview project, including interviewer selection and training, participant recruitment, development and formatting of interview guides and forms, obtaining approval from an institutional review board or other body related to research ethics, and so on. Because this book focuses mainly on analysis, I will not attempt to describe these practices in detail. However, because they are vital to the conduct of the interviewing enterprise, I refer readers to my earlier volume (Willis, 2005) and to a newly released guide that covers these elements (Collins, 2015).

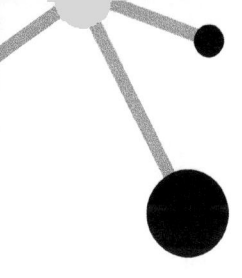

4

ANALYSIS STRATEGIES FOR THE COGNITIVE INTERVIEW

> *Qualitative analysis transforms data into findings. No formula exists for that transformation. Guidance, yes. But no recipe.*
>
> Adams, Khan, Raeside, and White (2007, p. 321)

4.1. Chapter Overview

In one sense, Chapters 1–3 were a warm-up for the key chapter on analysis, which is the core of this book. In this chapter I endeavor to (a) define what I mean by "analysis," in terms of its key components; (b) consider how various qualitative research traditions have implications regarding analysis; and then (c) present five analysis models applicable to cognitive testing results, with a discussion of the benefits and costs of each, as well as the context in which each may be most useful. These models are referred to as follows:

1. Text Summary
2. Cognitive coding

3. Question Feature Coding
4. Theme coding
5. Pattern Coding

I make no attempt to select an optimal analysis model, but rather present these as tools to be selected based on an assessment of the requirements of the investigation and on the fundamental attributes of each model.

4.2. Defining "Analysis"

The term "analysis" is classically vague, in that it means different things to different people. I define analysis as the series of steps that occur between data collection and the communication of what we have found. I therefore distinguish the sequential steps in the analysis continuum, as shown in Table 4.1.

These key steps can vary markedly in terms of how much attention is devoted to each (Sandelowski & Barroso, 2003) and in the specific methods applied. In the sections that follow, I will cover in some depth the way in which alternative analysis models differ with respect to Steps 2–4. However, given that these rely on a common set of data elements as input, I will first examine the fundamental step concerning the production of these data, and in particular, the *definition of the data unit that we endeavor to analyze*.

Table 4.1
Steps in the analysis sequence

Step 1. Definition of the *data* to be analyzed: What is the unit of analysis?
Step 2. Procedures for *processing* the data: How are these reduced into some type of summary of results that is informative?
Step 3. *Interpreting* results: How do we determine what our now-processed data tell us that is relevant to our research objectives?
Step 4. *Reporting* results: Although not technically "analysis"—this is closely tied to it.

4.3. Cognitive Interview Data: "Notes Versus Quotes"

At the outset of analysis, we need to answer the question: What are the data from the cognitive interview? To reiterate the introduction to this book, there are generally two forms of data, both of which are mainly in the form of words, as opposed to numbers: (a) original verbalizations by participants; and (b) interviewers' written notes from the individual cognitive interviews. Conrad, Blair, and Tracy (2000) entitled an article "Verbal Reports Are Data!"—and although it may not have been their main intent, their chosen title is suitable for making the case that we must look to the words that participants themselves have used—whether original transcriptions or by listening to recordings. That is, the data to be analyzed originate as the verbal reports or verbatim statements that our participants have provided and that were labeled by Ericsson and Simon (1980) as the *verbal protocol*.

Although this seems completely logical, from the perspective of classical qualitative research there is no clear requirement that these original words must necessarily comprise our raw data. Rather, anthropologists in particular make use of ethnographic field notes, which may contain verbatim quotes but also summarize their observations in the words of the researcher, as the first analysis step. It is these observations by the researcher that then become the data that are processed further. The analogous case within the world of cognitive testing would be for interviewers to write notes or otherwise make observations as they conduct the interview and to use these notes as the basic unit of analysis. Of course, they might supplement these notes by reviewing recordings or reading transcripts, but it is the *interviewer notes* that are regarded as the initial data unit. Many cognitive interviewing projects have relied upon such notes, especially because they are relatively quick and efficient to produce and obviate the need to completely review a recording of the entire interview.

Do we need to transcribe interviews, or at least listen to them again? The most comprehensive way to make sure we are relying on the participant's own words when commencing analysis– whether producing interviewer notes or verbatim quotes—is to work from a written transcription of the audio recording. Cognitive interviewers sometimes do transcribe every comment made (e.g., Napoles-Springer et al., 2006; O'Brien et al., 2013).

However, based on personal experience in working through the analysis of many cognitive interviews, I believe that transcription is usually unnecessary, and in some ways may even be insufficient, as it (normally) omits references to body language and other nonverbal cues. Short of transcribing, one might at least decide to listen to the recording of the entire interview. Although it is useful to listen again to every interview, and to take into account nonverbal cues by watching the video recording, this practice does require as much time as the original live interview and may increase costs unacceptably. A compromise would be to review only segments of the interview for which the original notes are unclear or where the interaction between interviewer and respondent was complex.

Because cognitive interviewers do frequently rely largely on interviewer notes that represent descriptions of what transpired during interviews, as opposed to a verbatim record of the exchange, analysis has already begun, at the time of data collection, given the interpretive nature of these notes. Acknowledging the importance of the quality of these notes, the next question that naturally arises is how to produce them in a way that they do reflect what occurred in the interview. Because this has not been well detailed and is a source of variation across practitioners, I describe several avenues, in Table 4.2, and suggest the strengths and limitations of each.

Besides considering resource requirements, another means for deciding the extent to which we rely on verbatim quotes versus notes, and exactly how to take the notes, is to consider what the analyst is going to do with these data. This is the topic of the next sections, which concern the second and third analysis steps: *processing* and *interpretation*.

4.4. Models of the Analysis of Cognitive Interviewing

All variants of cognitive interviewing analysis approaches make use of the data definition and production step described earlier. However, these approaches differ significantly in terms of how one summarizes and interprets those data. Figure 4.1 represents the results of my own qualitative analysis of qualitative approaches to analyzing cognitive interviewing results, based on a review of many cognitive testing reports and publications. This model consists of a tree diagram that organizes five specific approaches,

Table 4.2
Note-taking procedures in the cognitive interview

Procedure	Pros	Cons
(1) *Interviewer as note taker*: The cognitive interviewer takes written notes (live and/or through review of recording)	Quick and cost-effective	Interviewer may not take comprehensive notes due to demands of interviewing and note taking
(2) *Interviewer and observer as note takers*: The cognitive interviewer takes written notes, as does one or more collaborators who observe the interview (live and/or recording)	Provides "back-up" information by using a second analyst (i.e., assessment of interobserver reliability)	More resource intensive and time consuming than (1)
(3) *Observer as note taker*: The Observer(s) take notes; the cognitive interviewer only administers the cognitive probes	Interviewer can focus on conducting the interview, rather than on taking notes	May miss an opportunity to make use of the interviewer's written insights; may be difficult to coordinate probing and note taking, especially if both are done live

which I will describe in turn. Each relies on the raw data consisting of both (a) literal responses to target questions—for example, "excellent" (health); and (b) cognitive interview data consisting of interviewer notes and quotes (or, less frequently, verbatim transcripts). I end by discussing the relative strengths and limitations of each of the five approaches.

As a caveat, note that the flowchart is intended as a heuristic guide to clarify major differences in approaches and to guide selection of analysis procedures, rather than as a comprehensive or precise assemblage akin to the Periodic Table of the Chemical

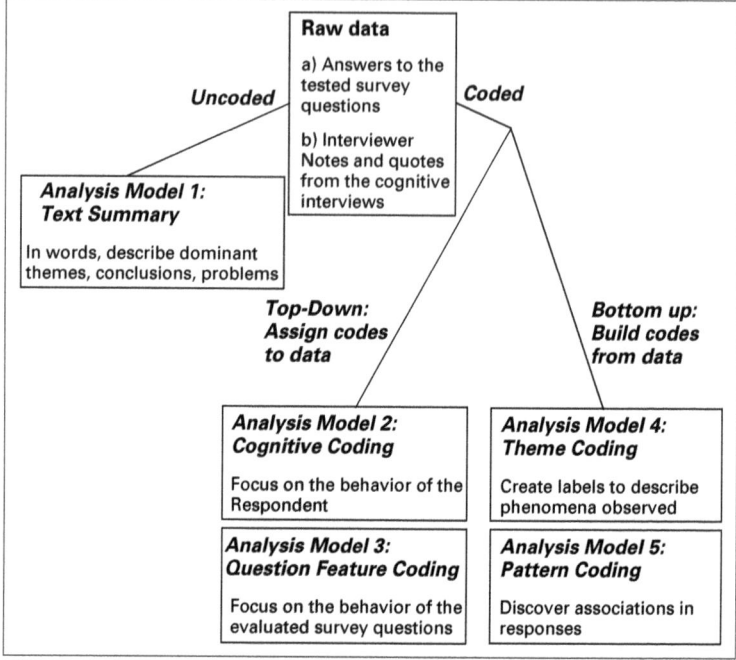

Figure 4.1. Five analysis models for cognitive interviews.

Elements. The basic models described are flexible, overlapping, and can be applied in imaginative ways that cross the somewhat artificial boundaries I describe. Motivated practitioners can (and should) produce variants or hybrids that borrow elements from each of these five basic skeletal representations, and in fact I will describe several.

4.5. Analysis Model 1: Text Summary

Put simply, the *Text Summary* involves the description of dominant themes, conclusions, and problems that are evidenced within a set of aggregated interviewer notes. Text summaries can exist at multiple levels: Where this distinction is critical, I will refer to an *Interviewer Text Summary* as the compilation of notes from one cognitive interviewer; and to a *Project Text Summary* where aggregation has been accomplished across all interviewers within a cognitive testing project. The Text Summary approach has dominated the practice of summarizing cognitive testing results, although it carries several labels: Sometimes this is simply known as "writing up the notes" (Fowler et al., 2013); is referred to by Izumi, Vandermause, and Benavides-Vaello (2013) as "summarized subjects' responses to each item"; and has been labeled "interaction analysis" (IA) by Napoles-Springer et al. (2006). The parallel term within the qualitative research literature, and which has served as an extension to the realm of cognitive interviewing by Miller et al. (2014) and by Chepp and Gray (2014), is *narrative summary*. However, despite the historical basis for usage of that term, I have selected "Text Summary" as the most general label, as a "narrative" is by definition a story, and text-based data from cognitive interviews consist not only of stories (which are represented by Tulving's [1972] notion of episodic memory) but also of facts and other forms of semantic memory. Further, the term "narrative" often refers to the verbatim story provided by each research participant, whereas "Text Summary" refers to aggregated comments of the cognitive interviewer(s).

By whatever name, text summarization attempts to identify consistent themes, as expressed in words. Text summaries parallel the practice of ethnography, where, as Boeije (2010) explains, extensive use is made of field notes. As an example, see Table 4.3.

In this case, the summaries created from interview notes are extremely brief and cover only the most salient elements. Text summaries may, however, contain much more detail, as in the following Interviewer Text Summary:

Across my four interviews, the term "health in general" simply meant physical health, and whether the participant had any kind of serious, chronic medical condition. One (45-year-old man) responded that his health is "excellent" because he does not have hypertension, heart disease, cancer, etc.—so he was talking in terms of absence of any health problems. A second (28-year-old man) said his health was "very good," because he is a runner and is in good shape. However, his health isn't Very Good or Excellent because he has been injured and is not quite in the shape he used to be. Further, a 70-year-old man said his health was "fair," because he has had ongoing trouble with a hip replacement that has gotten infected. Finally, another 85-year-old said "excellent" because "I got up this morning!" So overall, they seemed to be talking about

Table 4.3
Results of cognitive testing of the Health Information National Trends Survey (HINTS)

Evaluated (target) survey question:
Below are some ways people use the Internet. Some people have done these things, but other people have not. Please tell us whether or not you have done each of these things while using the Internet in the past 12 months:

- a. *Looked for information about quitting smoking?*
- b. *Bought medicine or vitamins online?*
- c. *Participated in an online support group for people with a similar health or medical issue?*
- d. *Used e-mail or the Internet to communicate with a doctor or a doctor's office?*
- e. *Used a Web site to help you with your diet, weight, or physical activity?*
- f. *Looked for a health care provider?*
- g. *Downloaded to a mobile device, such as an MP3 player, cell phone, tablet computer, or electronic book device?*
- h. *Visited a "social networking" site, such as "Facebook" or "LinkedIn"?*
- i. *Wrote in an online diary or "blog" (i.e., Web log)?*

Project Text Summary from interview notes:
1. Four participants expressed confusion whether subitems g–i only included that use for health-related reasons.
2. Two participants felt that the sentence "Some people have done these things but other people have not" was unnecessary.

Recommendations for question modification:
1. If g–i are not specifically limited to those uses related to health, then put these into a follow-up, separate item.
2. If they are intended to cover these uses just for health-related topics, the wording should be changed to state that.

Source: Adapted from Hicks and Cantor, 2011.

physical health, as none mentioned mood or feelings. If we want to get at the latter element, we may need to ask that more directly.

As another issue, I note that ratings of health tend to be relative—in particular, to age—rather than absolute. A young runner may define his health as "good" due to an injury, whereas an octogenarian may regard his health as "excellent" simply because he's still alive. If we want to "control" for the age factor, we might instead ask, "Compared to other people your age, would you say your health is Excellent... Poor?"

Note that both of the preceding examples make reference to the intent and measurement objectives of the investigator (both reflect the common situation in which the cognitive interviewers work for a client or research investigator). Under this analysis model, cognitive interviewing typically focuses on pretesting items in order to potentially modify them, according to a Reparative framework. As I have emphasized, the analytical methods invoked involve not only the participant's viewpoint but also that of the investigator, directly and by design. We conduct an analysis to determine the degree of overlap between two perspectives: (a) the investigator's intent and (b) the observed function of the items from the respondent point of view—as in the health insurance example of Chapter 1—to assess degree of common understanding.

A Venn diagram (Figure 4.2) illustrates this fundamental principle. Area A consists of the question objectives, or the researcher's conception of what the question means, and Area B is the set of respondent interpretations—or how the survey respondent conceptualizes the survey question. The overlap area (C) is shared meaning—anything outside of that is of necessity considered a

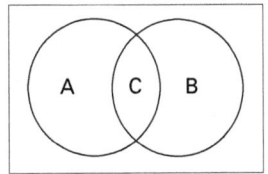

Figure 4.2. Venn diagram illustrating overlap of the Researcher's interpretation (A); the Respondent's interpretation (B); and the overlap between these (C).

"problem" with the question. This model explicitly encompasses the inspect-and-repair perspective I introduced in Chapter 2: Our approach to both the conduct of the interview and to analysis *is to focus on interpretation concerning this overlap*. We go into the testing process knowing what we believe the questions to mean (A) and then examine how closely the participants' perspectives (B) overlap with this. Based on verbal report methods, we determine whether we have attained a meeting of the minds, at the initial step of comprehension and communication. If not, we may modify the question, and test again, with the ultimate objective of cognitive testing to maximize the size of C, so that ideally the circles overlap completely.

This simple two-circle Venn diagram also serves to bring out another feature of the typical Reparative approach: We often pay much less attention to commenting on the (nonproblematic) area of overlap in C than we do to the (problematic) areas in A and B. To the extent that our attention and focus is on reconciling differences between A and B, these areas of overlap failure receive the lion's share of attention—we do not much worry about *why* there is agreement, as our concern, rather, is with why there is *failure* of agreement. This may explain why cognitive interviewers using a Text Summary approach have often been content to report within cognitive testing reports that "No problems with the question were found"—that there is in their estimation sufficient agreement, so there is no problem to resolve (i.e., we have completely merged A and B, and are left only with C).

The habit of simply stating "No problem was found" has been attacked as wholly insufficient (Miller et al, 2011; Ridolfo & Schoua-Glusberg, 2011), but I believe that those authors are viewing the cognitive interview according to a somewhat different (Descriptive) model. To the degree that we understand the objective of the item from the researcher's point of view, and consider the purpose of cognitive testing as creating survey items that convey that interpretation to survey respondents, it may make sense to pay more attention to areas of concern. In the interest of efficiency, we do not dwell on areas that have passed inspection (we do not care why they have—just that they have) and instead turn toward those that have failed the inspection. The Text Summary approach is well suited to this goal, as we can simply describe the areas that fail to overlap between ourselves and our participants.

Further, because we are not focused on gaining a full explanation concerning exactly how the question functions in all cases (e.g., where there is agreement), this also limits the amount of text produced to a manageable level.

As an example of this reasoning, consider the following target item and Text Summary based on cognitive testing:

> *Target item: The first time a doctor prescribes a drug for you, how often do you read the information leaflet that comes with the drugs? [Always/Often/ Sometimes/Rarely/Never]*
>
> *Text Summary*: Eleven of 27 respondents incorrectly defined the information leaflet, with 8 thinking it was the page the pharmacist stapled to the bag of prescriptions.
>
> *Recommendation*: Rephrase to say: *"The next few questions ask about the information leaflet that comes with prescribed drugs and medical devices. The information leaflet is the piece of folded paper inside the bottle or box."*

The cognitive interviewers focused on the failure of communication between the investigator and the respondent. The suggested repair attempts a meeting of the minds that reduces this conceptual distance. This simple example captures a wide range of typical cognitive interviewing results.

4.5.1. Beyond Failures to Communicate

The preceding discussion has cited comprehension, and shared understanding, as the cognitive process of interest. One can reasonably ask: To the extent that one does rely on cognitive theory, where are the other cognitive processes from the Tourangeau model described in Chapter 2: recall, decision, and response? A focus only on comprehension would seem to ignore critical elements of the survey response process model. In fact, under the Text Summary approach we do not necessarily limit ourselves to a consideration only of problems related to question meaning, interpretation, and communication. As a follow-up to determining whether the participants and investigators are in agreement concerning question meaning, we can then turn to the other key cognitive issues—whether participants can in fact recall the required information, enact the correct decision processes, and produce responses that are of the type we desire.

As an example of a retrieval problem, consider the following:

Target item: During the past 10 years, have you had a tetanus shot?

Text Summary: Everyone I interviewed could describe what a tetanus shot is and what it is for. But this is a very difficult question to answer—participants simply did not remember the last time they had a tetanus shot, even when they appeared sure they have gotten one, sometimes multiple times (most often after an injury that produced a deep cut). It is unclear that there is any way that we could rephrase the question to improve memory, unless we can drastically shorten the reference period—given that they understand the intent but simply cannot remember the last time they received the shot. It may be that we cannot expect to get accurate information with this long a timeframe, for an event that seems not to be "date encoded."

As opposed to retrieval processes, our summary may also describe problems related to the chosen response categories. For instance, testing of a tobacco survey across multiple language groups produced a common reaction (Willis et al., 2008):

Target item: How soon after you wake up do you typically smoke your first cigarette of the day? DO NOT READ: [ ] minutes [ ] hours

Text Summary: Because this is interviewer administered, and the respondent does not know he or she is supposed to report in minutes and hours, this tended to produce answers like "As soon as I open my eyes" or "before breakfast." If we want to force the type of answer we want, we have to say something like "How many minutes or hours after you wake up..." Or, if that is biasing, we can ask the question as it is but include a probe for the interviewer to use as necessary: "And how long would you say that is, after you wake up?"

Sometimes the Text Summary may make reference to multiple cognitive processes. Consider a further example of a question designed for young adult respondents (from Willis, 2005). Here the problem identified through cognitive testing is again not related only to interpretation or communication of the question intent but relates also to decision processes and to the mapping of the response to the required categories (i.e., the Response process within the Tourangeau model):

> *Target item: Do you think young people who smoke cigarettes have more friends?*
>
> a. Definitely yes
> b. Probably yes
> c. Probably not
> d. Definitely not
>
> *Text Summary*: The response categories produced consistent, major problems. Respondents tended to believe that "smoking makes no difference" in terms of the number of friends one has, and that none of the given categories adequately captured this opinion (very reasonably, they believed that a *not* response implied that smokers had fewer friends). The question might be rephrased: *"Do you believe that young people who smoke cigarettes have more friends, fewer friends, or the same number of friends as those who don't smoke?"* Further, there was a serious issue produced by the phrase "young people": One older teenager remarked that he did not believe that a 13-year-old who smokes necessarily has more friends. I propose that the use of "young people" is inappropriate –because this is not the way teenagers talk (e.g., I have never heard one say "I'm going to hang out with some other young people"). So this tended to be interpreted as "someone younger than you"—which represented a clear and undesired bias. To repair this defect, I would change the wording to include "people your age."

This example illustrates several auxiliary issues: First, contrary to the views of many parents, teenagers are capable of rational thought—their reasoning did appear to identify a legitimate defect of question construction. Second, it is important not to prematurely come to conclusions concerning question defects—as there may be several holes to patch.

Under the Text Summary model we can distinguish between what might be called cognitive *input error* (lack of comprehension that is appropriate to the goals of the investigation); *processing error* (e.g., inability to retrieve relevant data from storage); and *output error* (the person cannot or will not produce a response in the form matching the task requirements). Again, this approach adheres closely to the classical cognitive model, in a mechanistic sense. However, a recent extension of the approach—largely driven by an increased focus on cross-cultural research—has been to consider other factors that influence survey responses and, in particular, sociocultural contributions to question function (see Chapter 2). In particular, we look for errors in language translation, terms that have no easy translation, or other forms of cultural mismatch. For example, consider the examples in Table 4.4, where I have indicated the target question tested, the group the testing applies to, and then some comments that are consistent with the Text Summary approach to reporting pretesting results.

Table 4.4

Sample findings of cross-cultural investigations (examples are taken from Willis, et al, 2008; and from Willis & Zahnd, 2007)

Question Tested	Relevant Group(s)	Text Summary of Problems/Issues Identified
1. Have you ever smoked at least 100 cigarettes in your entire life?	Chinese, Koreans, Vietnamese	As translated, the phrase "in your entire life" came across as "in your ENTIRE life—from birth to death"—which is inappropriate as the participants are still alive. They tended to say things like "I don't know if I'll have 100 cigarettes before I die." We need to change this to somehow say "Until now, have you smoked at least 100 cigarettes?"
2. Overall, on a scale from 1 to 10, where 1 is not at all interested and 10 is extremely interested, how interested are you in quitting smoking?	Chinese, Koreans, Vietnamese	Asians were not familiar with the use of this scale and didn't readily answer with a number between 1 and 10. Change this to make the response task more explicit:

(continued)

Table 4.4 (continued)

		"Overall, on a scale from 1 to 10, where 1 is not at all interested and 10 is extremely interested, how interested are you in quitting smoking? Please indicate how interested you are in quitting by picking a number from 1 to 10."
3. Have you ever switched from a stronger to a lighter cigarette?	Chinese	Because at least some Chinese cigarettes are not labeled for tar or nicotine content, respondents who grew up in China could not answer this question—they literally did not know the strength of the cigarettes they had smoked.
4. Thinking about your race or ethnicity, how often have you felt treated badly or unfairly because or your race or ethnicity? Would you say never...all of the time?	Korean	12 of 27 Koreans had difficulty in answering the question: Overall, it was unclear what the reference period should be, and if they were intended to think about periods before coming to the United States, only periods since immigrating, or about one's entire life.

4.6. Top-Down Coding Approaches: Analysis Models 2 and 3

As an alternative major branch in the tree model depicted in Figure 4.1, coded analysis differs from uncoded analysis (e.g., text summarization) in that data processing does not involve (only) the production of a text-based description of what we have observed. Rather, we rely on a more compact descriptor, or *code*, that reduces data in a more formal manner than does the description of basic findings. Codes are normally applied to the target items we are testing because ultimately it is these items that are the units of analysis. However, the codes can be applied at either of two levels:

> (a) Most often: At the *individual* cognitive interview (participant) level: A code is applied to every item, for each interview conducted using the interview notes (e.g., 10 interviews involving 20 items will involve 10 × 20 = 200 coding decisions).
>
> (b) At the *aggregate* item level: A code is applied to every item, but only once all interviews have first been aggregated though use of a Text Summary (so, using the same example, the 10 interviews are first summarized in words, and a coding decision will be made once, for each of the 20 items).

The first branch in Figure 4.1, *top-down coding*, involves the development and application of potential coding categories prior to data analysis (Chi, 1997), which are also referred to as *deductive* codes. These can be viewed as ready-made bins into which we sort and place our results, and they are "top down" in the sense that the codes are not built up from the data but rather imposed by an existing theory or model which states that the observations can be fit to these codes. Blair and Brick (2010, p. 3746) suggest that a priori codes are especially useful because "a tailored frame is likely to be more effect[ive] in helping coders to identify problems of particular interest," which conveys the way in which such coding is normally associated with Reparative studies (i.e., those aiming to search for problems). At the most general level, top-down coding is not associated with any particular underlying theoretical orientation, and may derive from either a cognitive orientation or from the qualitative research tradition (e.g., see O'Brien et al., 2013). However, the nature of the codes assigned does vary according to the theoretical viewpoint of the analyst, which gives rise to two variants: *cognitive coding* and *question feature coding*, which I will describe in turn.

4.7. Analysis Model 2: Cognitive Coding

Cognitive coding approaches apply codes that are closely associated with the Tourangeau four-stage (or other cognitive) model, introduced in Chapter 2. The key characteristic of these codes is that they are devoted to the respondent's cognitive processes, and they attempt to chronicle instances of cognitive problems with the items (Drennan, 2003). Although several approaches are used, this model may consist merely of a formalization of the Text Summary approach, in which cognitive coding categories are made explicit. That is, either interviewer notes or the aggregate text summaries (described under Model 1) are reviewed, and one or more cognitive codes are assigned to each target item (e.g., comprehension, recall, decision/estimation, or response matching problem).

As an illustration, the following excerpt, taken from a testing report, illustrates how the Text Summary was used to indicate a problem that was assigned a cognitive code:

Item tested: In the past 12 months, how many sex partners have you had?

Interviewer note: The participant made a distinction between how many partners he had and the number of people with whom he had had sex, within the past 12 months (with the latter a larger number). To him, a partner is someone you have an ongoing relationship with, and it excludes casual relationships. So the use of the term "partner" tended to produce misinterpretation and did not capture the intent of "everyone you have had sex with."

Cognitive code assigned: Comprehension-Interpretation (C-I)

Willis, Schechter, and Whitaker (1999) assigned problem codes according to the Tourangeau four-stage model, based on the problems found by two cognitive laboratories: the National Center for Health Statistics (NCHS) and the National Opinion Research Center (NORC), for the same survey questionnaire on health questions. At both laboratories, it was found that the majority of problems fell into the category "Communication-Comprehension Problems," corresponding to the Tourangeau (1984) category of Comprehension (Table 4.5). There were also a fair number of problems that related to the Response process (Response categories) and fewer that related to Retrieval (Recall) or Judgment/Estimation (Bias). Significantly, although the investigation was intended to utilize only the four cognitive codes, the investigators developed a further category, which they labeled *Logical*

Table 4.5
Overall percentage of problem type codes assigned for cognitive interviews

	CO (Communication)	RE (Recall)	BI (Bias)	RC (Response Categories)	LO (Logical)	Total
NCHS Cognitive Interviews	70.5% (332)	11.0% (52)	1.9% (9)	12.1% (57)	4.5% (21)	100% (471)
NORC Cognitive Interviews	58.1% (358)	13.3% (82)	1.3% (8)	19.8% (122)	7.5% (56)	100% (616)

Note: Values in parentheses refer to code frequencies.
Source: Willis, Schechter, and Whitaker, 1999.

Problems, to encompass problems of a logical or structural basis that could not easily be fit into the four-stage cognitive model. I will expand this theme in the next section, but the main lesson from the study was the preponderance of failures to communicate meaning—a finding has been replicated several times (see Willis, 2005, for a review).

A second example of a cognitive coding scheme is provided by Presser and Blair (1994), who devoted three general codes to Comprehension issues: (1) difficulty understanding the question or remembering it as they answer; (2) understanding particular words or concepts; and (3) difficulties due to variation in understanding (which I interpret to be vagueness and which they label "boundary lines"). Interestingly, they lumped the remaining three cognitive categories, such that recalling, formulating, and reporting an answer were together. Although this seems like a violation of the Tourangeau formulation, the authors again found that most of the "action" was in the Comprehension-related categories.

On the other hand, there are likely to be types of questionnaires—those putting significant burdens on Recall/Retrieval processes (such as asking about lifetime events)—or those that ask very sensitive questions (and that therefore produce major problems at the Decision stage)—that would result in a distribution of problem codes that is much different, and for which noncomprehension codes would be vital. Fowler et al. (2013) conducted a Reparative study to evaluate and improve several items from a self-administered questionnaire on adherence to medication. The investigator trained cognitive interviewers to explicitly conduct probing sufficient to gather information relevant to each of the four cognitive stages of Comprehension, Retrieval, Decision-Judgment, and Response). Interestingly, unlike several previous studies using a cognitive coding framework, Comprehension problems were not found to dominate—and the problems identified were numerous across all four stages. This departure may be because the questions tested (e.g., "In the last 7 days, how often did you take your [name of medication] exactly as your doctor prescribed it?") placed fairly severe demands on retrieval and decision processes, relative to many typical health survey questions. However, another tantalizing possibility is that the procedure involved leading interviewers to focus on each cognitive stage, perhaps alleviating a bias toward investigation of comprehension processes in the (more usual) absence of such directions.

As a final example, Heesch, van Uffelen, Hill, and Brown (2010) applied a cognitive coding model in a cognitive interviewing-based study of physical activity questions in older adults. In this case, the cognitive coding scheme consisted of three categories, taken from Conrad and Blair (1996):

(a) *Understanding the intent* of the question (akin to Comprehension but in a way that additionally includes an appreciation of the researcher's objectives)
(b) *Performing the primary task*, involving retrieval of information from memory, mental arithmetic, and evaluation of a response (which effectively combines the Retrieval and Estimation-Judgment processes of the Tourangeau model)
(c) *Formatting the response* or *mapping* one's response to the prespecified response options provided by the survey (akin to Tourangeau's Response stage)

The authors in this case used the cognitive model as an orienting framework and organizational guide, as opposed to counting and quantifying the assigned codes. As such, they simply grouped their text summaries according to this overall framework, when reporting results. For instance, problems with understanding the intent included (a) confusion associated with "usual" and "on one of those days" when both were used as reference periods within the same question; and (b) failure to encode the restriction of reporting physical activities of 10 or more minutes.

4.7.1. Coding Schemes That Omit Text Summaries

For each of the examples listed earlier, cognitive coding involved reduction of text-based data to a set of simple codes. Yet, in their reports, each of these authors also chose to include text summaries as illustrative examples that supplemented the codes. That is, they found value in producing, retaining, and communicating written summaries, rather than relying on codes alone to convey the meaning associated with the cognitive testing results. Hence, coding involved an additional step that augmented text summaries, as opposed to replacing them. As an alternative, it is certainly possible to rely on codes and to dispense with text summarization altogether. One approach is to review the verbatim record of the cognitive interview, whether an auditory/visual recording or a written transcription, and to assign codes as they apply. As an example, the analyst could listen to interviews that demonstrate variability in understanding the term "sex partner" and directly assign the code "Comprehension-Communication problem." This practice parallels that of behavior coding (Fowler & Cannell, 1996), in which a small number of discrete codes are assigned to overt behaviors that are elicited as one listens to a fielded interview (e.g., codes are assigned when the respondent requests clarification, interrupts, or provides an uncodeable answer). Although this direct coding approach has appeared infrequently in the cognitive interviewing literature, I next describe a variant that makes heavy use of automated, computer-based coding.

4.7.2. Keyword-Based Automatic Cognitive Coding From Think-Aloud

A subcategory of cognitive coding that foregoes the production of text-based summaries is what I label *keyword-based coding*. It involves a brute force process of searching the results for particular keywords—that is, markers or indicators that are of analytic value. Because of the emphasis on particular words or phrases that emerged during the interview, this approach has been applied where think-aloud interviewing has been conducted, and the participant's verbatim verbal stream (as opposed to interviewer notes) constitutes the source data. The analyst uses a computerized search procedure to scan for specific terms that may be of interest because they indicate some type of difficulty with mental processing of the question. For example, "I don't know" may be a marker of knowledge or memory limitations, and if these are clustered around particular items, this could be useful to know. Bolton and Bronkhorst (1996) included the terms "don't remember," "can't think," "I'm trying to think," and so on, which were then grouped into a "Forget" category.

Presumably, if one can develop enough useful categories of this type, the programmed search algorithm could quickly dredge the raw data for such instances, count them, and even save the context in which they occurred. Again, note that such algorithmic approaches are not typically applied to interviewer notes or to summarized data (such as text summaries), but require literal transcripts. Further, given that these models lack a true "artificial intelligence" component, and therefore tend to fail to reach even a rudimentary level of human mental processing capability, they are extremely limited in making subtle determinations concerning whether the evidence at hand indicates that a true "problem" or that an interesting issue exists, given a particular phraseology or use of a key term. For this reason in particular, it again seems reasonable to conclude that cognitive coding schemes have greatest utility when they accompany, as opposed to supplant, text summaries.

4.8. Analysis Model 3: Question Feature Coding

The third major approach to the analysis of cognitive interviews depicted in Figure 4.1 also involves the use of a priori, top-down coding of cognitive interview results. *Question Feature Coding*, however, assigns codes according to a framework that is oriented toward the evaluated questions, as opposed to the mental world of the survey respondent. The objectives and approach are very similar, but the underlying analytic question posed is subtly different: Instead of implicitly assessing "What types of cognitive problems do people have with this question?" we turn this around to ask, "What features of this question cause people to have problems?" So, we rely on a categorical system that describes question features that may be problematic or otherwise remarkable. The focus on question characteristics such as wording and formatting is certainly not new, and it reaches back at least to the era of Payne (1951), who proposed a long list of rules to follow as part of the "Art of Asking Questions." To my knowledge, the first attempt to apply this art to the science of cognitive testing involved the addition of the category of *Logical Problems/Error in Assumptions* in questions to the four-stage cognitive model (Willis et al., 1991). Rather than focusing only on respondent cognitive problems, the focus was shifted to the issue of whether the item itself produced difficulty. This shift is most pronounced where the identified problems can be viewed as effectively separable from the mind of the respondent and therefore outside of the cognitive model; that is, where the logical premise of the question simply fails to "fit" the person's situation. It has been found that questions that make such erroneous assumptions are rampant—Table 4.6 gives a few examples that have emerged over the course of cognitive interviewing history.

As I detail next, question- (or more generally, questionnaire-) feature-oriented coding schemes have expanded to include a variety of question characteristics other than errors in logic and assumption. What these models have in common, though,

Table 4.6
Examples of logical problems/errors in assumptions found through cognitive testing

Survey Question	Problem With "Fit" to Many Respondents' Lives
Item: "Are you regularly exposed to loud noises, such as being at a rock concert, riding a motorcycle, or operating a chainsaw?" (Willis, 2005)	Limits consideration to high-risk activities engaged in by the young that may not be representative of the types of loud noise exposure in the elderly and those engaged in more passive endeavors
Item stem: "When you do your homework..."	"assumes that every student in every country has homework assigned and so can relate to this practice" (Lee, 2014, p. 232)
Item: "The last time you saw a doctor in the past 12 months, was this for a regular check-up or physical exam, or for some other reason?"	The respondent may not have visited a doctor in the past 12 months
Item: "Have you ever been treated unfairly in school because you are [self-reported racial/ethnic/national group]?"	The question assumes that the individual attended school in this country. However, for those schooled in Vietnam, it is illogical to ask, "Have you ever been treated unfairly in school because you are Vietnamese"

is a viewpoint that espouses a point of reference other than the purely cognitive, and that tends to consider the evaluated survey item, rather than the respondent, to be the focus of coding. Researchers promoting question-feature schemes tend not to be cognitive scientists but rather those trained specifically in questionnaire design. This perspective also appears to be associated with the school of sociology in which qualitative research is conducted according to a top-down approach to code assignment, such as the variant of the Framework coding approach described by Smith and Firth (2011).

On the other hand, this viewpoint is anathema to the school of qualitative research associated with Grounded Theory, especially the pure interpretivist view (see Chapter 2). Most significantly, the promotion of "logical problems" that codify the fit between the respondent and the background environment implies a strongly positivist view (e.g., that there are external realities beyond the precise manner in which the respondent views them—such as a health insurance program that carries an absolute set of "real" features. The interpretivist view described by Chepp and Gray (2014) instead promotes a constructivist stance, arguing that no such realities exist, and that it is meaningless to consider characteristics of survey questions apart from explicit consideration of how they are interpreted by respondents. I resurrect these theoretical issues not with the intent of resolving this debate but to clarify how choice of analysis model depends fundamentally on the analyst's background viewpoint concerning survey questions, scientific inquiry, and even the nature of the world. However, to keep the discussion grounded, I will return to a more descriptive level, and next I will describe several variants of Question Feature Coding systems in detail.

4.8.1. The Question Appraisal System

A system designed to identify a range of problems in survey questions—itself informed through cognitive interviewing results—is the Question Appraisal System (QAS) first introduced by Willis and Lessler (1999); an updated version is summarized in Table 4.7. Although originally designed for the identification of potential problems with survey questions through an expert review process (see Willis, 2005), the QAS can also be used as a checklist model

Table 4.7
The Question Appraisal System (QAS-2009).

STEP 1—READING: Determine whether it is difficult for the interviewers to read the question uniformly to all respondents

1a. **WHAT TO READ**: Interviewer may have difficulty determining what *parts* of the question should be read.	YES NO
1b. **MISSING INFORMATION**: Information the interviewer needs to administer the question is *not* contained in the question.	YES NO
1c. **HOW TO READ**: Question is *not* fully scripted and therefore difficult to read.	YES NO

STEP 2—INSTRUCTIONS: Look for problems with any introductions, instructions, or explanations from the *respondent's* point of view.

2a. **CONFLICTING OR INACCURATE INSTRUCTIONS**, introductions, or explanations.	YES NO
2b. **COMPLICATED INSTRUCTIONS**, introductions, or explanations.	YES NO

STEP 3—CLARITY: Identify problems related to communicating the *intent or meaning* of the question to the respondent.

3a. **WORDING**: Question is lengthy, awkward, ungrammatical, or contains complicated syntax.	YES NO
3b. **TECHNICAL TERM(S)** are undefined, unclear, or complex.	YES NO
3c. **VAGUE:** There are multiple ways to interpret the question or to decide what is to be included or excluded.	YES NO
3d. **REFERENCE PERIODS** are missing, not well specified, or in conflict.	YES NO

STEP 4—ASSUMPTIONS: Determine whether there are problems with assumptions made or the underlying logic.

4a. **INAPPROPRIATE ASSUMPTIONS** are made about the respondent or about his/her living situation.	YES NO

(*continued*)

Table 4.7 (*continued*)

4b. **ASSUMES CONSTANT BEHAVIOR** or experience for situations that vary.	YES	NO
4c. **DOUBLE-BARRELED**: Contains more than one implicit question.	YES	NO
STEP 5—KNOWLEDGE/MEMORY: Check whether respondents are likely to *not know* or have trouble *remembering* information.		
5a. **KNOWLEDGE** may not exist: Respondent is unlikely to *know* the answer to a factual question.	YES	NO
5b. **ATTITUDE** may not exist: Respondent is unlikely to have formed the attitude being asked about.	YES	NO
5c. **RECALL** failure: Respondent may not *remember* the information asked for.	YES	NO
5d. **COMPUTATION** problem: The question requires a difficult mental calculation.	YES	NO
STEP 6—SENSITIVITY/BIAS: Assess questions for sensitive nature or wording, and for bias.		
6a. **SENSITIVE CONTENT** (general): The question asks about a topic that is embarrassing, very private, or that involves illegal behavior.	YES	NO
6b. **SENSITIVE WORDING** (specific): Given that the general topic is sensitive, the wording should be improved to minimize sensitivity.	YES	NO
6c. **SOCIALLY ACCEPTABLE** response is implied by the question.	YES	NO
STEP 7—RESPONSE CATEGORIES: Assess the adequacy of the range of responses to be recorded.		
7a. **OPEN-ENDED QUESTION** that is inappropriate or difficult.	YES	NO
7b. **MISMATCH** between question and response categories.	YES	NO
7c. **TECHNICAL TERM(S)** are undefined, unclear, or complex.	YES	NO

Table 4.7 (continued)		
7d. **VAGUE** response categories are subject to multiple interpretations.	YES	NO
7e. **OVERLAPPING** response categories.	YES	NO
7f. **MISSING** eligible responses in response categories.	YES	NO
7g. **ILLOGICAL ORDER** of response categories.	YES	NO
STEP 8—OTHER PROBLEMS: Look for problems not identified in Steps 1–7.		
8. Other problems not previously identified.	YES	NO

for coding cognitive interviewing results (Wilson, Whitehead, & Whitaker, 2000).

The QAS consists of eight major coding categories, each containing several subcategories, for a total of 27 possible codes. Although designed for interviewer-administered (specifically telephone) questionnaire administration, the QAS has also been applied as a coding scheme relevant to self-administration (Buers et al., 2013).

Table 4.8 contains several excerpts from the QAS manual, and illustrates how these codes were assigned to particular observed problems with survey questions. Note that the table includes not only the codes but also explanatory comments (that are analogous to the Text Summary comments already described).

Assignment of QAS codes has not generally been done in production cognitive interviewing, in part due to the burden of assigning each of a relatively large number of codes to every problem that has been identified. Rather, the QAS is most applicable for purposes of methodological research concerning the results of cognitive interviewing studies. For example, Rothgeb, Forsyth, and Willis (2007) applied QAS codes to a series of cognitive testing results as part of an experimental study to compare the types of results obtained across laboratories. The assignment of codes was therefore not for the purpose of providing the basis for item revision, but simply to be able to compare results where these should, in theory, be similar.

Table 4.8

Examples of coding QAS categories (with text comments)

Question Evaluated	QAS Code Assigned	Comments
Which of the following best describes whether you have a smoke alarm in your home? You own a smoke alarm, and it is installed and working; you own a smoke alarm, but it is broken or not installed; you own a smoke alarm but the battery is missing; you don't own a smoke alarm because it is too expensive; you don't own a smoke alarm because you don't think it is necessary; or you don't own a smoke alarm for some other reason?	3a. Clarity (Wording)	The question is (clearly!) too long.
Have you had your blood tested for the AIDS virus?	3c. Clarity (Vague)	It is unclear whether this means: "Did I take the initiative in deciding to have my blood tested?" versus "Was it tested as part of any type of blood test?" Sometimes respondents will say that "I needed it tested for my job—but I didn't go out of my way to have it done." If the issue of interest is the act of testing, it might be better to simply ask, "As far as you know, has your blood ever been tested for the AIDS virus?"

How often do you take part in community organizations, meetings, or other activities involving Hispanic people or culture?	3c. Clarity (Vague)	What is to be included here? If I have a meeting at work with two people who happen to be Hispanic, does that count? For this question to work as it is (probably) intended, it would need to ask specifically about "activities that focus on Hispanic culture or people of Hispanic origin."
Before your last pregnancy, had you stopped using all methods of birth control?	3d. Clarity (Reference Period)	How long before pregnancy? Do we mean days, months, years, or something else? Depending on the reference period of interest, the question could instead start with: "During the 3 months before that pregnancy…."
Thinking about your most recent mammogram, how much did it cost, regardless of who paid for it? Include just the cost of the X-ray itself and not any fee charged by the doctor at the X-ray facility, or the cost for an office visit where the test was ordered.	5a. Knowledge (May Not Exist)	Respondents have no way of disentangling the cost of the test from the cost of the office visit.

4.8.2. The O'Brien, Bereket, Swinton, and Solomon Coding System

A second top-down, question-feature-based coding system was utilized in a questionnaire testing project (involving an HIV Disability survey) by O'Brien et al. (2013), based on Feinstein's (1987) Theory of Sensibility. Interestingly, neither the Feinstein coding system nor the qualitative approach described by O'Brien at al. makes any reference to the field of cognitive interviewing as applied to questionnaire design. Rather, the study can be viewed as an independent attempt by qualitative researchers to achieve the goal of understanding the functioning of survey questions. The coding system contained 10 major categories, which are summarized in Table 4.9. The codes tend to vary from the very specific (appropriateness of the title assigned to the questionnaire) to the very general (problems with the formatting of the instrument as a whole). Unlike the coding schemes I have described, the level of analysis is mainly the questionnaire, as opposed to each specific question. This broad level of analysis does provide the basis for an overall assessment that may be missing from coding schemes that are very question specific. On the other hand, the general nature of the codes may not induce the investigator to focus on each item, in terms of its individual merits.

A final significant feature of the O'Brien coding scheme is the manner in which it effectively directs the procedures used for probing and data collection: As I have pointed out, to some extent the nature of the analysis drives choice of data collection procedures. In this case, the focus on explicitly requesting participant opinions of the questionnaire (which could be labeled "participant-based expert review") departs from the approach taken by most cognitive interviewers, who assess participant reactions to survey questions but without directly asking for a critique of the questions.

4.9. Hybrid Coding Schemes

Coding schemes need not be either purely devoted to either cognitive categories (i.e., the Tourangeau model) or question feature categories (as the QAS). It can be argued, in fact, that a pure approach is unrealistic because there is not necessarily a clean division between the characteristics of the respondent's cognitive processing that create problems and the characteristics of the

Table 4.9
Survey question coding scheme developed by O'Brien, Bereket, Swinton, and Solomon (2013) based on the Feinstein (1987) Framework of Sensitivity

Code Label	Description
1. Overall impressions of the questionnaire instrument	Questionnaire-level (rather than specific-question-level) critique by the participants
2. Perceived purpose of the questionnaire	Questionnaire-level perceptions of purpose and intended users of the data collected
3. Face Validity	Determination of whether the individual questions are clear, and whether the overall instrument makes sense to the participant
4. Content Validity	How suitable the questionnaire items are; which are unsuitable; which items should be modified or re-ordered; what items should be added
5. Ease of Usage	Ease of administration; length of time, effort, discomfort associated with completing the questionnaire; clarity of instructions
6. Response Sets	Appropriateness of response options contained in closed-ended questions
7. Format of Instrument	Appropriateness of the formatting of the overall questionnaire
8. Episodic Component	Capacity of the instrument for assessing the dynamic/fluctuating nature of the topic (disability)
9. Title of Instrument	Participant perspectives on the title of the instrument chosen by the researchers
10. Additional Emerging Themes	Other themes that do not fit the above code categories

question. For example, the QAS category "Recall failure" is virtually identical to the Retrieval process from the Tourangeau model (and this seems not at all surprising, given that the distinction between saying, "The respondent experiences a recall problem" and "The question has a feature related to recall which results in a problem" is largely semantic).

An initial step toward a hybridization of cognitive and question-featural models was that by Watt et al. (2008), who developed a patient-reported outcome instrument for thyroid patients, relying on cognitive interviews to detect and remediate potential sources of error. Their coding scheme included the four classical Tourangeau categories of Comprehension, Retrieval, Judgment, and Response; and also included a Logical category that included "problems in the inherent logic or structure of the questionnaire, such as implicit assumptions"; plus one code labeled "Acceptability" (akin to sensitivity); and one called Coverage (failure to include elements important to respondents). Similarly to several other studies cited earlier, the most frequently used category was Comprehension (across 31 interviews involving 99 items, 54 comprehension issues were identified), whereas only a single Retrieval issue was found, 23 Judgment-related problems, and 28 Response problems. The researchers also report—in Text Summary fashion—the nature of many of these comprehension problems. Interestingly, they were able to document a decrease in the number of problems identified as iterative rounds were completed, after questionnaire revision, suggesting the success of the Reparative objective.

Several other authors have found it valuable to expand a Tourangeau-type system to include question-feature codes. As a follow-up to their cognitive coding scheme described earlier, Willis et al. (1999) created a more detailed breakdown of the types of communication problems experienced, and the more precise codes included a level of specificity that represented distinctions based on question characteristics. Referring back to Table 4.5, the NCHS interview Comprehension/Communication (CO) cognitive category was subdivided into the following question feature code subsets (the percentage of total CO problems [70.5%] falling into each new category is indicated in parentheses):

(a) IN: Administration problems for the interviewer (0.6%)
(b) LE: Problems due to question length (1.7%)

(c) TE: Problems with specific terms in the question (21.4%)
(d) DI: Problems related to overall difficulty to understand the question (11.9%)
(e) VA: Problems related to question vagueness (25.5%)
(f) Uncodeable/other (9.3%)

This subdivision provides considerable specificity concerning the nature of the Comprehension-Communication problems identified. Mainly, questions were either vague—not difficult to understand but containing multiple meanings—or they contained terms that were not well understood by participants. This level of analysis provides some degree of hair splitting, as far as the nature of the difficulties, and perhaps provides direction toward question modification to a degree substantially greater than does a simple four-category coding system.

A further model that I consider a top-down-coding hybrid between cognitive and question-feature approaches is that proposed by Levine, Fowler, and Brown (2005). The six coding categories within that model are illustrated in Table 4.10. The

Table 4.10
Levine, Fowler, and Brown (2005) coding system for the classification of questionnaire problems

Code Label	Description
1. Comprehension	Items with unclear or ambiguous terms; failure to understand the questions consistently
2. Knowledge	Items for which respondents lacked information to answer a question
3. Inapplicable	Items measuring construct that is inapplicable for many respondents (e.g., made assumptions)
4. Construct	Items failed to measure the intended construct
5. Subtle	Items making discriminations that are too subtle for many respondents
6. General	Several other general issues associated with the development of a questionnaire

first two codes– Comprehension and Knowledge—are consistent with the original Tourangeau cognitive model and focus on respondent processes. The Inapplicable code matches the question-feature-based Logical-Structural designation introduced by Willis et al. (1991). The final three codes: Construct, Subtle, and General, have analogs within the QAS. In their comparison of the QAS and the Levine et al. system, Buers et al. (2013) noted that the systems operate similarly, but that they favored the QAS, in part because it contains built-in suggestions for question modification once problem codes are assigned, a feature well suited to their applied (Reparative) objective.

The Cognitive Classification Scheme (CCS) evolved through the work of Forsyth, Rothgeb, and Willis (2004) and is presented in Table 4.11. Note that the types of problem categories bear significant resemblance to the QAS: In particular, it contains roughly the same number of codes, and the *Comprehension and communication* category spawns the most (16 in all). Because four of the major categories correspond to Comprehension, Retrieval, Judgment, and Response, this model can be viewed as a hybrid that contains elements of both cognitive and question-feature coding. However, the most detailed, lowest level codes do focus on characteristics of the questions—as opposed to characteristics of the respondent's cognitive processes (e.g., "Shortage of cues"; "Undefined terms"). Application of this model to cognitive interviewing results would be similar to endeavors that utilize the QAS—each substantive cognitive interview result is assigned one or more codes, to characterize the nature of the flaw being described.

4.10. Cross-Culturally Oriented, Top-Down Coding Schemes

Finally, several coding schemes are hybrids in a different sense, in that they also bring into the coding mix sociocultural and linguistic elements that are integral components of the survey response process. These have been developed by researchers who work in the cross-cultural cognitive interviewing area—and present a useful case study of how parallel development by independent researchers can result in convergence toward a strikingly similar outcome. In the United States, Willis and Zahnd

Table 4.11
Problem Classification Coding Scheme (CCS)

Problem Codes

1. Comprehension and Communication

Interviewer Difficulties
1. Inaccurate instructions
2. Complicated instruction
3. Difficult to administer

Question Content
4. Vague topic/term
5. Complex topic
6. Topic carried over from earlier question
7. Undefined term(s)

Question Structure
8. Transition needed
9. Unclear respondent instruction
10. Question too long
11. Complex, awkward syntax
12. Erroneous assumption
13. Several questions

Reference Period
14. Carried over from earlier question
15. Undefined
16. Unanchored or rolling

2. Memory Retrieval
17. Shortage of cues
18. High detail required or information unavailable
19. Long recall period

3. Judgment and Evaluation
20. Complex estimation
21. Potentially sensitive or desirability bias

4. Response Selection

Response Terminology
22. Undefined term(s)

(continued)

Table 4.11 (*continued*)
23. Vague term(s)
Response Units
24. Responses use wrong units
25. Unclear what response options are
Response Structure
26. Overlapping categories
27. Missing categories
5. Other
28. Something else
Source: Reprinted with permission from Forsyth, Rothgeb, Willis (2004, p. 530).

(2007) conducted a series of cognitive interviews of Koreans and non-Koreans involving a range of health topics and classified the results according to a simple model that appeared to capture the major types of defects identified. They labeled these as (a) Translation problems, (b) Problems of cultural adaptation, and (c) Generic problems of questionnaire design, within a *General Cross-Cultural Problem Classification* scheme. Table 4.12 illustrates an example of each type of problem.

Meanwhile, in the United Kingdom, Fitzgerald, Widdop, Gray, and Collins (2011) conducted similar cross-cultural cognitive interviewing and produced the *Cross-National Error Source Typology* (CNEST). The CNEST categories are depicted in Table 4.13 (reordered but consistent with Fitzgerald et al., 2011, Table 1). Note the marked similarity between the Willis-Zahnd and the Fitzgerald models—in fact, the only substantive difference, apart from labeling, is that the CNEST subdivides the major Translation category into (a) errors of translation and (b) difficult to translate. I consider this further distinction to be of value, so the CNEST system constitutes a modest improvement over the Willis-Zahnd model. However, the major point is the fact that these models developed independently (at least in original form) but have evolved to almost an identical state would seem to validate the general approach.

Table 4.12
Types of problems identified by Willis and Zahnd (2007) within a cross-cultural study: General Cross-Cultural Problem Classification

Type of Problem	Question Tested	Description of Problem
Translation problem	Would you say that in general your health is excellent, very good, good, fair, or poor?	In Korean, several response categories overlapped: Participants could not distinguish between the translated versions of "excellent" and "very good"; or between the translations of "good" and "fair."
Problem of cultural adaptation	During the past 12 months, did you either delay or not get a medicine that a doctor prescribed for you?	Monolingual Koreans tended to be poor, and received very limited medical attention. They did not delay obtaining medicine, but only because they tended not to have any medicines prescribed to them in the first place. This situation differed markedly from that of non-Koreans, who could report this meaningfully because they had received prescriptions for medications.
Generic problem of questionnaire design	In the past 12 months, how much of a problem, if any, was it to get a specialist you are happy with? Was it a big problem, a small problem, or not a problem?	It turned out that some individuals within both Korean and non-Korean groups had in fact not needed a specialist in the past 12 months, so the question makes an erroneous assumption. This is true in Korean as it is in English.

Table 4.13
CNEST model of cross-cultural problems with survey questions, from Fitzgerald, et al. (2011)

Type of Problem	Description
Translation problems: (a) Resulting from translation error (b) Resulting from source questionnaire design	(a) Errors stem from the translation process (i.e., a translator making a mistake or selecting an inappropriate word or phrase) (b) Features of the source question, such as use of vague quantifiers to describe answer scale points, are difficult/impossible to translate in a way that preserves functional equivalence
Cultural portability	The concept being measured does not exist in all countries. Or the concept exists but in a form that prevents the proposed measurement approach from being used (i.e., you can't simply write a better question or improve the translation)
Poor source question design	All or part of the source question has been poorly designed, resulting in measurement error

Note that both the Willis-Zahnd and CNEST coding schemes are very general, in that the category "poor source question design" is an all-encompassing category that fails to differential the exact type of problem. However, it is easy to envision combining a more detailed question coding scheme, such as the QAS or CCS, with the QNEST, in order to produce a more comprehensive coding scheme within cross-cultural cognitive interviewing investigations. Consistent with this logic, Lee (2014) introduced The Appraisal System for Cross-National Surveys, which extended the QAS to the cross-cultural domain (see Table 4.14).

4.11. How Do We Select a Top-Down Coding Scheme?

Beyond simply providing a potentially bewildering compendium of alternative coding schemes to be applied to cognitive

Table 4.14
The Appraisal System for Cross-National Surveys

Survey Features	Sources of Potential Problems
Instruction	Ambiguous
	Complicated
	Undefined or ill defined
	Conflicting
Substance/concept	Unclear
	Complicated
	Implicit assumption
	Multiple questions (i.e., asking a few things in one question)
	Multiple interpretations (i.e., a concept contains multiple meanings)
	Sensitive information (e.g., weight or potential legal consequences)
	Culturally inappropriate
Vocabulary/sentence	Awkward or uncommon
	Undefined/unclear/confusing
	Technical terms without providing definition
	Inappropriate for respondents (e.g., age, education level)
	Multiple definitions (e.g., "park")
	Lengthy or complex sentences
	Culturally inappropriate
	Lack of cultural equivalence
Reference points	Missing
	Vague (e.g., "in recent years")
	Complex
	Conflicting
	Unanchored, undefined boundary (e.g., "lifetime")
	Weakly anchored, uncertain boundary (e.g., "in your school days")

(continued)

Table 4.14 (*continued*)

Survey Features	Sources of Potential Problems
	Time period too short or too long
	Culturally inappropriate
	Lack of cultural equivalence
Item format	Poorly matched between the question content and item format
	Poorly matched between the question content and response category
	Unclear, conflicting, or confusing
	Respondents' attention and motivation problem
	Inappropriate for respondents (e.g., age, education level)
	Uncommon or unfamiliar format for a particular culture
	Potential response bias
Translation/adaptation	Awkward or uncommon expressions
	Unclear words/sentences
	Words requiring adaptation
Response category	Illogical order
	Ill-defined boundary setting
	Ill-defined category intervals
	Nonexclusive (i.e., overlapping categories)
	Nonexhaustive (i.e., missing categories)
	Ambiguous terms (e.g., nearly always, always)
	Culturally inappropriate or ineffective sets
Task performance	Memory or retrieval problem
	Too challenging—reading comprehension or complex calculation
	Requiring too much detail of an event or information
	Nonreachable answers (e.g., father's income, last election)

(*continued*)

Table 4.14 (*continued*)

Survey Features	Sources of Potential Problems
	Social desirability
	Perceived consequences (e.g., teachers may get to see the answer)
	Respondents' attention and motivation problem
	Refusal to answer

Source: Reprinted with permission from Lee (2014), p. 231.

interviewing results, it would be useful to provide guidance in the selection of one of these. To do so, I review the major dimensions on which these differ: (a) complexity, in terms of sheer number of codes; and (b) focus, in particular on *cognition*, versus on *question*, versus *culture/society*.

Complexity: Being more mechanical than conceptual in nature, complexity is perhaps the more straightforward issue. An overall conundrum concerning "how many codes to use" is not unique to cognitive interviewing but plagues a range of sciences that attempt to affix labels to discrete observations. The advantages of a small set of codes is that they are easier for the analyst to learn, remember, and apply coherently and reliably (again, I cite the persistent theme that analysis is itself a cognitive activity limited by the capacity of the human brain). However, coding systems that force a lot of the world into one bin (e.g., "Comprehension error") tend to produce very blunt instruments with limited measurement resolution—many phenomena that may be very different in nuanced ways effectively fall into the same conceptual container.

Alternatively, the use of a large set of codes is correspondingly difficult and cognitive complex, and it tends to lead to a disappointing degree of correspondence in code assignment, either within coder, or across multiple coders (e.g., intracoder and intercoder reliabilities). However, the use of a multitude of codes does result in finer distinctions, and it can produce a more sharply delineated description of different varieties of reality. By way of metaphor, having only vanilla, chocolate, and strawberry ice cream may make differentiating these very easy, but it does present a less interesting variety of flavor dimensions than does having 50 varieties. Of course, those favoring the simple three-flavor model might ask whether consumers can really tell the difference between, say, boysenberry and elderberry, and whether much of the advertised variety is lost to failures of meaningful perceptual differentiation.

Perhaps one way to resolve the question of number of codes is to consider the purpose of the investigation, as well as the auxiliary types of information to be gathered. To the extent that codes are to be supplemented by rich qualitative information, it may not matter so much how fine-grained the assigned code is—the virtues of the Text Summary may remediate problems caused by blunt coding. On the other hand, where rich qualitative summaries are not able to be used, and where we rely only on the codes (e.g., where so many interviews are done that we cannot make use of all of the text data), then we may require a more fine-grained coding level. Further, the choice of codes also depends on pragmatic issues, such as the amount of training that coders are able to be given, and whether coders are previously experienced with the coding system. I have found that new coders can typically handle at most a half-dozen codes, whereas those with a long history of applying a coding scheme such as the QAS may be well versed in the application of dozens of codes.

Focus: (1) Cognition versus (2) Question–structure versus (3) Cultural and society. The more qualitative issues concerning choice of coding approach may be especially interesting, because they speak to issues of underlying philosophy and conceptual approach, especially regarding what we believe we are searching for when we do go through the results of cognitive testing with our analytic fine-tooth comb. In reviewing the historical basis for cognitive interviewing, I have indicated how this began as an investigation of the cognitive characteristics of the individual (e.g., mechanistic comprehension of the item)—but how later developments embellished the Tourangeau (1984) cognitive model in several ways. For one, question designers began to focus on the characteristics of the question as they influence cognition—giving rise to models like the QAS. Additionally, by including interviewer-oriented codes, the QAS approach recognized the inclusion of the interviewer within the implicit model being represented (at least for administration modes, such as telephone, that include an interviewer).

The second additional strand, which existed somewhat in the background at all times, was the inclusion of both cultural elements that give rise to differential responses to the items (and hence codes that involve cultural group membership, e.g., Hispanic versus non-Hispanic), and social-structural elements that emphasize the background context that the question must account for. As a first step, analysts found it necessary to develop a Logical-Structural code to describe how questions that function in one structural context may not apply in another (e.g., questions on health insurance that apply in the United States will be flawed when used in Canada). Following this, authors such as Fitzgerald et al. and Willis and Zahnd found a need to incorporate linguistically-related categories involving problems with translation.

The logical extension to this reasoning would be a comprehensive model like Lee's (2014), which incorporates cognitive, question feature, and linguistic/sociocultural coding categories. Taken together, the ascendancy of codes pertaining to each of these facets implicitly fuels a model of questionnaire structure recognizing the interaction of multiple facets within a total system, involving:

(a) The individual respondent and his or her attendant cognitive processing
(b) The survey question and its associated characteristics
(c) The background sociocultural and physical environment in which the individual is administered the question—which includes the interviewer, for interviewer-administered questionnaires; and implicitly, the investigator (see Figure 4.3)

To the extent that this model applies to the target items being evaluated through cognitive interviewing, a natural conclusion may be that no coding system focused on just one of these elements will be adequate. It would seem that an integrated coding scheme that addresses each of these levels, as by Lee (2014), would be the most effective in drawing attention to the variety of issues at hand. That is, sometimes the problems we address will be associated most closely with features of the survey question

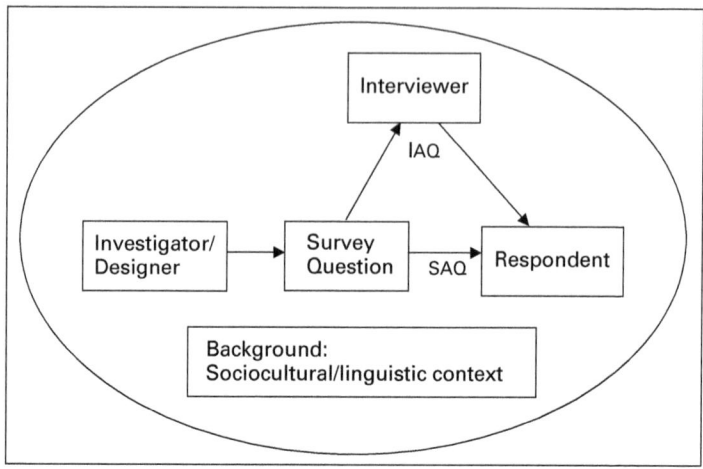

Figure 4.3. Model of the complex interaction between survey investigator/designer, interviewer, instrument, and respondent, within a sociocultural and linguistic context, for both Interviewer Administered Questionnaires (IAQ) and Self-Administered Questionnaires (SAQ).

(e.g., it is too long and should be shortened); other times the issue may be with the respondent's capacities (e.g., people cannot remember the last time they had a tetanus shot—and this cannot be resolved through question restructuring). At still other times, it is the context of the interview, or in which the respondent exists, that may be the most salient element (e.g., individuals of a particular culture will refuse to assent to answering survey questions on a particular topic unless the process is vetted by a respected elder). Finally, we must not forget the interviewer, in the case of an interviewer-administered questionnaire, as that person serves as the bridge between survey question and respondent (and by extension, between the investigator and the respondent). Capturing all of these factors through a set of top-down, deductive codes requires a comprehensive system that both anticipates, and accounts for, the contributions of each of these. There is no single psychological, sociological, or qualitative research tradition that can serve as a direct model or guide to either the conduct or code-based analysis of cognitive interviews. What is vital is that whatever system we apply is adequate for capturing the myriad findings from our cognitive testing process.

4.12. Bottom-Up Coding: Inductive Approaches to Coding (Analysis Models 4 and 5)

Another school of analysis that relies on coding is based on a very different philosophy than that underlying the QAS, CCS, CNEST, or other top-down coding schemes. This alternative explicitly rejects the assignment of preexisting codes. Rather, one begins with the raw data and builds codes from the *ground up* based on intensive analysis of these data (Chi, 1997). Both remaining analysis models represented in Figure 4.1, which I have named *Theme Coding* and *Pattern Coding*, tend to rely on bottom-up coding. The procedures used in the conduct of the cognitive interviews, or even in the early phases of analysis, may be somewhat similar to the Text Summary approach, where the cognitive interviewing results are mined for meaningful information, but without either the contributions or the constraints of a coding scheme to guide this analysis activity. Hence, either quotes, or notes, in some combination, are the basis for these codes, sometimes also labeled *themes* or *patterns*. However, rather than achieving data reduction through (only) the production of a text-based summary, the analyst instead develops codes to represent key findings and applies these to each occurrence within an interview that is deemed worthy of note.

4.13. Analysis Model 4: Theme Coding

Theme coding is closely associated with the Interpretivist viewpoint introduced in Chapter 2. Interpretivists adopt an analysis process deriving from Grounded Theory, which is the qualitative research tradition that appears to have the most widespread application to the analysis of cognitive interviews (e.g., Miller, Willson, & Chepp, 2014; Ridolfo & Schoua-Glusberg, 2011) and in fact has been described as "one of the most popular research designs in the world" (Birks & Mills, 2011, p. 1). Under Theme coding, discrete labels are developed and applied to segments of data from the cognitive interviews. Themes may be brief keyword-type summaries (of just a few words) or may constitute sentence-length descriptions (e.g., in a cognitive testing study of end-of-life care [EoLC], Daveson et al. [2011] developed themes including: "Priorities and preferences are determined dynamically during EoLC" and "EoLC preferences regarding place of terminal care, place of death, and other choices may change over time"). Finally, the codes may consist literally of participants' verbatim quotes—so-called in vivo codes.

Consistent with an Interpretivist philosophy, ground-up coding seeks to elucidate common elements within the data by beginning without preconceived notions or schemes concerning the assignment of codes—either their number or their nature. At each analytic step, the researcher identifies the themes and then collects more data that can then be related—according to a Constant Comparative basis (Glaser & Strauss, 1967)—with data already collected, in a way that is strongly reflective of the Bayesian approach discussed in Chapter 3. The descriptive framework that is in built up for the dataset is custom designed for the investigation, and hence there is no expectation that this will produce a singular, common scheme (such as the four-stage Cognitive Coding scheme) that will be applicable to other survey items, even within the same questionnaire or cognitive interviewing project.

As a concrete example of Theme coding, consider one of my favorite examples: *"Would you say that your health in general is excellent, very good, good, fair, or poor?"* An analyst may be interested in developing a set of codes that encapsulate the cognitive interviewing results, but without worrying about assignment to either a Cognitive coding or a Question Features coding system. Rather, the intent is to develop codes that are dependent *only on the data* at hand. Applying this approach to the results of a set of cognitive interviews involving the general health question, the researcher may develop the following conceptions of general health, across several cultures:

(a) Code: Physical health
   Sample quotes from cognitive interviews:
   "I'm pretty healthy—I don't have high blood pressure or cancer or anything serious like that."
   "I haven't been sick a day in the past ten years—been healthy as a horse."
(b) Code: Mental/Emotional health
   Sample quotes from cognitive interviews:
   "I said 'fair' because I've been pretty depressed lately, and that just brings me down and makes it hard to do anything."

"Not so good anymore—I tend to forget things a lot, like going into a room and then forgetting why I went there."
(c) Code: Spiritual health
Sample quotes from cognitive interviews:
"Excellent—because I feel like I'm where I should be in the world—like I'm a healthy part of it."
"I have a connection to God—that's the best way to be healthy, because then you don't need to worry about things like disease or whether your arm or leg hurts."

Note that the conceptual model of interpretation concerning "health in general" that results in codes for (a) physical, (b) mental/emotional, and (c) spiritual varieties would have no obvious application to a survey question on opinions about immigration, which presumably would produce a set of codes specific to that item.

4.13.1. Why Select a Theme Coding Approach?

Although one may certainly develop themes for any type of study, they most closely adhere to a model in which the intent is Descriptive (reverse engineering) research. This view stems from the argument that the purpose of qualitative research is to uncover the ways that people give meaning to their social world (Silverman, 2001). In application to cognitive testing, instead of focusing on problem detection—that is, on targeting "bad" questions that require repair, and otherwise largely accepting questions without problems as unremarkable, we consider *all* tested items to equally be fair game for analysis. The key objective is to collect information not only about what goes wrong but also includes what goes right—and more generally, what happens, period, when the question is asked (Miller, 2003, 2011; Ridolfo & Schoua-Glusberg, 2011). That is, *apart from worrying about problems, how do the tested individuals think about and react to the questions, and how do the questions apply to them in a wider sense, in a way that takes into account context and social location?*

As such, at least in pure (or perhaps extreme) form, we focus on the item consumer's interpretation—and not on that of the investigator. The emphasis on removing researcher objectives recapitulates a key theme often expressed by qualitative researchers, in which we recognize investigator expectation and bias as contaminants, to be acknowledged but also actively avoided (although as Emmel [2013] points out, qualitative research traditions vary markedly in their views of the degree to which the investigator should be actively removed from this process). Following this logic, there is no attempt to create a match between the intent of the investigator and the interpretation of the cognitive interview participant—we focus solely on the latter. In essence, when a survey question is evaluated, the interviewer's task is to focus on capturing as much information as possible about what the respondent believes it to be asking, and how it is interpreted.

Because the intent of Theme coding is not to focus on the investigator, the objective of the investigation is not primarily to find problems with the item but to disentangle it and represent its inherent components, according to an Interpretivist framework. Ridolfo and Schoua-Glusberg (2011) have described this approach as determining "what a question captures"—and this well describes the notion of determining the range of interpretations that may be subsumed under a singular wording, across a range of survey respondents. This focus on an unbiased analytic approach to understand item functioning is implicit in any cognitive interviewing analysis that purports to promote a complete understanding of respondent reaction and interpretation, but without endeavoring to necessarily "repair" the item.

Referring to the Venn diagram from Figure 4.2 once again, an analysis approach focusing on what the question captures does not, within the testing and analysis phase, focus on the meaning of the item from the investigator's point of view (A), nor are we concerned with the match between investigator and respondent conceptualization that is represented by the overlap area (C). Rather, in this case the mental world of the analyst is very different: Our job is not problem solving, or constantly trying to evaluate an item against a standard consisting of its purpose within the current investigation. Rather, our goal is to understand one limited part of the world, concerning conceptualization of a specific set of survey items. We are finished when we fully understand the range of respondent perceptions associated with those items (B).

What do we do with these results? It is, of course, interesting to know "what a question captures"—but how does this help us?

Ultimately this information is useful to the extent that it provides a ready compendium of items that one can select, depending on the specific objective. Returning to our Venn diagram, to make effective use of these results, the investigator can consider the degree to which the item meets the requirements of a particular study—that is, whether area (A), corresponding to our own interpretation, in fact overlaps enough with (B), the description of question function—that this item can be considered to be fit for use. Critically, our definition of (A) may vary, from survey to survey, such that the issue of whether the item is "good" or "bad" depends on the simple judgment, *what do we need it to do?* In this way, we do consider the overlap between our own (investigator) understanding and that of the recipients of the item. However, this match is seen as variable, as the investigator's view may depend on the particular study, so in effect there is no single study objective (A) but, rather, multiple potential variants $(A_1, A_2 \ldots A_n)$—which overlap with (B) to varying extents. The key point is that *whether the item presents problems is specific to the investigation, rather than an immutable characteristic of the item.* This view recapitulates Oppenheim's (1966) suggestion that an item may have multiple validities, depending on the measurement objective (see Chapter 2).

Given this perspective, an investigator may determine that the general health item is fine (e.g., "fit for use") because we may not care especially what variety of health our respondents are thinking about—a response of Excellent is so different from Poor that it is adequate for apportioning individuals to categories representing extremes of self-reported health status. On the other hand, for a survey endeavoring to assess cross-cultural differences, the investigator may decide that the global item is insufficient, because it simply incorporates too many varied conceptual elements for resultant survey data to be unambiguously interpreted. It is for this reason that the Centers for Disease Control and Prevention, Behavioral Risk Factor Surveillance System (CDC-BRFSS) decided (I believe on the basis of cognitive testing results) to administer separate items on physical and mental/emotional health—as "health in general" captures too much to be useful as a singular item. Theme coding would be ideal for making such determinations.

To illustrate related variants of Theme coding, I provide two additional examples. The first comes from Miller, Willson, and Maitland (2008), who explicitly make use of a Venn diagram—analogous to what I have referred to as area (B) in Figure 4.2—partitioned into segments representing distinctions with respect to item conceptualization. Miller and her colleagues have applied this approach to create what I label *pie-chart coding*: For a range of concepts, they create a circle (such as that in Figure 4.4), which can then be subdivided into the key components that are found to constitute this conceptual whole—a type of "Table of the Elements" with respect to this concept. For instance, the question: "*Overall, during the past 4 weeks, how much difficulty did you have with thinking clearly and solving daily problems?*" revealed six interpretations). Looking at this simple example, the analyst may be tempted to code Interpretations 1 and 3 into a "more serious" category (which could be labeled "Chronic limitation or health problem") and the others into a "less serious" category ("Activities/problems of daily life"). If, based on more extensive testing, it turned out that these two categories describe what the question captures, then this would be viewed as the key cognitive interviewing result.

Other means exist, beyond pie-chart coding, to arrange, organize, and represent thematic codes, including the use of hierarchical representations to organize concepts. Miller et al. (2014) present a series of flowcharts that illustrate successively more complex relationship inherent in the coded data. As an illustration, the simplest of these consists of a figure that summarizes findings from testing the item "Does (child) have difficulty hearing?" by reporting two types of activities mentioned by participants: (a) literal hearing, and (b) listening; and then subdividing (a) into (i) hearing in a noisy environment, and (ii) hearing in a quiet environment (Figure 4.5). This type of visual scheme helps the analyst to both understand and convey potentially complex relationships between the components that together comprise an evaluated concept.

This information can be used to understand the function of the question either within the current investigation or for future uses of the item to achieve particular objectives. Of course, one can take the next logical step and consider whether the evaluated item needs to be modified (repaired) so as to alter, or to restrict, this range of interpretations in order to satisfy the objectives of the

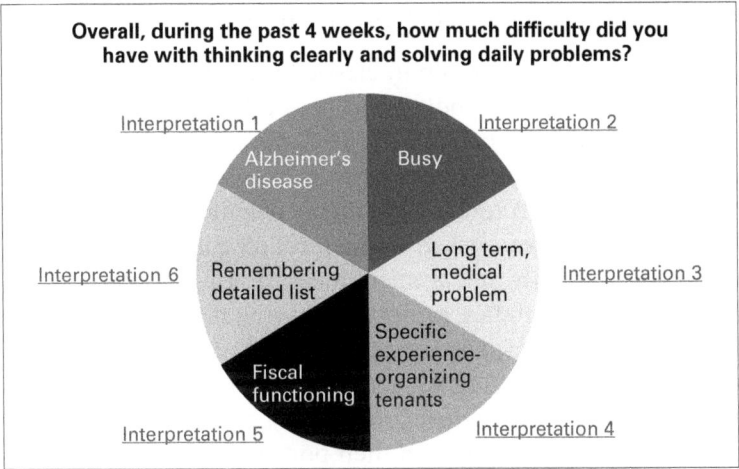

Figure 4.4. Example of use of Pie-Chart Coding to identify what a question captures, using Theme Coding. Source: Willis & Miller (2008).

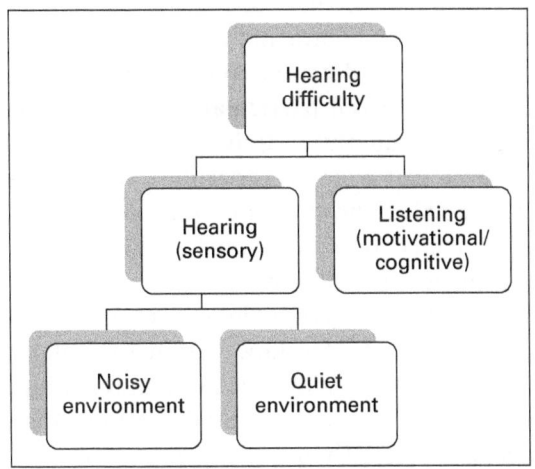

Figure 4.5. Flowchart organization of themes uncovered by Miller, Willson, Chepp, and Padilla (2014) through cognitive testing of the item "Does (child) have difficulty hearing?"

investigation. This decision, however, may be left to the research investigator (e.g., the client, sponsor, or design team), rather than the cognitive testing staff. In such cases, disentanglement of the concept—to appreciate fully what the question captures—is the goal, and therefore the product, of cognitive testing.

4.13.2. Mixed Approach to the Use of Theme Coding

As I noted earlier, although in classic form a Grounded Theory perspective on Theme coding will have a Descriptive base, it is also possible to code themes within a Reparative study. An example consists of a cognitive interviewing investigation by Knafl and colleagues (2007). A total of 27 parents of children with chronic health condition were asked to interpret 65 questionnaire items comprising a family management measure. Unlike many cognitive interviewing studies, rather than having respondents answer the target questions, the investigators asked them to directly interpret the meaning of each question. A systematic coding sheet was used to summarize their comments.

To enable data reduction of their body of comments, the analysts conducted a systematic "item review" following qualitative research procedures described by Miles and Huberman (1994). First, verbatim transcriptions of all participant responses were produced, and then a listing was made, for each item, of the related comments. The comments were appended with several items of demographic data, as contextual information. The authors then summarized participant interpretations of each item, by applying inductively derived (bottom-up) codes. The codes that developed from considering a wide range of such comments resembled those of the Question Feature Coding approach described earlier: (a) limited applicability, (b) unclear reference, (c) unclear perspective, and (d) problems with wording or tone. Finally, the analysts looked across all of the comments for each item, to see how varied the interpretations were, and developed a decision rule for item retention: "Thirty-one items were retained without modification. Across the 31 retained items, no more than one parent provided an idiosyncratic interpretation of the item, one that varied substantially from all other respondents" (p. 230). In effect, the researchers applied the logic of a Reparative investigation but without top-down constraints on code production.

This example serves the wider purpose of illustrating how coding and analysis approaches may borrow elements from the different models in Figure 4.1. I caution the practitioner not to fall into the trap of thinking that "Qualitative researchers do things one way, and cognitive psychologists do them another way." In particular, both Reparative and Descriptive studies can make use of a variety of coding approaches. There may be a tendency to follow what others in the same disciplinary field have done in the past, but that limitation is self-imposed. This point is most salient with respect to the notion of code assignment: We might do this via a number of ways—both top-down and bottom-up—even within the same investigation. Further, we may combine Reparative and Descriptive elements.

4.14. Analysis Model 5: Pattern Coding

The analysis procedure that I choose to refer to as Pattern Coding bears close resemblance to the *Framework approach* advocated by Miles and Huberman (1994) and extended by Spencer, Ritchie, and O'Conner (2003); it can also be referred to as *matrix coding*. Whatever term one favors, I consider this analysis procedure to involve, at its root, searching for "patterns in the data." Although every analysis procedure for cognitive interviews can be thought of as attending to patterns, this approach is the one most actively targeted toward the detection of relationships across, and between, the various elements we assess—involving not only the item tested but also other survey items, the participants' characteristics, and background sociocultural context. The term *pattern* therefore fits well as a one-word reference to convey the notion that our emphasis is not so much on naming, labeling, or assigning codes, but rather on describing *how item functioning varies as a function of these other factors*. Although I include Pattern Coding as a ground-up procedure, as this appears to be the normative application, there is no restriction such that this approach could not also be carried out in a top-down manner.

4.14.1. Using Data Displays to Portray Patterns

A key characteristic of the Pattern Coding approach is to create what Miles and Huberman (1984) labeled a *data display*. This concept is critical to the qualitative research tradition: In order to make trends in the data viewable by the analyst (again, implicitly invoking the cognitive aspects of data analysis), the data must be placed in a format in which relationships and trends can be clearly identified. A data display is a way of indicating, by use of table or other display, what we have found, or what Miles and Huberman (1984, p. 21) describe as an "organized assembly of information that permits conclusion drawing and action taking." They argue that although a frequent form of reduction for qualitative data has been summative text, this produces a cumbersome and poorly structured array that overwhelms the analyst's processing system and can create biases. Displays, on the other hand, may be matrices, graphs, networks, or charts—that "assemble organized information in an immediately accessible, compact form, so that the analyst can see what is happening and either draw justified conclusions or move on to the next-step analysis the display suggests may be useful" (p. 21).

The earlier table in this book (Table 1.1 in Chapter 1), depicting a two-by-two illustration of having or not having health insurance, as both reported by the participant and as conceptualized by the researcher, is in essence a data display. The cells within the display can then be used for both quantitative purposes (to count each type of relationship), and for qualitative purposes by including rich contextual information, so that it is possible to make reference to the specific information or behavior underlying the assignment to that cell in the table. For cognitive interviews, especially those having a Reparative emphasis, it seems that this type of display—that focuses on both the participant and researcher conceptualizations, respectively—is naturally useful.

4.14.2. Example of Pattern Coding

Within a very large cognitive interviewing investigation—the most extensive I have encountered—Miller et al. (2010) examined six core questions on various forms of physical, sensory, and mental disability, using a very structured cognitive interviewing guide, to 1,290 participants across 15 countries in Central and South America, Asia, and Africa. As well as administering the to-be-tested questions, they presented additional scripted probe questions (what Willis, 2005, refers to as Anticipated probes) to provide additional explanatory information. Because their focus was on cross-cultural comparability, a major emphasis was placed on how questions are interpreted—and also whether these interpretations matched the investigator intent. As such, the approach was initially Descriptive but ultimately included at least the inspection element of a Reparative investigation. The evaluated multipart question focused on various forms of disability:

> *The next questions ask about difficulties you may have doing certain activities because of a HEALTH PROBLEM.*
> *Do you have difficulty seeing, even if wearing glasses?*
> *Do you have difficulty hearing, even if using a hearing aid?*
> *Do you have difficulty walking or climbing steps?*
> *Do you have difficulty remembering or concentrating?*
> *Do you have difficulty (with self-care such as) washing all over or dressing?*
> *Using your usual (customary) language, do you have difficulty communicating, for example understanding or being understood?*

The authors provide a detailed description of the analysis concerning the first item in the series, involving difficulty with seeing. Analysis was conducted by comparing answers given by the respondents to this item with the responses to two additional follow-up probes that asked (1) whether the person wore glasses and (2) whether he or she had difficulty seeing either near or far. By relating the responses to these questions and probes, the analysts attended to *patterns* of responses that indicated either consistency or inconsistency for each participant. With respect to the vision item, the eight patterns (A through H) in the data were recorded (Table 4.15).

Note, first, that similarly to Theme coding as described earlier, all of the collected data are considered—and not only those that are problematic and indicate a need for repair. In essence, this strategy—using a data display to portray all of the data, as Miles and Huberman (1984) advocated decades ago—is similar to the example concerning health insurance that was introduced in Chapter 1 as an example of the type of qualitative data that are available from cognitive interviewing. This analysis strategy also considers explicitly where cognitive interview participants may be providing conflicting information—between the tested item and the answers to probes—as has been a common practice (Willis, 2005). Hence, there is nothing particularly radical about the logic applied. Mainly, what is noteworthy is that we are extremely

Table 4.15
Illustration of Patterns of responses to tested items and cognitive probes

	Pattern (n: %)	Answer to tested question: Do you have difficulty seeing, even if wearing glasses?	Wears glasses?	Does follow-up probe indicate difficulty with near or far vision?
Consistent (969, *83.3%*)	A (468, *40.2%*)	No	No	No
	B (149, *12.8%*)	No	Yes	No
	C (183, *15.7%*)	Yes	No	Yes
	D (169, *14.5%*)	Yes	Yes	Yes
Inconsistent (194, *16.7%*)	E (119, *10.2%*)	Yes	Yes	No
	F (30, *2.6%*)	Yes	No	No
	G (21, *1.8%*)	No	Yes	Yes
	H (24, *2.0%*)	No	No	Yes

Source: Miller, K., Mont, D., Maitland, A., Altman, B., & Madans, J. (2010).

systematic in considering the patterns observed, across all interviews. Further, we actively consider the implications of each of these patterns, with respect to the measurement properties of the item.

Miller et al. considered Patterns A through D in Table 4.15 to be consistent and rational. Persons who answer the evaluated question ("Do you have difficulty seeing, even with glasses?") with a *No* may, upon further probing, indicate that they do not wear glasses, and that they do not have any type of problem with seeing either near or far (Pattern A). Similarly, a person answering *No* to the initial question on difficulty may wear glasses, and when probed indicate no visual acuity problems because the glasses successfully correct his or her vision (B). Patterns C and D are the inverse cases: The individual supports a *Yes* answer to the target item (difficulty seeing) by indicating that he or she either lacks glasses and therefore has problems seeing near or far (C), or else has glasses yet still experiences near/far problems (D).

E–H, on the other hand, represent inconsistent patterns of response between tested questions and follow-up probes. Pattern E consists of a person who reports (a) *Yes* to the tested question about having difficulty seeing, and (b) wearing glasses, yet (c) no difficulty seeing near or far, implying that the glasses successfully correct the person's vision. Pattern F differs in that the individual initially reports difficulty seeing, does not wear glasses, yet when probed also gives no indication of a problem with near or far vision. For Patterns G and H, the individual indicates no difficulty with vision, but both those with glasses (G) and those without (H) do later indicate some problem related to near/far vision.

The patterns with which these frequencies occurred were quantified: 83.3% were found to be consistent. Inconsistent cases (16.7%) were further divided into those (n = 149, or 12.8%) that were regarded as false positives (i.e., Patterns E and F, who reported difficulty with vision, yet no problems when probed about near-far difficulty), and 3.8% false negatives (G and H, who reported no difficulty, yet who later did indicate problems with near/far vision). The causes of discrepancies were in turn ascertained by digging even deeper, making use of information obtained from two additional follow-up probe questions also asked of all participants (following the original source, data for these do not appear in Table 4.15):

1. [With your glasses], how much effort do you have to put into seeing?
2. [With your glasses], how often do you have difficulty seeing well?

Based on these additional probes, Miller et al. considered 53.7% of the initial false positives (80 of 149) to be truly false, as the participants indicated that they put little effort into seeing and had little difficulty seeing well. Most of these cases (71 of 80) were found to be contained in just one pattern: (E), corresponding to a visual problem that is corrected by glasses. The analysts concluded that these people, who did wear (perfectly adequate) glasses, had reported problems seeing simply because they did not hear (or ignored) the phrase "even when wearing glasses" in the initial question. As a consequence, they believed that they should answer as if not wearing them.

False-positive reports involving pattern (F), although infrequent ($n = 30$), were different: These were people who initially reported difficulty seeing, wore no glasses, yet also reported no problems seeing either near or far. However, they did answer the final cognitive probes by indicating that they had to expend effort and often had difficulty seeing well. These individuals were interpreted as those with a vision problem unrelated to nearsightedness or farsightedness, such as night blindness or injury to one eye. Unlike Pattern E, which indicated a problematic response to the evaluated question, Pattern F was not interpreted by the research team as a defect—but rather as an advantage, as it indicated that the initial question served to detect visual difficulties other than those related to basic acuity.

Note how the authors in this case made use of the probe questions strategically, as they compared results, developed hypotheses, and then made use of responses to further probes to support or refute these, or to obtain clarifying information. It is because of this systematic, investigative "interrogation" of the data that I consider this approach to be bottom up in nature, as it makes use of the information at hand. It certainly would be possible to name and specify every potential pattern up front, consistent with a top-down coding approach. That, however, could produce a huge number of patterns to identify and decode. It seems more efficient to follow the path blazed by Miller et al., in regarding the qualitative data as a puzzle to be solved once they are collected, consistent with the investigative methods typically advocated by qualitative researchers.

The overall advantage of systematically examining patterns for consistency versus inconsistency, across items, is that the researcher can understand the various ways in which the evaluated questions are interpreted, and to perhaps obtain evidence of issues that may be creating problems resulting in survey response error (or if not literally error, a discrepancy between interviewer and respondent interpretations). Intensive (and perhaps even tedious) analyses of this nature may make clear the functioning, and perhaps the limitations, of the evaluated questions, in the Descriptive sense. Beyond this, however, it seems that within-participant inconsistencies also represent problems with the items that perhaps cry out for attention. That is, if participants are internally inconsistent, or are found to produce conflicts with the answers to further probe questions, one might reasonably argue that we have crossed the line from the purely Descriptive to the Reparative. By analogy, even if we have not endeavored to fix leaks, it does seem that the boat in this case has some large holes in it. Thus, a clear understanding of how the question functions in this case indicates that, to some extent, it is malfunctioning—respondents are likely to fail to adequately encode the phrase "even when wearing glasses"—which I regard as a clear problem. In many cases, the distinction between what is purely Descriptive versus Reparative is hazy—we aim to understand but cannot help but to inspect. Whether the damage is repaired is up to the researcher.

To summarize: Pattern Coding is intriguing because it illustrates a mixing of concepts and elements key to analysis of cognitive interviewing results:

1. It contains elements of both Descriptive and Reparative research, and it involves elements of both pure empiricism (i.e., looking at what respondents say, think, and do) and also the interleaving of investigator objectives, as well as hypothesis generation, using our prior knowledge of questionnaire function to guide our interpretations.
2. The Pattern Coding approach is cross-cutting, in that it explicitly forces us to consider the consistency of results across tested survey items, between the response provided by the participant to the target item and those to the probes used to study those items, and across defined participant subgroups. In fact, it is the Pattern approach that perhaps puts the most demand on the full set of cognitive processes the analyst must bring to bear.

4.15. Strengths and Limitations of Each of the Five Key Analysis Approaches

I have deferred a discussion of the relative benefits and costs of each analysis approach until describing them. Figure 4.6 summarizes key strengths and limitations of each of the five models I have defined, and serves as a guide to the following in-depth

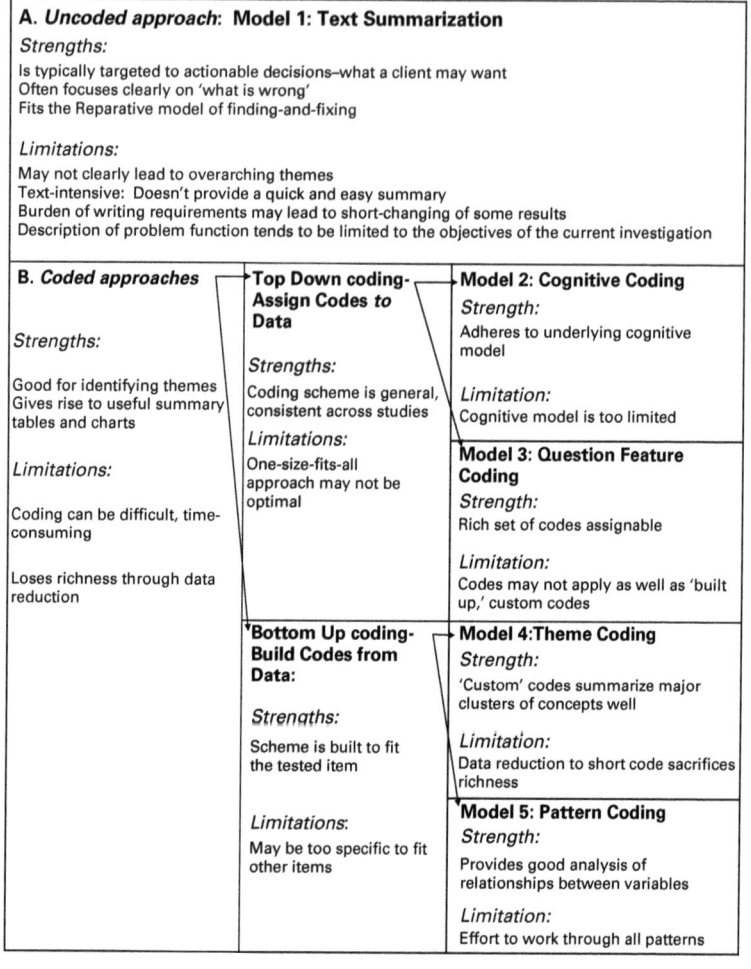

Figure 4.6. Strengths and limitations of five models for the analysis of cognitive interviews.

discussion. To begin, one must decide which of the two major branches in the tree illustrated in Figure 4.1 to follow: Do we use a simple Text Summary approach that avoids coding and categorization, or do we insist that results of cognitive interviews include categories that are associated with a coding scheme? If we do categorize our data or produce codes, as opposed to providing only text-based description on a question-by-question basis, should we follow the approach of the psychological and questionnaire design orientations, which emphasize extant coding schemes that can be used as ready-made templates? Or should we work only from the ground up, according to the more inductive Theme coding model? Further, how comprehensive should the analysis be? Do we work through all of our data to completely describe the reactions to our evaluated items, whether positive or negative? Or should we cut to the chase and focus on what does not work, as opposed to worrying also about what does?

4.15.1. Strengths and Limitations of Model 1: Text Summary

Strengths:

> *Efficiency:* Text-based summaries are fairly quick to complete, and—although I do not want to underrepresent the amount of work invariably involved—are relatively low burden on the analyst. Because no coding is done, one need not be concerned with the meticulous process of either assigning codes (if top down) or developing them (if bottom up). As such, there is also no need to be concerned about computation of interrater code reliability; with the effectiveness of whatever coding scheme is used; or with training of analysts to apply the codes.
>
> *Richness of data:* The focus on text—that is, words—can be a significant strength. By virtue of describing results in prose, including quotes from interviews, and what has been called "thick description" (Lincoln & Guba, 1985), the analyst can retain a richness, and a context, that only comes from a detailed summarization. The use of codes (e.g., the question is coded as having a Recall problem) necessarily involves data reduction in a way that at least some information is lost (e.g., recall of what, in particular?). This is an especially important problem when the objective of our testing is Reparative—to locate specific deficiencies with targeted questions and then to address them. The more detailed information we have, the easier it is to diagnose and then fix the problem.

Limitations of the Text Summary:

> *Volume:* As Miles et al. (2014) point out, written summaries tend to produce a large volume of material that is difficult to

process by the human analyst. Pages of written notes may be impossible to sort through to make efficient use of, impeding our attempts to "get to the bottom line."

Incomplete analysis: Because notes get long and laborious, there is a tendency to cut corners and fail to write everything up (i.e., analysis satisficing). This may be one reason that analysts choose to focus on problems, as opposed to a full description of question functioning. Although there is certainly no inherent reason why we cannot produce a Text Summary for everything the question captures, I have seen that this simply does not tend to happen, and the descriptions become very problem focused and therefore limited in scope.

Lack of a grounding framework: When one uses a coding system, the particular codes used force the analyst to pay attention to recurrent behavior or results that represent an underlying consistency. In fact, this is a key reason that coding is used—two participants may describe their views on mental health using different words, but both may be reasonably categorized as understanding the concept identically. Recognizing such consistencies may be more difficult when we are simply summarizing in strings of text, absent the intermediate step of developing a coding category that allows us to step back and take a tree-top view.

4.15.2. Strengths and Limitations of Model 2: Cognitive Coding

Strengths:

1. *Suitability for quantification*: Once we conduct coding of results into prescribed cognitive categories, we can easily tabulate the codes to produce a degree of quantification that is often missing from qualitative research. This becomes especially useful when submitting reports on cognitive interviewing results to academic journals, which often expect numeric data, and even statistical analysis, for an otherwise qualitative investigation. As such, a statement such as "62.5% of problems observed were within the Comprehension category, and this was significantly greater

($p < .05$) than the frequency of Recall problems (22.5%)" has some attraction, as it "looks like science."

2. *Comparability across investigations:* Cognitive coding categories (e.g., the Tourangeau cognitive categories) can be used across investigation, laboratories, and testing context, allowing an assessment of comparability of results. For example, both Presser and Blair (1994) and Willis (2005) found that Comprehension codes dominated. Such results can be useful in advancing the science by helping to establish what cognitive interviewing is most useful for; or perhaps in describing the relative magnitude of various types of problems inherent in survey questionnaires.
3. *Reliance on theoretical underpinning*: To reiterate, the fields of questionnaire design generally, and cognitive interviewing specifically, have sometimes been criticized as devoid of a common underlying theory as a driving force. In part, this has produced a great degree of enthusiasm for the Tourangeau cognitive model, as it engages at least rudimentary cognitive theory. A coding system that makes use of such codes has merit, to the extent that it incorporates theory.

Limitations:

1. *One-size-fits-all approach*: Adoption of a cognitively oriented coding scheme assumes that a unified system applies across topics, respondents, specific question types, and so on. Proponents of the reverse view—for example, from Grounded Theory—are likely to take issue with this and to suggest that the "truth" should be contained within the dataset, and not imposed on it by preset coding categories.
2. *Loss of information through coding*: Because coding involves data reduction, specific information is invariably lost. I have already stated my view that a four-process cognitive coding scheme is limited in "getting to the root of the problem."
3. *A limited range of codes*: A purely cognitive coding scheme, by definition, omits anything regarded as other than cognitive in nature.

4.15.3. Strengths and Limitations of Model 3: Question Feature Coding

Strengths:

> The benefits of coding systems that are oriented toward features of the evaluated items are similar to those that emphasize cognitive processes. The codes produced are suitable for quantification, as coding frequencies can be reported. Further, code frequencies can be compared across investigations using the same system. One departure may be with respect to theory—as it cannot be claimed that feature-based systems rely on a theoretical orientation, as does cognitive theory. However, even if bereft of theory, the adoption of a general-purpose model, such as those that document question-design defects, as the QAS and CCS, do represent attempts at modeling errors associated with survey questions, and these models tend to be similar in positing question characteristics that create difficulty, and therefore serve as a lens through which to interpret our testing results.

Limitations:

> Like the advantages, the drawbacks of Question-Feature coding are similar to those of Cognitive coding. The singular approach of a top-down system may constrain what can be coded, and therefore learned, from the empirical qualitative data. Further, as for any type of code that involves data reduction, detailed levels of information are invariably lost.

4.15.4. Strengths and Limitations of Model 4: Theme Coding

Strengths:

1. *Fit to the data*: Because codes are developed from the ground up, they invariably fit the analyzed dataset well. We end up with a set of codes that describe what each evaluated question captures (i.e., to the extent that our data are extensive and rich enough to provide this information).
2. *Description of full question function*: As a related benefit, but with a different emphasis, the Theme codes can be used

to fully describe question functioning in a way that the question's fitness for use can be assessed across a range of potential objectives. The now familiar question "Would you say your health in general is Excellent... Poor?" might give rise to themes describing (a) physical health; (b) mental/emotional health; (c) spiritual health; or even (d) financial health. An investigator armed with this information can then decide how useful this question is for fulfilling a particular requirement, or whether it may be necessary to decompose it into its various elements in order to measure these separately.

Limitations:

1. *Lack of generalizability*: As discussed, although bottom-up, custom-built codes may apply well for a particular survey question, they tend to be specific to that question. Hence, the codes developed for the general health question would not apply to another item asking about satisfaction with one's employment situation. Whether this is seen as a defect depends on our intent—if we want the codes to be universal, this would be a drawback. Blair and Brick (2010) have suggested that the time and labor involved in the establishment of a new coding scheme for each additional questionnaire (or question) may be excessive and favor the alternative of a harmonized, top-down system.
2. *Loss of information through coding*: Just as for top-down codes, grounded codes may result in the loss of some specific information pertinent to question inspection and repair. In particular, although Theme coding tends to be very effective in capturing the range of interpretations, it may not be as effective in accounting for cognitive processes other than those pertaining to question comprehension. Given severe retrieval-based problems (e.g., if the question asks, "How was your health during March, 1970?" it may not be of interest to determine how the question is interpreted, but rather whether respondents can remember the answer. It may be possible to generalize a theme-based coding system to account for discoveries such as retrieval failure, and Miller (2011) has argued that such processes can be subsumed under the

rubric of interpretive processes. On the other hand, there are defensible reasons for separating Recall, Decision, and Response processes from the interpretive processes associated with Comprehension in the Tourangeau cognitive model, and a case can be made for viewing them as different subspecies, within the questionnaire-related animal kingdom.

4.15.5. Strengths and Limitations of Model 5: Pattern Coding

Strengths:

1. *In-depth focus on question function*: The systematic dissection of patterns between the responses to evaluated survey questions, and those to further probe questions or other survey items, provides a richly structured way to assess question function. By working through the degree to which information provided is consistent, for every case, the researcher is not likely to miss interesting and useful information.
2. *Suitability for both Descriptive and Reparative purposes*: Assessing all the patterns both consistent and inconsistent—satisfies the Descriptive research emphasis on "what the question captures." As a natural extension, more focused attention on the inconsistent patterns gives rise to hypotheses concerning why the question is problematic in the current context, which also satisfies the common mechanical requirements of Reparative pretesting. That is, attending to patterns that either conform to, or violate, the investigator's expectations, produces results that conform to the requirements of a Reparative study.
3. *Providing structure to the cognitive interview*: By virtue of its reliance on tables, charts, or other data displays, a Pattern approach requires that specific types of information be gathered during the cognitive interview—or cells will end up with missing data. That is, if we neglect to probe appropriately to determine whether the participant was appropriately using the reference period—or appropriately interpreted the phrase "even when wearing

glasses"—then this will be evident when the table is completed and that information is conspicuously missing. Thus, it makes sense to create the table headings first and to use these as a guide to probing, which leads the interviewer to ensure that all appropriate information has been obtained in each interview.
4. *Suitability for large investigations.* A feature that derives directly from (3) is that the process of (a) setting up a table, (b) obtaining concurrence concerning its use across interviewers, and (b) relying on this as both a data collection guide and an analysis tool, helps significantly in cases where many interviews (e.g., hundreds) are to be conducted across a range of researchers or laboratories. Development of a structured table—prior to the conduct of the interviews—may go a long way toward maintenance of the analyst's sanity (or at the least, minimizes cognitive fatigue).

Limitations:

1. *Effort required.* It clearly requires time and energy to work through and map all of the patterns intrinsic in the data. If applied to every question, this could be quite a task to accomplish.
2. *Providing too much structure to the interview.* The strength mentioned earlier—the structure provided a priori by the establishment of a table or chart that gives rise to patterns—can be a weakness to the extent that it restricts imaginative probing. Given that structured probing is *Anticipatory* in nature (Willis, 2005), it focuses on issues that are sought out prior to the interview, based on researcher expectation. The danger associated with this approach is that unexpected issues that are in evidence during the interview are less well represented (i.e., those best detected through *reactive, emergent* probes that are constructed during the interview). One can avoid this problem by resisting the temptation to *only* address "what is to be filled into the table"—and to retain a capacity for modifying the table subsequent to data collection, in order to represent unexpected findings. This more fluid approach, of course, may negate the advantage of structuring the interviews so that "everyone is looking for the same

things"—and is therefore likely to reduce strict comparability of results.

4.16. Which Coding System Is Best?

One way to answer the "Which is best?" question is to object that this choice is not in any way forced upon us: We can utilize multiple approaches within any investigation. The analyst might decide that there are several questions for which we will focus on Text Summarization, emphasizing observed problems for respondents from the start, and others for which it will be very informative to conduct ground-up coding to determine what the question captures (see the Case Studies in Chapter 7). Even within the qualitative research tradition, it is not the case that codes are necessarily completely ground up or top down, and this may vary over the course of an investigation, as more data are collected, codes are developed, and then are established and used within later rounds, or in later investigations (Miles et al., 2014). For example, O'Brien et al. (2013) initiated their qualitative-research-based coding project with a set of a priori codes, but revised these throughout the course of data collection and analysis. Similarly, even those who have adhered to a cognitively based theoretical orientation, such as Willis et al. (1991), have sometimes found it useful to assign observations that failed to fit into established code categories to a newly defined (Logical-Structural) category, that is developed in ground-up fashion from the data.

A second way to answer the question concerning "Which coding system is best?" is with the question: "Best for what?" Note that there are vast differences in the approaches used in interpretation of qualitative research results generally—and not only of cognitive interviewing—and that this is not necessarily a defect, as this provides us with a tool chest of potential solutions. In determining which approach to take, the answer must depend on the objectives, practical aspects like time and resources, nature of the materials tested, respondent populations, and so on. To be more specific, the principal considerations that I would use to guide these decisions are as follows:

Coding requires time, effort, and resources: If the investigators are in a hurry—in full production mode—then there may be little time to do more than to create quick Text Summaries.

For example, we may say that *"None of the participants I interviewed could understand this question because it is very long and complicated, and I suggest breaking it into two simpler questions."* The analysis in this case is very targeted and specific, and it does not attempt to fully determine everything that the question captures. For evaluated questions for which the interviewer observed nothing remarkable indicating that there is some type of problem—however defined—we may simply note "no problems noted" and focus our energies on those questions that are found to be problematic.

Looking to the future requires attention to the present. If, rather than simply working to get the project done, we instead carry out cognitive interviewing in a way that the results are to have meaningful application to future investigations, or to inform the science of questionnaire design and evaluation more fully, then a more intensive, systematic approach is appropriate. This does not mean that one cannot do Text Summary analysis and must instead code every result. It does mean, however, that we should fully investigate and document as much as possible, with respect to *each tested item*. That is, if we are going to the trouble to conduct cognitive interviews, we may as well fully explain everything that occurred when testing each item.

I recommend going beyond simply concluding, for any evaluated survey items, that "no problems were noted"—and explain *why* we are saying that. Put another way, we must fully elaborate the nonproblematic findings as much as the problematic ones—given that the problem/no-problem distinction, or threshold, may be different in a future study where the objectives, or the population surveyed, are different. Especially if our underlying philosophy is not that question are either "good" or "bad," but rather that they are fit for some uses more than for others, then it is logical that our pretesting approaches, and their analysis, reflect this viewpoint.

Documentation is vital. If one does decide to adopt a minimalistic inspection-and-repair point of view, it may be allowable (or at least excusable) to forego elaborate and extensive description of problem function and choose to simply state that *"The question works"*—that is, it satisfies the current requirements. However, it is imperative to at least indicate, for the record, *our basis for stating this*. Did we in fact inspect the target item, or were there no problems because it was not asked during the cognitive interview? (This is a not infrequent consequence of attempting to test a questionnaire that is too long, such that only selected questions are actually tested.) Or was the item asked during cognitive testing but left relatively unprobed because it was not one of the questions deemed critical to evaluate? Finally, if the item was tested in a meaningful sense, can we at least provide a summary that explains how the item was interpreted, with respect to the intended interpretation: In effect: *"The intent of the item was to measure X—in each case it was evaluated, probed participants described an interpretation that was consistent with that meaning and contained no elements other than the one intended."*

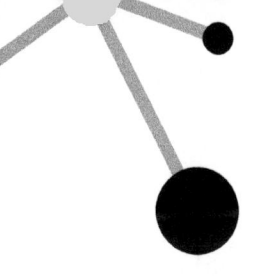

CRITICAL ISSUES IN ANALYSIS OF COGNITIVE INTERVIEWING RESULTS

5.1. Chapter Overview

In Chapter 4, I identified five general approaches to analysis and their relative benefits and drawbacks. Even after considering these and deciding on an approach, there are still several analysis issues to consider. In this chapter, I therefore cover, in turn, the following:

> Issue 1: How should we combine or aggregate data across multiple interviewers?
> Issue 2: Does sample size influence what we can do analytically?
> Issue 3: How do we deal with multiple levels of analysis: within interview, across interview, and across subgroups? Concerning the latter: Can the findings concerning problems with survey questions be compared across cultures or linguistic groups?
> Issue 4: Can we rely on our background expertise to help us with analysis?
> Issue 5: Can we rely on the computer to help us with analysis?

5.2. Issue 1: Combining Data Across Interviews

I have considered the raw materials of coding—what it is that gets coded, assuming any coding is performed—mainly at a relatively low level: the individual cognitive interview, or within a single cognitive interviewer. However, it is common to utilize multiple cognitive *interviewers* to conduct the interviews, such that streams of data consisting of interpretations across interviewers must be combined, perhaps across several laboratories or interviewing teams. For several reasons, I believe that relying on an interviewing team, as opposed to a single interviewer, is a positive feature—especially from the point of view of the individuals who are able to distribute the interviewing load but also for reasons detailed elsewhere (Willis, 2005). However, given that cognitive interviewing is a flexible qualitative endeavor, it does beg the question of how the data from different interviewers—and even from collaborating cognitive laboratories—can be effectively combined and analyzed. In particular:

- Should interviewers conduct their analyses independently, and then compare and combine?
- Or should they come together and collaborate in the analysis from the start?
- Should interviewers meet and discuss their results prior to writing them up?

At first glance, the obvious answer may that analysis should be done independently, to avoid contamination; that collaboration too early in the analysis stage violates basic principles of science. In particular, we might regard such efforts as contaminating if they cause analysts to change their approach to the interpretation of their data. So we might question the legitimacy of having interviewers "compare notes," prior to coming to their own judgments. Further, we might ask why any interviewer would alter the description of what he or she has seen in the interviews, based on what someone else has seen.

5.3. Successive Aggregation

In fact, one model of analysis of multiple interviewers' cognitive interviews has for some time followed a model that allows for a degree of independence. The *Successive Aggregation* of results, as the term implies, involves the combination of sets of independently analyzed interviews that are reconciled once they are aggregated at the highest level. As a metaphor, consider a set of builders who will be working together to create a boat and who work independently to prefabricate its major structures. They may all come together with their work done and contribute their part to the larger whole—which is coordinated by an overall project analyst. Analysis of cognitive interviews has often followed a similar sequence (e.g., Lee, 2014). A set of interviewers writes up their own results and delivers them to a coordinating researcher, who then acts as an adjudicator to fashion these into a single, coherent set intended to fit together seamlessly.

More precisely: Under the Successive Aggregation model, if for a hypothetical project, three interviewers within each of three cognitive testing laboratories each conducts four interviews, there will be 36 interviews to combine. So this can proceed in steps, as summarized in Figure 5.1.

Aggregation Step 1: Summarizing within-interviewer. Each interviewer "writes up" his or her own results, combining across all four interviews, to produce an Interviewer Text Summary, as

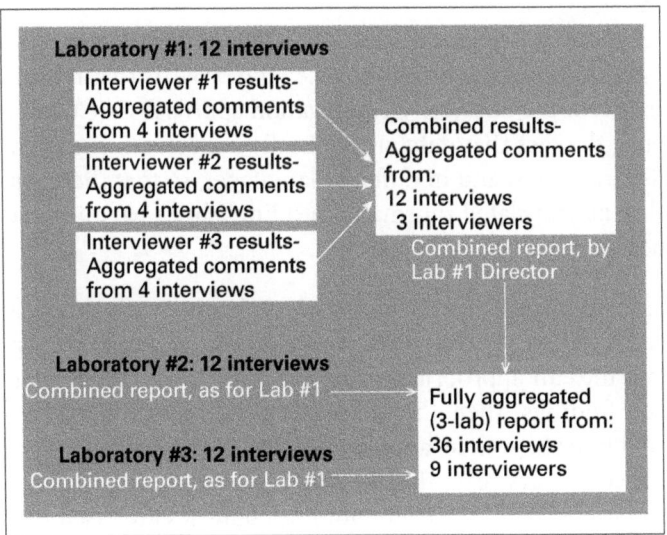

Figure 5.1. Successive Aggregation of results over three laboratories (9 interviews each) to produce 36 total interviews.

defined in Chapter 4. For example, Interviewer 1 within Lab 1 may state that *"For the question asking about dental sealants, two of my participants believed these to be fillings, which is not the correct interpretation."* Each of the interviewers would produce such a summary, resulting in a total of three interviewer-level text summaries within each lab.

Aggregation Step 2: Summarizing within-laboratory. Within each of Labs 1, 2, and 3, the three interviewers submit their report to a higher level analyst. That person summarizes across the interviewers within each lab, resulting in three lab-level reports (e.g., a summary from Lab 1 may be that *"Of 12 tested participants, 6 erroneously identified a 'dental sealant' as a filling; we should consider providing a definition."*

Aggregation Step 3: Summarizing across laboratories: The analysts from the three laboratories convene to compare the lab-level reports and to produce a final Project Text Summary across all the interviews. This report may state that *"Across all three cognitive laboratories, we obtained evidence that the term 'dental sealant' is not well understood; 15 of the 36 participants believed this to consist of getting a cavity filled. We propose including a definition, using wording such as '... a dental sealant is a protective covering over the teeth at a dental office, to prevent decay.'"*

Lee (2014) advocates the use of a data compilation procedure for cross-national cognitive interviewing projects that reflects an extension of the Successive Aggregation approach. Lee takes into account the fact that data are normally collected across a range of disparate sites, and in different languages, so that these results need to be translated (normally into English) as part of the data reduction process:

> ...the first part of the data analysis begins with the local team members in the target countries, who record the verbal data into an appropriate form and summarize their interview findings. Then, the various interview results are translated into the source language and then "transferred" to the source country team. In the second part of the analysis, the data inputs collected from multiple countries are assembled and further analyzed in the source country. (p. 234).

If all works as it should, this sequence will result in positive changes to the target items. Further, it is somewhat reassuring that this process retains a capacity for built-in checking on the reliability of results—if each of the laboratories has independently identified the same problem, then this could be seen as a very positive feature that lends credence to our results.

5.3.1. Illustration of Successive Aggregation

Several years ago, I conducted an experiment to test the proposition that independent assessment across cognitive interviews would reveal similar results (Willis, 2009). If so, this would serve to validate cognitive interviewing (i.e., by showing that results are consistent, rather than idiosyncratic). More specifically, the finding that independent analysis gives rise to similar results specifically buttresses the use of a Successive Aggregation approach.

Case Study: Parallel Cognitive Interviews

(a) *Objective*: To determine whether independent assessment by different cognitive laboratories would produce similar overall results. Specifically, a self-administered paper questionnaire asking respondents about their degree of concern about cancer was tested in four independent labs, in four languages.

(b) *Design*: Researchers at four laboratories—The National Cancer Institute, Westat, the National Center for Health Statistics (NCHS), and the Public Health Institute in California (PHI)—each agreed to conduct cognitive testing on the same instrument, using their usual procedures. Table 5.1 illustrates the design and the number of interviews carried out at each laboratory.

(c) *Materials*: The questionnaire evaluated was a "Concern About Cancer" questionnaire designed to assess the respondent's perceptions concerning breast (women) or prostate (men) cancer. In particular, the objective was to determine how concerned individuals are about developing this type of cancer. The questionnaire

Table 5.1
Between-laboratory cognitive interviewing study: Number of cognitive interviews conducted by each of the four laboratories, in each of four languages

	Language of Administration				
	English	Spanish	Chinese	Korean	Total
NCI	16	9	0	0	**25**
Westat	18	36	9	9	**72**
NCHS	15	0	0	0	**15**
PHI	18	0	0	18	**36**
Total	**67**	**45**	**9**	**27**	**148**

followed a common convention for self-administered instruments, by relying on a matrix approach that presented a series of statements, and required a judgment of "feelings of concern now" (Not at all...Extremely), with respect to each of several items (Figure 5.2). The questionnaire contained both an instruction at the top (asking the respondent to circle his or her response indicating degree of concern) and a bolded FEELINGS OF CONCERN NOW heading at the top of the response categories. The individual items to be rated in this way were selected to cover various components of potential concern, including that of developing the cancer, effects that the cancer would have on the body, and of dying. The questionnaire was translated into Spanish, Chinese, and Korean.

(d) *Cognitive testing objectives*: The stated cognitive interviewing objectives were to determine:
- Ease (or difficulty) of completing this task
- Any comprehension problems related to the items or to the overall task
- Degree of perceived duplication across items
- Potential sensitivity of any items or of the overall questionnaire

Please circle the single number (on a scale from 1 to 5) that best describes how concerned you feel right now about the following things:

	FEELINGS OF CONCERN NOW				
	Not at all	Hardly	Somewhat	Very much	Extremely
1. Breast cancer occurring in me	1	2	3	4	5
2. My family's history of cancer	1	2	3	4	5
3. What I can do to prevent breast cancer	1	2	3	4	5
4. Breast cancer hiding silently in my body	1	2	3	4	5
5. Not being able to avoid getting breast cancer	1	2	3	4	5
6. How I would feel if I had breast cancer	1	2	3	4	5
7. My chances of getting breast cancer in the future	1	2	3	4	5
8. Getting breast cancer without my knowing it	1	2	3	4	5
9. Finding out if I have breast cancer	1	2	3	4	5
10. What I can do to detect breast cancer early	1	2	3	4	5
11. Inheriting cancer from my "genes"	1	2	3	4	5
12. What having breast cancer would do to my body	1	2	3	4	5
13. Symptoms or signs of breast cancer in me	1	2	3	4	5
14. My chances of dying of breast cancer	1	2	3	4	5
15. How I would deal with breast cancer if I got it	1	2	3	4	5
16. Things I do that affect my risk of breast cancer (e.g., activities, habits, lifestyle, diet)	1	2	3	4	5

Figure 5.2. Cancer Risk Perception questions evaluated in between-laboratory cognitive interviewing study (first 16 items).

- Knowledge of breast/prostate cancer by women and men, respectively
- The reference periods that participants used

(e) *Cognitive testing procedures*:
All interviewers were asked to conduct an expert review of the instrument prior to cognitive testing, in order to predict the types of problems likely to occur. Then, for the cognitive testing phase, because the questionnaire was intended for members of the general public who had not experienced breast or prostate cancer, each laboratory used its usual recruitment procedures to locate participants from the general population, excluding those who had one of these cancers. Interviews were conducted using whatever specific procedures the organizations chose to use for a paper-based, self-administered instrument. Investigators across the laboratories engaged in a mix of concurrent and retrospective probing techniques. No further constraints were put on testing procedures, and no communication was allowed between laboratory staffs during the recruitment, interviewing, and analysis phases. Analysis was also conducted according to the usual procedures engaged by each lab—in all cases, a Text Summary approach was taken.

(f) *Results.* Comparison of the summarized written reports submitted by each of the four laboratory staffs produced a clear picture. Although none of the researchers involved had anticipated this in the expert review process, all observed a major defect, hinging on participants' interpretation of the overall task. This can be described by first considering the designers' assumptions: That the respondent will read the instructions at the top, appreciate the requirement to assess each item with respect to his or her current feelings of "concern," and then choose a response between 1 and 5 for each of the vertically listed items.

This was not what was found. Instead, cognitive probing revealed that many participants, across all laboratories, and in all languages, chose a strategy that departed markedly: They initially ignored the instruction, as well as the bolded reminder to think about FEELINGS OF CONCERN NOW, and simply responded to each item in whatever manner they chose. Specifically, participants tended to alter, and to simplify, the task by answering each item in terms of some dimension (other than that of "concern") that could take a value of "Not at all" to "Extremely." So, for the item: "What having breast cancer would do to my body" (Item 12), a typical response was Very Much (4); and when probed (e.g., "Why did you choose that?"), a participant explained that it was "Because cancer would do very much to my body." Similarly, for "My chances of dying from breast cancer" (Item 14), a participant chose Somewhat (3) and explained that she had "somewhat" of a chance of dying from breast cancer. Men's responses for the prostate cancer version showed a strikingly similar pattern.

(g) *Interpretation.* Overall, participants' comprehension tended not to focus on concern about cancer but instead on some other, self-defined consideration. What is of most interest for this exercise was not precisely what was wrong with the questionnaire (although the designer was surely interested!)—but rather the fact that each of the four within-laboratory cognitive interviewing reports contained an overall assessment stating that, in effect, "*The questionnaire approach did not measure perceptions of degree of 'Concern' about (X), because the critical element of Concern was very often ignored.*" Put differently, participants had an overwhelming tendency to answer a different question than the one the researchers believed they were posing—and this tendency was identical across gender and sociocultural group. Further, this fatal flaw had not been identified based on prior expert review, indicating that it was certainly not so obvious that "anyone could have seen that." Most significant was the fact that this illustration was reassuring from a methodological viewpoint: At least for one case study, the answer to the question: "Do independent cognitive labs that assess and then analyze the same instrument come to similar conclusions?" was unambiguously *yes*.

5.3.2. A Failure of Successive Aggregation

The robust results of the Cancer Risk Factor questionnaire testing exercise may be seen as putting to rest the question of how analysts should behave—they should, of course, be independent. However, a wise person one stated that "Sometimes the opposite of a profound truth is another great truth"—and in that sense, there is also evidence that our attempts to maintain analytic independence can be counterproductive. An example—equally compelling as the one I just described—is provided by Miller (described in Willis & Miller, 2008), who worked with colleagues in a multicountry investigation to evaluate survey questions on disability status through cognitive interviewing.

This case study involves a comparative study, across five countries, that applied cognitive interviewing to evaluate disability questions—for example, pertaining to walking. Investigators in the United States, Canada, England, Italy, and Australia all independently tested questions such as:

> *Overall, during the past 4 weeks, how much difficulty did you have with walking long distances, for example 500 (yards/meters) [as appropriate to country]?*

Procedures for analysis and interpretation followed a standard Successive Aggregation model: Each site summarized its own findings, and then sent them to the central coordinator in the United States for compilation. Interestingly, and somewhat distressingly, the results varied greatly. The Italian investigators reported no difficulty with comprehension of the 500-yard/meter measures, whereas findings from the United States, Canada, and Australia suggested serious interpretation problems with participant knowledge of how far this is. It was unclear what to make of these results: Was this a cultural or country-specific phenomenon, such that Italians happen to be better at estimating such distances? Or perhaps it was due to the specific demographic characteristics of the participants who were tested in each cognitive laboratory, as the Italian participants were found as a group to be especially well educated. However, so were the Canadians.

Ultimately, the investigators decided that it was impossible to tell why these disparities had occurred, because there were simply too many potential sources of variation between sites, concerning both the way the testing was carried out and in the nature of the procedures used for data analysis. Further, it appeared that there were important differences in the degree to which results were based on empirical evidence (what was actually observed), as opposed to expert opinion (what the investigators believed concerning question function). Even where empirical evidence was relied upon, there was great variation in who conducted the review of the interviews and the criteria used for establishing whether a problem exists (e.g., in at least one interview versus in multiple interviews). Ultimately, given that it was not possible to reconcile these differences, the team had great difficulty in reaching a consensus concerning what to conclude, concerning how questions functioned and whether they required repair.

5.4. Collaborative Analysis

Based on such experiences, Miller revised her perspective on how analysis should be done—especially for cross-cultural and multinational projects that involve a range of investigators. In essence, the approach she came to advocate relies on reducing the degree of independence between laboratories or sites, both in how the interviews are conducted and how they are analyzed. In particular, she and her colleagues introduced what I will refer to as a *collaborative analysis* (or *joint* analysis), which requires that each analytic step that results in data reduction, beginning at the individual interview level, involves researchers from across the range of sites or interviewing teams, rather than only from within each site (Miller et al., 2011). So, in contrast to Successive Aggregation, the compilation of results is conducted so that the cognitive interviewers and central coordinators are involved at the earliest stages of analysis, in a way that forces harmonized, systematic review of these results. This analytic strategy reiterates key features of qualitative data analysis as promoted by Miles and Huberman (1984), and relies heavily on the use of data displays to depict the results of every interview, for every tested item.

5.4.1. Charting

One example of use of collaborative analysis involves use of a *charting* approach to data display. In this case—also involving multicountry cognitive testing of disability questions, Miller and colleagues (described in Willis & Miller, 2008) began with questions to be tested across locations:

> *Overall during the past 4 weeks, how much difficulty did you have in recognizing the face of someone 4 yards away? (None, Mild, Moderate, Severe, Extreme)*

As is common for cognitive interview studies, the results consisted of text-based comments from individual interviewers. However, conduct and analysis now utilized a data display—the chart—that became the central driver of the investigation. Table 5.2 illustrates the chart used (in simplified form, for illustrative purposes). Across the top this lists the key items of information to be collected, and summarized, for each cognitive interview. In this case, the interviewer was instructed to gather information on the following:

(a) The answer given to the tested question (e.g., Severe Difficulty)
(b) The activity the participant reported being involved in at the time, as ascertained by additional probing by the cognitive interviewer
(c) Whether it was necessary for the interviewer to repeat the question, for the participant to indicate that he or she understood it
(d) Whether, in the interviewer's judgment, the participant illustrated successful comprehension of the critical distance measure (in this case, 4 yards)
(e) Whether, again based on interviewer judgment, the participant accurately comprehended the (4-week) time period involved

The requirements of this *top-row listing* serve to guide the interviewers in their initial task, and illustrate how the nature of analysis can be used to drive initial data collection. Subsequent to completing the interviews, the chart is used to enter information for each tested participant (P1, P2, and P3) at each location.

Table 5.2
Example of a Charting approach to the listing of cognitive testing results

Participant ID	Open/ Verbatim Response	Activity Reported	Repeated Question?	Knew/ Used Distance Measure?	Knew/ Used Time Period?
P1	"Not any"	Watching TV	No	Yes	N/A
P2	"A lot of difficulty"	Seeing someone a block away	No	No	Yes
P3	"I don't know what you mean"	Recognizing a friend: Could be a sight or a memory question	Yes	No	No

Source: Willis & Miller (2008).

A similar chart would be developed for every target survey question—but perhaps with differing top-row variables, depending on the nature of the information deemed to be of importance in understanding the functioning of that question.

Readers will recognize this chart to be a data display produced by the Pattern Coding and analysis strategy described in the previous chapter, and that logic is certainly inherent in this approach. The figure illustrates the results from only three participants—clearly this listing could get very long, once all participants from all the sites are included. However, this form of data display does facilitate the task of making sense of results—at the lowest level—and for deciding, as a collaborative group, what to make of each outcome, prior to aggregating these into a summary judgment.

For example, Participant 1 reported no difficulty recognizing the face of someone 4 yards away. However, although the individual illustrated no apparent problem in understanding what 4 yards is (as he or she used the measure correctly), the activity listed involved watching television. Given that recognizing a person on the television depends fundamentally on the degree of magnification of the face, this has little value as a measure of visual acuity and is clearly outside the scope of interpretation intended by the designers. Hence, this represents an unambiguous problem with interpretation by that participant.

The second participant reported difficulty in recognizing someone but, upon probing, described a situation involving someone "a block away." Under the assumption that there are no 4-yard geographical blocks—in any of the countries involved—the interviewer understandably came to the conclusion that this individual had not adequately encoded the intended measure—again indicating a comprehension/interpretation difficulty.

Finally, Participant 3 could not answer the question—saying, "I don't know what you mean." Probing then revealed that this individual was unsure of the intended meaning, as this could refer to "recognizing someone" in terms of knowing who this person is (e.g., seeing one's dentist in street clothes and recognizing who this familiar-looking person is). Or the meaning could refer to whether that person could be seen clearly. So the participant felt that the question could either pertain to knowledge, or vision, but failed to make this clear. Upon reflection, this seems a valid (and insightful) observation, and again indicates a potential problem with the question, but one that is somewhat different from that experienced by the first two participants.

Presumably, over a large number of tested participants, there would be a number of rows without any remarkable results—as it is uncommon that a question is so problematic that every participant provides evidence of difficulty. However, the types of patterns illustrated here do provide fairly systematic evidence that can be evaluated by each investigator—in a way that hopefully avoids idiosyncratic analytic interpretations. Parenthetically, although the use of this data display involves a Pattern-based analysis approach, this is not necessarily a defining feature of collaborative analysis. The data display selected could just as well involve an open area for completely uncoded comments or a place in which one of a number of codes (Cognitive or Question-Feature based) could be entered, and so on. The key feature of this approach is that no matter how the analysis of lowest level data is accomplished, it leads the research team to consider the meaning of the data "in the weeds"—rather than only at the tree-top level once data are accumulated, aggregated, and synthesized.

5.5. Deciding Between Successive Aggregation and Collaborative Harmonized Analysis

I have detailed two alternative approaches to data reduction, but eventually one must make a choice between these. This can be a very complex judgment because of the potential advantages to each. Clearly, if independent investigators do come to similar conclusions by working independently (as in the Cancer Risk Factor example), this is reassuring and reinforces the value of seeking reliability of independent judgment. Further, independent analysis avoids the possibility of "groupthink" that might occur when everyone is looking at the same data, or where the group is swayed by one very persuasive individual. On the other hand, Miller's experience with a failure of independent testing to produce coherent results is also compelling—and points to the potential value of a collaborative approach to the conduct of the analysis of qualitative data.

I believe that one resolution to this conundrum is to recognize that the pitfalls we face, concerning subjectivity of analysis, may depend heavily on the degree of experience of the parties involved in the testing. For the Cancer Risk Factor study, all cognitive laboratories—and interviewers conducting the testing—were highly trained and experienced. On the other hand, multinational studies such as the one that Miller describes, typically involve staff who are somewhat new to the cognitive testing endeavor. Hence, it may make sense to make use of the major advantages of Successive Aggregation of results—independence and potential for convergence of observation—for cases in which interviewers are highly experienced and regarded as trustworthy. On the other hand, given a set of interviewers sporting a wide range of experience, it may be better to rein in the horses, so to speak, and to rely on a collaborative approach that is led by an experienced investigator.

Finally, if one is conducting cognitive interviews in multiple languages, this introduces one additional consideration in choosing between an aggregated and a collaborative approach, concerning when to translate the results of cognitive interviews into a common language (typically, English). The aggregation model tends to lead researchers to conduct early stages of data reduction and analysis in the original language (e.g., Spanish)—and to only translate the summarized findings into English. This is efficient, as it saves the time and cost of translating all of the lowest level data into English prior to aggregating it. On the other hand, this precludes English speakers from having access to this level. A proponent of the collaborative model, on the other hand, would advocate translation of the original interviewer notes before placing these all into the data display, which facilitates the process of parallel, harmonized analysis—yet at a cost that can be significant. As for many endeavors in life, the researcher must consider the range of tradeoffs presented, related to cost and quality issues, in deciding on an optimal strategy.

5.6. Collaboration and Researcher Communication

The discussion immediately above brings up a more general challenge concerning interaction among staff, no matter what analysis model is being used, and points to the value of ongoing, intensive communication and collaboration throughout the analysis and interpretation processes (as advocated generally for qualitative research projects; Adams et al., 2007). Cognitive interviewing has sometimes been practiced as an assembly-line process in which the researchers endeavor to "get as much testing done as possible" by developing a cognitive guide, enlisting a group of interviewers, and then unleashing them with the admonition to return when they have evaluated the questions. This scenario follows a common practice in medical research in particular, in which a set of senior investigators develop a research protocol and enlist research associates to administer it, as for a clinical study of therapeutic drug safety. The research associates then are instructed to carefully note any adverse events that occur.

Especially under the Successive Aggregation approach, it may seem that such a model should naturally apply to cognitive interviews—with the analog to medical adverse events being, of course, adverse events involving survey questions—or what I have labeled as "problems." This model might be feasible, and it could be used to conduct a large number of interviews, if we can enlist enough research assistants. Be cautioned, however, that it may present serious limitations and lead to misguided, erroneous results. In a real-world situation, interviewers are often called upon to do more than simply conduct the interviews and observe problems that occur—even within a strongly Reparative investigation where detecting problems is the whole focus. To the extent that interviewers must necessarily engage in a process of interpreting what they have seen in the context of what is desired—that is, the measurement objectives of the investigation—it can be a nontrivial endeavor to come to unambiguous interpretations.

Resurrecting material from an earlier chapter, it is challenging to establish whether the participant's interpretation (Area B in our Venn diagram from Figure 4.2) matches the intent of the investigator (Area A). Such judgments are greatly enhanced through having a clear understanding of the objectives of the investigation, often obtained through a series of discussions with other staff throughout the testing process. In conducting any analysis, the fundamental question needs to be: "What is it we are after with this question?" I have often found that the judgment of whether a particular finding is a problem or not depends fundamentally on a clear understanding of what types of findings are viewed as problematic and which are not—in the context of the particular investigation.

Further, our understanding of the intent of the question can be subdivided into (a) communicative intent, or what the item is designed to include/exclude; and (b) analytic intent, or how it is going to be analyzed (e.g., what other variable it is to be related to). So a question on general health status may be fine for purposes of prediction of mortality, but it may need to be divided into subcomponents if we want to know, for example, whether users of a particular drug have lower levels of self-reported mental health but not physical health. As a general thesis: Interpretation of results depends fundamentally on communications that prepare us to decide which findings constitute actual problems and which do not.

To illustrate, another personal case study: The investigators developed a questionnaire intended to assess the prevalence of diagnosed mental health conditions, and this began with a checklist of items such as depression, bipolar disorder, obsessive-compulsive disorder, and so on. The question evaluated through cognitive testing asked, "*Has anyone in the family ever been told by a doctor or health professional that they had (EACH CONDITION)?*". I found myself arriving late to the study, for one reason or another, and found detected I believed to be a problem: Persons whom I tested had a tendency to respond YES, but upon probing, it turned out that several had included relatively minor forms of depression that are commonplace, and that did not seem as though they should count as true disorders. A reasonable conclusion seemed to be that the question was overly sensitive and likely to produce many false positives. This did seem to be a reasonable (even obvious) comment to make to the investigators.

The situation turned out to be less straightforward, however. Upon further discussion with the designers, I discovered that the questionnaire was intended to be followed by a more detailed and intensive, yet-to-be-developed section asking about the severity and impact of each condition—in order to weed out those that did not pass a particular threshold (I no longer remember why testing was not delayed until that critical section had been prepared). As such, the initial questions I had tested were intended as a screener to cast a wide net, and to err on the side of overinclusion, to later be winnowed down by the (as yet missing) items. Had I been armed with this knowledge earlier, I would have interpreted my findings in a way that acknowledged this plan. In particular, false positives would have seemed less of a concern. If, on the other hand, I had discovered that the question appeared to cast an insufficient net—that it let true positives fall through via *No* responses—that would certainly have been worthy of noting and communicating. It is this type of communication process that makes interviewers effective in considering the ramifications of their findings.

In short, a problem may not always be a problem—this depends on what the question is supposed to be doing for us. The best way to make these subtle judgments is to be engaged in the process, starting where the cognitive interviewing guide, and its analysis plan, are developed. Such intensive engagement is one of the costs of qualitative research, where the results do not necessarily speak for themselves. I would argue that cognitive testing is a clear example of such a situation. Based on this argument, a strong case can be made for a collaborative approach not only within the analysis stage but through the conduct of the entire cognitive testing process, from start to end. *Optimally, even if a Successive Aggregation model is followed, it may be best to relax requirements concerning independence and to encourage continuous communication between and across each analysis stage.*

5.7. Issue 2: Sample Size and Analysis

Sample size has often been discussed in terms of logistical requirements—unsurprisingly, more interviews require more work (Willis, 2005). Further, I have already discussed sample size in Chapter 3, when discussing critical issues in the *conduct* of cognitive interviews. With respect to the subsequent *analysis* of the results, we must also consider sample size, in particular to answer the question: *How large a sample do we need to conduct any particular type of analysis?* As I stated earlier, setting an appropriate number of participant interviews (not really a "sample" in the statistical sense, although that term is normally used) is a contentious and unsettled issue. Cognitive theory is not particularly helpful in settling this debate. Further, qualitative research, as a source of theoretical guidance, provides inconsistent guidance. On the one hand, in discussing analysis, Boeije (2010, p. 36) points out that samples for qualitative research projects are generally small, and that we do not seek statistical representation. On the other hand, as we have seen, several authors have stressed the need to conduct enough interviews to achieve saturation.

With respect to analysis, one can certainly make the argument that the use of very small samples inhibits analysis procedures which attempt any meaningful quantification of the results. In particular, with only a few interviews, it makes little sense to count up qualitative results in such a way that frequency distributions can be used to make general conclusions; few would argue that the finding of two comprehension problems within a 10-participant study is indicative of a 20% rate of comprehension failure in the general population. Partly for this reason, projects involving small samples tend to rely on simple Text Summary description, as this is the least quantitative of the various analysis models, and often makes little reference to the frequencies with which particular outcomes were observed (e.g., the report may say that "a few" or "some" participants behaved in a particular manner). For many studies, the qualitative nature of the results is taken to an extreme, in which little or no quantification of results is done—and I believe that this is a direct result of the use of small samples.

The counterargument is that testing should occur until saturation, in which no new information it obtained. Under this requirement, we certainly should have enough data to conduct analysis that incorporates a degree of quantification. However, note that saturation has a special meaning in the qualitative research literature that derives from the overwhelmingly nonquantitative nature of that science, and that may itself limit quantification. Within a classical Grounded Theory orientation, saturation is achieved when no new *coding categories* are discovered. This makes sense if one is attempting to cover the landscape, in determining what the question captures in a conceptual sense; we may find, for example, that there are eight dominant interpretations of a particular target survey item.

However, if one's analysis aim is to determine the *frequency* with which each potential interpretation occurs, then the general principle of saturation is less helpful. Even after assessing that, say, three major interpretations represent the comprehension of a particular survey item, the investigators may still be interesting in determining, *Which is the most frequent understanding?* As an extreme example, if the true distribution of Interpretations A, B, and C is 33% each, that presents a different case than when the percentages are 95%, 3%, and 2%, respectively. In the latter case, one might decide that the item can be used, as is, as the observed distribution represents a state of almost universal interpretation. However, the former, more equal distribution would certainly not lead to that conclusion.

Optimally, analysts of cognitive interviews do make use of the weight of such quantitative frequency distributions. If we find that 10 of 12 participants completely fail to understand our tested question (e.g., by saying "Huh?"), this is worth paying attention to. An argument can therefore be made that, to the extent that we are interested not only in how many different interpretations exist but in how frequently each is likely to occur, more interviews truly are better—perhaps even beyond the point of saturation in the classical sense. This is admittedly a somewhat hypothetical argument, as cognitive interviewers normally do not debate how far beyond saturation to test in order to attain meaningful frequency distributions, given that we infrequently are able to even reach saturation (Blair & Conrad, 2011; Miller, 2011). The critical point, however, is that setting sample size to enhance the analyzability of the obtained data is not simply a matter of applying a singular principle (e.g., "achieve saturation") but in determining what level of precision we require for our analysis. In some cases, this does not require as many as needed for saturation; in others (as when we want to obtain meaningful frequency distributions concerning item interpretation), it may even exceed that number.

Overall, in conducting the analysis, the investigator should keep in mind several guidelines:

(a) The larger the sample, the less we will need to rely on our own judgment in interpreting the significance of either individual interviews or of the entire investigation.
(b) Conversely, small samples put a premium on determining the relative meaningfulness of each interview that has been conducted—an idiosyncratic participant could certainly have an outsized influence where only a handful of interviews are done.
(c) To develop a theme I develop earlier, some types of problems are of a logical or structural nature involving the survey question and therefore are to some extent sample independent—if a problem makes an erroneous assumption that affects a class of individuals, then one member of that class should be sufficient for identifying the problem.
(d) On the other hand, as Blair and Conrad (2006) point out, even for such "critical cases," the probability of detecting the problem will increase to the extent that more interviews are conducted.

5.8. Issue 3: Levels of Analysis

I have discussed aggregation of results, and the size of the interview set that is analyzed, in quantitative terms. An associated

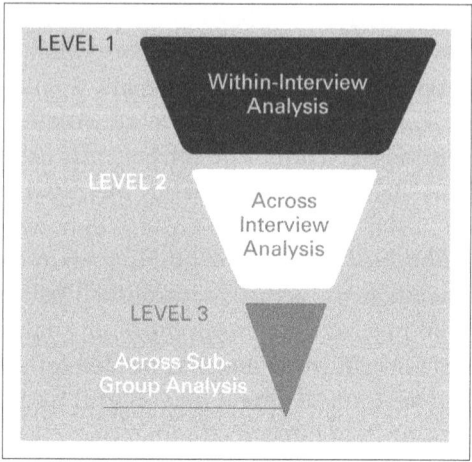

Figure 5.3. Levels of analysis within the cognitive interview.
Source: Miller, Fitzgerald, Padilla, Willson, Widdop, Caspar, Dimov, Gray, Nunes, Prüfer, Schöbi, & Schoua-Glusberg (2011).

issue concerns the qualitative differences across various levels of analysis (Boeije, 2002). Miller et al. (2011) make an explicit distinction between what goes on *within* an interview, what occurs *across* multiple interviews, and what happens across *subgroups* that are interviewed—as depicted in Figure 5.3. Cognitive interviewing normally involves the comparison of findings both within and across all of these levels, consistent with fundamental notions from the Constant Comparison Method. Especially because of what I consider to be the considerable cognitive demands on the analyst, especially when one attempts what Miller et al. (2014) refer to as a *complete analysis* that endeavors to cover all of these levels, it is imperative to consider each, in turn.

5.8.1. Within-Interview Analysis

The question of "what goes on within an interview" can have several meanings, including:

(a) What is it that we make of a single individual's reaction to each target survey question, in isolation from other questions?

(b) How do we relate what has occurred *across* questions that are contained in this interview?

The first of these is subsumed by much of the preceding discussion. The latter is not, however, and brings up some interesting challenges. In analyzing individual questions, there is a tendency—especially when applying codes—to focus on the item itself, in isolation from the effects of other items in the questionnaire. However, it is well known that there are interactional effects between items—or context effects—that influence responding (Tourangeau Rips, & Rasinski, 2000). For example, an item about health conditions that follows a long string about income and employment may produce hesitation because of the change in topic. It is important to notice these effects and to be "aware of what is around" when making conclusions about item function. Note that, to some extent, a Pattern-based analysis (see Chapter 4) is concerned explicitly with across-question effects, as it considers the consistency of responses across target items.

5.8.2. Between-Interview Analysis

The second level of analysis, concerning between-interview effects, concerns the extent to which results, interpretations, or patterns are similar across individuals. This is, of course, the crux of any attempt to summarize across cognitive interviews, and it is most explicitly represented by the thematic, pie-chart approach described in Chapter 4. Such analyses ascertain consistency across individuals, and they give rise to considerations such as adequacy of the sample size for assessing reliability, the nature of sample selection, and any other issues that pertain to compare-and-contrast analyses involving the individual interviews.

5.8.3. Between-Group Analysis

The third level of analysis—between group—is exemplified by the Cancer Risk Scale testing presented earlier, in which results are assessed with respect to multiple defined groups. So we may talk about the ways in which English speakers versus Spanish speakers process the question. As surveys become increasingly cross-cultural, between-group analysis is a vital component of the overall approach to viewing and interpreting our findings. It is not automatically the case, however, that cognitive interviewing is necessarily useful at this level. In particular, practitioners of what is variably referred to as cross-cultural, multilingual, or comparative cognitive testing must face a vexing question: *Can the findings from cognitive testing concerning problems with survey questions be compared across cultures or linguistic groups?*

The potential impediments to such comparisons fall into several categories. Some are, of course, procedural: With independent bilingual interviewers who may be conducting interviews differently, can the results really be compared? Assuming these differences can be controlled through the use of careful attention to monitoring and ongoing communication through fully collaborative analysis, the question still remains of whether different subgroups are directly comparable, with respect to the results of cognitive interviews. It has been found that cultural groups tend to differ reliably in such behaviors as tendency to acquiesce or to provide explanations that accompany their answers to survey questions (Marin, Gamba, & Marin, 1992). As such, it is not unrealistic to believe that they may also react differently within a cognitive interviewing environment, and that the obtained data may differ not because of differential reactions to evaluated survey questions, but rather reflect disparate tendencies concerning how these reactions are communicated to the cognitive interviewer.

There is some evidence that members of disparate groups do react differentially to the cognitive interview requirements (Pan, Landreth, Park, Hinsdale-Shouse, & Schoua-Glusberg, 2010). Goerman (2006) notes that both Spanish and Asian-language speakers have experienced difficulties with several types of probes used in cognitive interviews, especially those requesting paraphrasing of question meaning. Further, Pan et al. (2014) found that monolingual Chinese participants produced nonproductive responses to paraphrase probes at much higher levels than did bilingual Chinese-English speakers or monolingual English speakers.

The conduct of cross-cultural cognitive interviewing does remain a significant challenge. However, note that there are some categories of findings that may be—if not immune—arguably resistant to such problems. If we adopt the strategy (such as that of the QAS coding system described in Chapter 2) of classifying some problems as errors of assumption, it may be found that some questions simply make logical assumptions that do not hold for certain groups, and that this will come across clearly in the analysis of the cognitive interviews. For example, in asking about a history of racial and ethnic discrimination, cognitive testing revealed significantly more problems with questions on lifetime unfair treatment in various contexts for immigrants than for those born in the United States (Shariff-Marco et al., 2009). This turned out to be in part because immigrants were forced to reconcile two very different situations in creating a single response: treatment in the country of origin versus treatment within the United States. As such, the issue of comparability of behavior across groups within the cognitive interviews becomes less significant—as it was clear that structural differences in society (as opposed to interpretation issues) were at work, and that these could be readily identified.

5.8.4. Other Breakdown Levels

There are additional ways in which the data can be broken down, with further analysis levels defined. Although Miller does not discuss a between-interviewer level, I often find it useful to separate interviews that have been done by a particular interviewer from those conducted by the others. Again, between-interviewer analysis allows us to determine degree of convergence of results. Note that this level will be more salient, and more strongly differentiated, for a Successive Aggregation approach, than for a collaborative analysis approach—simply because the former puts emphasis on summarizing results within each interviewer, whereas the latter treats all interviews as similarly as possible, no matter who the interviewer happened to have been.

At a further analytic level, we might also be interested in the across-laboratory level, where we are interested in whether the same procedures may give rise to *house effects* that produce differences in results (as for the cancer risk study, discussed earlier). Note also that the distinction made earlier concerning question interaction at the individual level (e.g., order effects) can also be elevated to other levels. We may endeavor to determine whether an interaction between target items is found to apply variably across subgroups, such that the context of asking one question before another is more important for one language or cultural group than another. If this notion seems esoteric or far fetched, consider findings by Lee and Grant (2009) that asking the general health question before, versus after, a checklist of health conditions appeared to produce differential responding for Hispanics and non-Hispanics (specifically, for Hispanics, self-rated health was worse when asked before chronic conditions than when asked after them). The bottom line is that there are a number of ways to break down the data—some more of substantive interest and others (e.g., interviewer effects) of methodological interest—but all have their place in the realm of analysis.

5.9. Issue 4: Can We Rely on Our Background Expertise to Help Us With Analysis?

A particularly contentious issue concerns the sources that we are allowed—and disallowed—to use as we conduct the analysis and make decisions. In particular: To what extent can we rely on our own knowledge related to questionnaire design—so-called expert review—as opposed to only attending to the empirical data? In their chapter on analysis techniques, Miller Willson, and Chepp (2014) are unequivocal in their admonition that: "Expert opinion or self-imposed analyst interpretation—both common pitfalls—should be avoided" (p. 48). For example, we should never claim that a question is double-barreled or that it contains two parts with separate interpretations. Rather, such a statement should only derive from the empirical evidence obtained through cognitive testing.

I believe that these authors make an excellent point—but that it should not be overgeneralized to the point of asserting that expert knowledge should be banished from the cognitive testing process. Rather, there are at least three ways that expert review is effectively applied: (1) searching for problems, (2) deciding whether a problem exists, and (3) repairing items:

1. *Using expert opinion to search for problems:* I reiterate that conduct and analysis of cognitive interviews cannot be

separated, and that these are interlinked and dynamic—especially across iterative testing rounds. As such, the use of expert opinion commences at the time that we design the cognitive probes we administer in the interviews. I have argued (Willis, 2005) that having a notion of how survey questions function—expert knowledge—is fundamental to driving probing activities. For example, knowing that a question containing multiple concepts (e.g., it appears to be double-barreled) can be problematic will lead us to probe about comprehension of this item. At the time of analysis, we will likely be on the lookout for such problems, given that we have decided to actively probe for them. Put more generally, we may engage in *theory-driven analysis,* particularly where we rely on our knowledge of the literature related to questionnaire design to examine hypotheses concerning item function. To the extent that we believe that we are competent designers, we rely on this knowledge throughout the analysis process, and this is not only permissible but key to our success.

2. *Using expert opinion to decide whether a problem exists in Reparative studies.* I believe that this is the case that Miller et al. (2014) have in mind, and I agree that we should rely on empirical data to make these decisions: *What we find in the interview concerning an item's function should trump what we believe about its function.* If expert review tells us that an item is double-barreled, but the cognitive interviews suggest it is not, then we should conclude that it is not. I still maintain, however, that where there are *no* observations based on data to the contrary, the cognitive interviewer—or analyst—can serve as an expert questionnaire designer who is fully capable of making useful suggestions. An illustration of this is the simple question:

> ***In what grade are you?*** [] 6th [] 7th [] 8th [] 9th [] 10th [] 11th [] 12th [] Ungraded or other grade

The cognitive interview report for this item stated that:

> *Our results were very consistent: Participants were not bothered by the Ungraded category. They believed this*

> to mean that someone had dropped out or had graduated from school. Although there were no obvious problems in understanding the question, it is somewhat awkward and might be better as "What grade are you in?"

The first part of the Text Summary indicated that there were no obvious problems with the "Ungraded" category, based on the empirical data, and gave an indication of how this element had been interpreted. However, following this, the opinion is ventured that the wording could perhaps be made less unwieldy and more like regular speech. I see no problem with providing such opinions, expert reviews, or musings—as long as *they (a) do not conflict with the empirical results and (b) are identified explicitly as opinions.* If there is no confusion concerning the nature of the statement, then it can be taken for what it is—a suggestion that comes only from the mind of the interviewer and/or analyst, as opposed to the cognitive interview participants. These comments can be ignored if they are viewed as substandard, or inappropriate. More often, I have found such suggestions to be useful and to reflect a major function of cognitive interviewing that is not widely appreciated.

Most generally, in identifying problems, the analyst must go beyond the data at hand in a strictly empirical sense, to adopt a perspective that is informed by our assessment of the strengths and limitations of the testing process. I make the following recommendations as to how to make this judgment, whether conceptualized as "expert opinion," "the cognitive aspects of data analysis," or just "thinking through what we can conclude based on what we have found":

(a) Consider the implications of *outlier cases*—participants who stand outside the norm and provide unique information: Is this an individual who behaved in a bizarre manner that is outside the range of typical behavior of survey respondents? Or does the participant represent a situation that is uniquely valuable, in that he or she provides insight into a situation not otherwise anticipated or experienced? The former might be deleted from the dataset; the latter should not be. To some extent, we have to evaluate each case as to its information value, rather than treating them as equal, as in a quantitative study.

(b) Consider the contribution of *interviewer behavior*: An interviewer comment may emanate from a probe that is biased, or the interviewer's own opinions, rather than empirical information. Sometimes this can only be determined by reviewing the recorded interview, but it can also be examined by requiring that interviewers include in their summaries the probes they asked, as context, and the participant behaviors and comments that support each conclusion.

(c) Consider the *similarity of interviewer results*—and reasons for discrepancies. If interview results seem to be in conflict, this calls for a "levels of analysis" approach that strives to compare across the interviewer level and also the participant subgroup level: Are differences seemingly due to interviewer, to discrepant types of individuals they interviewed, or something else? Although this may represent a classic experimental confound, if one interviewer interviewed Hispanics and the other non-Hispanics, it is important to consider whether obtained differences were due to the interviewer or to the subgroup studied.

(d) Consider whether or not the interviews constituted *appropriate tests of the target questions*. Just assuming that "the questions were tested" is not meaningful, for example, if items on "other tobacco products" such as cigars and pipes were not evaluated because no users of these were included in the interviews.

3. *Using expert opinion to fix problems in Reparative studies*. Finally, we cannot escape the imperative of expert knowledge to help with the most difficult aspect of finding and fixing—once we have observed

that there are clear difficulties with comprehension, or other common problems, we must make decisions about how to modify the questions. In cases where we are "going back into the lab" for testing, we must have some notion in mind of how we will go about improving the situation. Having determined that "In the past 12 months, how many sex partners have you had?" is problematic due to interpretations of "sex partner" as including only "regular partners" rather than a one-time event, I may invoke my expert questionnaire design skills to craft an alternative such as "... how many people have you had sex with?" Whether this version also fails, I will need to be in a position to provide expert advice to my client as to how to proceed next.

To summarize my view on expert review, most simply: We must be good at "hearing data," but we must speak up as well.

5.10. Issue 5: Using Analysis Programs for Cognitive Interviews

Analysis of cognitive interviews is intensive, rich, multifaceted, and, as those who have done this know, a lot of work. To reduce the burden on the analyst, researchers have increasingly made use of the data manipulation and organizational capacities of the computer, in order to either develop or adapt qualitative analysis programs. Several software applications have been created to assist with the analysis of qualitative research—sometimes labeled CAQDAS, for computer aided/assisted qualitative data analysis software. I will describe several of these, beginning with ones that have been designed for qualitative interviewing generically, and then a special-purpose approach system (Q-Notes) designed specifically for the analysis of cognitive interviews. Although these programs do not conduct the analysis in the same sense that statistical analysis programs do for quantitative data, they take advantage of the computer's impressive ability to quickly grind through data for purposes of storing, searching, sorting, segmenting, and data reduction generally.

5.10.1. General Qualitative Analysis Programs

Although general qualitative analysis programs differ in their features and functions, a common theme is that they attempt to assist the researcher to sift through data in a way that (a) saves time relative to unaided analysis and (b) assists one in seeing patterns that one might not otherwise detect. A central theme in qualitative analysis that is carried to these programs is the use of a *node*, which can be viewed as a type of container into which information may be kept. Nodes can be used to represent codes, and the information that "fits" a particular code is stored in that node. Coding can generally be done either by making use of a top-down coding system, or from the bottom up. Information can also be *tagged*, which allows it to be connected with a code or other type of written observation or summary.

A core feature of qualitative analysis programs is that they perform a code-and-retrieve function that is integral to qualitative analysis—that is, a key segment (such as a comment indicating a misunderstanding of a survey question by a tested participant) can be coded as a Comprehension/Interpretation Problem. Later, that segment can be retrieved, as when there is a desire to access all segments associated with that particular code for summative analysis. Additionally, *attributes* can normally be stored with key units—participants can be assigned the attributes of age, gender, and educational level, so that results may be sorted or viewed for a subset—such as for only men, and so on.

Although there are a number of currently available programs for analysis of qualitative data, a few appear to dominate. The International Institute for Qualitative Methodology (IIQM) currently provides training on two proprietary programs: Atlas.ti, by Scientific Software Development GmbH (www.atlasti.com) and NVivo (see Heesch et al., 2010), an evolutionary successor to the earlier (but still used) NU*DIST program (see Napoles-Springer et al., 2006), from QSR International (www.qsrinternational.com). These may be the most frequently accessed programs for qualitative research analysis, generally. There are, however, other programs, such as QDA Miner (www.provalisresearch.com) and MAXQDA (www.maxqda.com) that also have adherents within the world of qualitative research analysis, and that may be especially appropriate in application to cognitive interviewing analysis, as they both have an explicit focus on interview-based data collection, including the survey interview, and provide for results that are at the item (survey question) level of organization, as opposed to at the case (person) level. Further, ambitious researchers have also attempted to fashion systems for the analysis of mixed (qualitative and quantitative) data, of the type produced by cognitive interviewing, through the imaginative combination of software programs—as the integration of analysis based on a combination of Atlas.ti and SPSS, with further incorporation of a Microsoft Access relational database system (Annechino, Antin, & Lee, 2010).

It is difficult to choose a single best option, especially as the authors of these programs produce new releases fairly often, and each release tends to include major new features, so that reviews quickly become somewhat dated. For example, Lewis (2004) published a comprehensive review of NVivo 2.0 and Atlas.ti 5.0, based on hands-on testing of each, but subsequently NVivo released versions 7, 8, 9, and 10; and Atlas.ti is, as of this writing, at version 7. However, certain programs may have natural advantages for the analysis of cognitive interview data. QDA Miner, in particular, appears to have been designed expressly to handle data consisting of a large number of short segments of text (e.g., open-ended responses to survey questions). Therefore, it can be used to capture critical data, including the text of each tested question, the comments made when testing the survey questions, and the metadata—or contextual data about the survey question being tested (e.g., participant characteristics for each interview). Overall, general purpose qualitative research analysis software is built to handle a wide range of approaches, including those based on ethnography, Grounded Theory, conversation analysis, phenomenology, and mixed-methods research—so they are presumably capable of being adopted for cognitive interviewing data as well.

5.10.2. Analysis Software for Cognitive Interviews: Q-Notes

Because cognitive interviews represent a particular type of qualitative investigation, staff at the National Center for Health Statistics (NCHS) are, as of this writing, in the process of developing and evaluating a system, labeled *Q-Notes* (https://wwwn.cdc.gov/qnotes/)—the first systematic attempt to develop an analysis support program for cognitive interviewing results. Q-Notes is especially useful for large-scale analysis involving many interviews, or multiple testing sites or organizations. Q-Notes includes a capacity to create documentation and store it in standardized form, to allow collaboration across interviewers or testing locations, to provide access to the data for project staff as the project is being conducted, and to secure stored data in deidentified form.

Q-Notes also allows researchers to build codes or more expansive themes (i.e., from Theme Coding) from the data throughout the study, or afterward, both at the level of the evaluated item and also at a more general level (e.g., concerning the topic under study). Because codes can be applied at any time (or not at all), the system is flexible enough to support text summaries, as well as both bottom-up (Grounded Theory) and top-down coding schemes. Further, Q-Notes can be used for Reparative (diagnose and repair), and for Descriptive (reverse engineering) approaches to analysis.

The Q-Notes system also features a capacity for linking to digitally recorded interviewing segments, so that the user can view these as the analysis is conducted. It is therefore possible to review every interaction involving a particular target item, across interviews, facilitating comparison of results in a straightforward manner. Further, the system is custom-designed to carry out the major steps involved in conducting analysis, and it includes a range of information and utilities:

- A capacity for entering background information about the project: its topic, description, types of demographic information to be collected (age, gender, education, language spoken), interviewer names, and so on
- Specifying the wording of each target survey question tested, including instructions, response categories, and skip patters (sequencing instructions)
- For each participant tested, entering demographic information, responses to each target question, and open-ended text comments by interviewers, at a question-specific level

- Entry of codes and themes at either the question level or the project level
- Procedures to facilitate analysis, including (a) viewing all data for a particular participant (for within-interview analysis), (b) viewing all data for a single question, across participants (for across-interview analysis), and viewing data according to participant group (for subgroup-level analysis)

Chapter 7 contains a case study of cognitive interview analysis which contains depictions of the types of output that are obtained using the Q-Notes system.

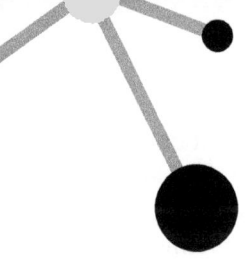

WRITING THE COGNITIVE INTERVIEWING REPORT

6.1. Chapter Overview

I have discussed analysis in terms of defining the unit of analysis, deciding whether the data to be analyzed are coded, and considering which of several analysis models to use. I have also discussed the issue of data reduction, in terms of whether analysts work independently or collaboratively and on the interpretation step. What is left, as the final vital step, is the write-up and dissemination of the cognitive testing results. In this chapter, I cover two elements of reporting:

(a) How to write a cognitive testing report, using the *Cognitive Interviewing Reporting Framework* (CIRF)
(b) How we can include those reports in a widely accessible archive of results, by placing them in the *Q-Bank* database of cognitive testing reports

6.2. A Persistent Challenge: Insufficient Documentation

Cognitive interviewing practitioners have—with justification—been criticized for producing reports that are skeletal and insufficient, as they may neglect key pieces of information (Miller, 2011). A lack of critical detail is important for several reasons. For one, a lack of transparency in how conclusions were arrived at, given the data collected, violates the fundamental premise of scientific investigation that researchers clarify their methods. More generally, lack of procedural detail impedes other researchers from attempting a replication of the results or from adopting the results to new projects.

6.3. The Cognitive Interviewing Reporting Framework

To address these critiques, Hennie Boeije at Utrecht University initiated the concept of developing a reporting system, to be modeled on existing quality checklists and reporting frameworks developed for in qualitative research, that attempts to systematize the write-up of cognitive interviewing studies. The resulting *Cognitive Interviewing Reporting Framework,* or *CIRF* (Boeije & Willis, 2013), along with several case studies that apply the system to cognitive testing projects, are contained in a special issue of *Methodology*, a journal devoted to novel research methods. The CIRF emphasizes key elements that are frequently overlooked in the write-up of cognitive testing results, such as (a) background development of the questionnaire; (b) rationale for participant selection and sample size; (c) the basis for selection of the variant of cognitive probing used, and (d) the background training and level of expertise of the interviewers selected.

Boeije and Willis (2013) propose that it is premature to bring the different cognitive interviewing practices in line with a single standard—as there are a number of ways to both conduct the interview and to analyze the resulting data. Further, we follow both Sandelowski and Barroso (2002) and Seale (1999) in believing that demonstrating the "quality" of qualitative research is a challenging endeavour without commonly accepted criteria. At the least, however, practitioners should all agree to fashion reports in a way that makes clear what was actually done and, in particular, how conclusions were made. To that end, a flexible reporting system that captures the different varieties would be a useful tool. Table 6.1 illustrates the CIRF checklist form, and the key elements of the system follow.

Table 6.1
Cognitive Interviewing Reporting Format (CIRF): Checklist of Major Elements to Include in a Cognitive Interviewing Report

CIRF Element	Description
(1) Research Objectives	(a) Clearly define the research objectives (b) Provide a review of the relevant background literature
(2) Research Design	Describe the features of the overall research design
(3) Ethics	Describe any review by a body such as an Institutional Review Board (IRB)
(4) Participant Selection	Including information on recruitment sources and procedures
(5) Data Collection	Include details relevant to interviewing procedures
(6) Data Analysis	Provide key details of the type discussed in this book
(7) Findings	Include a systematic summarization of results
(8) Conclusions, Implications, and Discussion	Discuss the overall impact of the cognitive interviewing project
(9) Strengths and Limitations	Include appropriate critique of the methods used, including caveats
(10) Report Format	Use a structured format to facilitate ease of reading, e.g.: (a) Executive Summary; (b) Introduction; (c) Design and Methods; (d) Findings; (e) Conclusions and Implications, with limitations; (f) Appendix materials, including Interview Guide

Source: Boeije & Willis (2013).

6.3.1. Element 1: Research Objectives

6.3.1.1. Clearly Define the Research Objectives

As stated in Chapter 2, cognitive interviewing projects tend to fall into the categories of (a) pretesting prior to question finalization—Reparative efforts; and (b) quality assessment to assess functioning of existing questions—Descriptive studies. Also, the objectives may be to test generally (i.e., to understand how cognitive processing of the questions might be related to the potential response error, based on a Tourangeau four-stage model). Or the purpose may be more specific: for example, "For a set of questions on patient reported outcomes, cognitive interviews will be used mainly to assess the functioning of 7-day versus 1-month reference periods." Another critical element to include would be the degree to which modifications to questions will be allowed versus constrained (as where trends over time are important, and changes will be made only if serious flaws or limitations are observed).

6.3.1.2. Provide a Review of the Relevant Background Literature

Background literature may not necessarily consist of published articles, but often includes "gray literature" such as previous cognitive testing reports related to the same items. At the least, there should be background concerning whether the evaluated questions are novel or have been used previously, and whether they have been adapted from an existing instrument. Particularly for purposes of classifying findings and establishing coding schemes for analysis, it is useful to specify the theoretical perspective that underlies the study. Often this is the well-known four-stage cognitive model (Tourangeau, 1984). Cross-cultural studies might rely on relevant classification schemes such as those by Fitzgerald et al. (2011), which divide results into (a) terms/concepts that have been translated erroneously, (b) those that do not translate easily, (c) challenges of cross-cultural adaptation of key concepts, and (d) generic problems with the questions, independently of translation to other languages (see Chapter 4).

6.3.2. Element 2: Research Design

Cognitive interviewing investigations do not often feature a true experimental design with assignment of research participants to multiple conditions, although there are exceptions, such as a study by Willis and Zahnd (2007) involving systematic variation in both subgroup studied (Korean versus non-Korean) and level of acculturation to the United States (low versus high). Or there may be a research design that relies on a specific variant of cognitive testing, such as the Three-Step-Test Interview (TSTI) (Hak, van der Veer, & Ommundsen, 2006). Finally, an investigation may involve the comparison or coordination of cognitive testing with some other procedure, such as mixed-method studies involving psychometric evaluation of survey pretest data (Reeve et al., 2011). In each of these cases, the nature of the design should be specified.

6.3.3. Element 3: Ethics

Increasingly, journal article editors require evidence that a research investigation has been reviewed by an Institutional Review Board or other body responsible for ethical or administrative review of human subjects research. If only for that reason, it is advisable to include some information concerning that review process. For cognitive interviewing studies that involve sensitive topics, such as illicit drug use or sexual behavior, the inclusion of information concerning privacy during the interview, and confidentiality with respect to data collected, is vital.

6.3.4. Element 4: Participant Selection

Selection of participants in cognitive interviewing studies normally involves a recruitment process, and describing this process helps to establish the credibility of the study, in demonstrating that appropriate processes and sources were used to obtain participants. Further, from a longer term perspective, details concerning recruitment processes can aid future researchers in determining what mechanisms may be effective. The investigators should indicate the following:

- The subpopulations or subgroups that were sought (e.g., cigarette smokers, users of chewing tobacco and snuff, and nonsmokers; or those with at most a high school education)
- Any organizations that were used as a recruitment source (e.g., elderly center, health clinic)
- Media or other means used to contact potential participants (e.g., newspaper ads, fliers, word of mouth, or use of Internet-based procedures)

- Demographic characteristics of those successfully recruited (within a table, normally presenting frequency distributions or means for age, gender, educational level, income, or other basic demographic data)
- Information concerning number of calls/recruitment attempts made, and yield
- Total sample size, with a discussion of how the total number of conducted interviews was determined—whether based on resources available or through a desire to produce saturation in which all major results or patterns could be obtained or observed (see Chapter 3)
- Whether the nature of participant selection altered over the course of the investigation (as is typical of many qualitative research projects; see Emmel, 2013)

6.3.5. Element 5: Data Collection

Details of the procedural nuts and bolts should be included:

- How many cognitive interviewers were used to conduct interviews?
- What types of individuals conducted the interviews, in terms of professional orientation and training?
- If novice interviewers were used, how were they trained to conduct the interviews?
- Were interviews (video/audio) recorded?
- What type of cognitive interviewing procedure was used? In particular, describe the mix of think-aloud and verbal probing.
- If verbal probing was used, how were probes constructed? Were they standardized (i.e., Anticipated and Conditional probes), or were interviewers given latitude in their design and implementation (e.g., Spontaneous and Emergent probes) (see Willis, 2005)?
- What rules governed how probing was done? Were probes administered for each question, only if a problem was noted, or was some other procedure used?
- Was probing done concurrently or retrospectively, or as a hybrid of these approaches?

- Were notes taken during the interview, or afterward, and were these by a single cognitive interviewer?
- Was the interview done by the interviewer alone or observed by other staff? Was this done within the same physical setting or via remote viewing?
- How many interviews were conducted in a round before a process of review and modification? How many total rounds were conducted?
- Was the interviewing guide adjusted throughout the course of the investigation for any reason?

6.3.6. Element 6: Data Analysis

- What was the basic unit of analysis—interviewer notes or verbatim participant quotes?
- What type of coding, if any, was done?
- If data were coded, was this done according to a top-down coding system, a grounded/bottom-up approach, or as a combination of these (see Chapter 4)?
- How many analysts were involved in the analysis? Did these include the cognitive interviewer?
- How were results compared, across interviewer, and across testing locations or organizations?
- What other comparisons were made in conducting analysis, such as between demographic groups?
- Was any type of software used in the analysis (such as Q-Notes)?
- Was data aggregation done according to a Successive Aggregation model or through collaborative review (see Chapter 5)?
- Were results reviewed or adjudicated by a separate individual or group, especially where there were disagreements?
- If assignment to code categories was done, were measures of intercoder reliability computed?
- Were suggestions for question modification made (according to a Reparative model), or was the study strictly Descriptive?
- Were any other sources of data used in the analysis, such as field pretest results, psychometric results, and so on?

6.3.7. Element 7: Findings

- The results of the investigation should be presented in sufficient detail that these will be transparent to readers. In particular, it is important to provide a full rendering of what was observed, as opposed to only "cherry picking" select examples.
- In presenting evidence for the findings, researchers should rely on quotes to illustrate points.
- If the focus of the investigation includes the level of the individual survey question (item) level, as opposed to only the global questionnaire level (which is the usual case), results should be provided for each item in the questionnaire that was evaluated. If certain items were skipped or otherwise untested, this should be explained, rather than implying that items were evaluated but no issues observed.
- For each item that was tested, the report should attempt to provide some information about what the item captures. Although a client may mainly be interested in knowing that "no problems were found, given the measurement objectives," it is always extremely helpful to go beyond this level and to provide as much explicit information as possible about what the item *did* succeed in measuring.
- Indicate where there was variation in results, according to participant subgroup membership or other important distinctions (e.g., that a question made sense for current but not for former smokers).

6.3.8. Element 8: Conclusions, Implications, and Discussion

Overall, the report should indicate the extent to which the study in fact addressed the research objectives. In particular:

- Were the results clear enough, in terms of the functioning of the evaluated items, or is more/different testing required?
- Were the participants who were tested adequate? If not, what groups or characteristics were missing?
- Discuss findings and solutions in the light of any previous evidence: If testing of the items had occurred previously, how did the current results compare?

- Were any *general principles of question design* developed? Was there evidence from the study that particular question characteristics or formats tend to produce problems, especially for specific subgroups?

6.3.9. Element 9: Strengths and Limitations

- Discuss strengths and limitations of the design and conduct of the cognitive interviewing study and provide appropriate caveats.
- Discuss potential for generalization to any wider population from which the participant groups were drawn, and the potential applicability to other contexts.
- Based on the manner in which the study was conducted, were there any methodological contributions to the wider science of cognitive interviewing or item pretesting?

6.3.10. Element 10: Report Format

Researchers should use a logical, structured format for organising the report. One common approach consists of sequential sections:

(a) Executive summary
(b) Introduction
(c) Design and data collection methods, including information on participants
(d) Findings
(e) Conclusions and implications, including the strengths and limitations
(f) Appendix materials, including the interview guide used (i.e., target items, along with a listing of cognitive probes administered)

6.4. Q-Bank: A Repository of Cognitive Testing Reports

Finally, with respect to reporting, Boeije and Willis (2013) also note that research findings are only useful if they are available. To this end, a group of US federal interagency researchers have developed a database for the storage of cognitive testing results.

Q-Bank is a publicly available resource (http://wwwn.cdc.gov/qbank/home.aspx) that chronicles the results of cognitive testing, by including entire testing reports, as well as a searchable index of individual survey questions evaluated within those reports. The survey questions are searchable by survey question, topic, and several other features, and link to the full PDF-format texts of the associated cognitive testing reports. Practitioners can use Q-Bank to determine how tested questions have fared, potentially obviating the need to reinvent the wheel by testing these anew, or by at least providing useful background and context for additional cognitive testing.

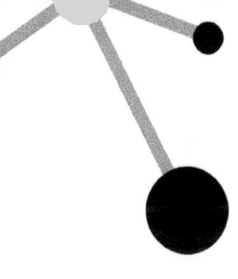

CASE STUDIES IN ANALYSIS

7.1. Chapter Overview

I have talked at some length about analysis philosophy and about variations on this theme. However, when confronted with real data, as opposed to general principles and guidelines, the analyst must make a multitude of decisions concerning exactly how to proceed with the analysis, once a general approach is laid out. This chapter will present three specific examples, relying on a case-study approach that provides sufficient depth that the reader can appreciate the way in which multiple decisions are made with respect to a set of items as they move through the analysis stage. The first example involves the interpretation of notes from a small set of cognitive interviews. A second example takes a different approach and indicates how several of the divergent analysis models I have described in Chapter 4 can be applied selectively to different questions within the same dataset. Finally, a third case systematically applies several analysis models to the same set of target items, to elucidate the differences in these approaches when they are viewed in parallel.

7.2. Case Study 1. Reviewing an Interviewer Text Summary: Analysis in the Trenches

Analysis of cognitive interviewing results can be made systematic, guided by theory, conducted by well-trained and experienced researchers, assisted by software, and otherwise make use of effective practices. Yet be warned that this is still challenging, and it may involve a strong dose of judgment that directly and unavoidably involves the cognitive aspects of data analysis. Consider the following example of a project with a strong Reparative orientation. The analyst is presented with the compilation of results from three interviews conducted by a single interviewer (an Interviewer Text Summary) and is faced with making an assessment of "how things worked" and whether there were any observed problems to potentially be followed up. The format of this (tiny) report is characteristic of an approach that is often used: It includes the accumlated write-up of the interview notes from the investigation, interspersed within a copy of the target items, and the probes that were included in the cognitive testing guide.

As an exercise, the reader can (a) review the background notes in Part 1 (immediately below), then the cognitive testing report that includes the Text Summary of three interviewer notes in Part 2 (Table 7.1), and finally, make conclusions concerning whether the items exhibit clear problems, relative to the measurement objectives of the study. Circling back to my previous discussion of *Successive Aggregation* of results, this report could be one of several contributions to a final product, once the reports of other interviewers are included. Or, based on this one report, the analyst may decide to consult with the design team for further clarification before other cognitive interviews are attempted.

Case Study 1, Part 1: Investigator notes describing the background for cognitive testing (notes supplied by the design team as a guide to conducting the cognitive interviews)

1. Overall objective of the questionnaire: Assess respondent's attitude toward eating fruits/vegetables (F/V) from a health perspective. The designers have chosen to use a multi-item attitudinal (5-point agree/disagree) scale, to develop the *F/V eating index.*

2. Question-by-question measurement objectives are as follows:

　Item a. Eating fruits and vegetables will help me live a healthy life.
　　The objective is to determine the extent to which the respondent believes F/V consumption is related to overall health.
　Item b. I eat more fruits and vegetables than other people I know.
　　The objective is to determine the extent to which the respondent believes himself/herself to be higher than a normative level of F/V consumption.
　Item c. Generally, I like sweet foods.
　　The objective is to determine the degree to which respondent reports favoring sugar-laden foods—a risk factor for unhealthy diet.
　Item d. I eat enough fruits and vegetables to keep me healthy.
　　The objective is to determine if the respondent believes his/her F/V intake is sufficient to maintain overall health.
　Item e. I enjoy trying new foods.
　　The objective is to determine respondent's dietary flexibility, in terms of willingness to change to foods other than those normally consumed.
　　In addition, two items have been added from a social desirability scale, to control for acquiescence bias (i.e., if he/she responds YES, this is an indication of positively biased responses, throughout the instrument):
　f. I never hesitate to go out of my way to help someone in trouble.
　g. I have never intensely disliked anyone.

Analysis: What Would We Make of These Data?

At this point, it is useful to put oneself in the position of the analyst trying to make sense of these data. First, let's critique the approach taken by the interviewer as a whole, from an analysis standpoint. Inevitably, the analyst not only derives meaning from the results but is also afforded an opportunity to review the

Table 7.1

Case Study 1, Part 2: Cognitive Testing Report Containing Interviewer Text Summary

Three interviews were conducted by interviewer GB. Comments are in italics and are written in under each target question →

INSTRUCTIONS: I will read a number of statements. For each, please give me a 1 through 5 answer, where 1 is strongly disagree, and 5 is strongly agree (GIVE RESPONDENT CARD WITH RESPONSE CATEGORIES).

	STRONGLY DISAGREE				STRONGLY AGREE
	1	2	3	4	5
a. Eating fruits and vegetables will help me live a healthy life. Probes: Why do you say that? What does "live a health life" mean, to you? What fruits and vegetables were you thinking of? *(GB) All three of my participants referred to the show card. Without that, I doubt that the response categories would have worked at all. Note that there's research (Alwin & Krosnick,1991) indicating that ALL scale categories should have verbal labels—and NOT just the endpoints, so I would consider doing that (e.g., somewhat agree…). All three participants strongly agreed (5), and said that of course eating fruits and vegetables makes one healthy. They mentioned hearing this through the media and from doctors. By "healthy life" they were thinking of both avoiding disease and living a long time. When I asked what types of fruits and vegetables they were thinking about, one started mentioning a string of both fruit and vegetable types, which I interpreted as being prompted by the probe as opposed to necessarily what she had said initially, and the other two just said they weren't thinking of any type in particular.*					

	STRONGLY DISAGREE				STRONGLY AGREE
So overall this item produced no obvious problems, though I wonder whether it's so "easy" that we'll get near total agreement (that is, if we find that 98% of every demographic group agrees, is that useful information?).					
b. I eat more fruits and vegetables than other people I know.	1	2	3	4	5
Probes: Why do you say that? What other people are you thinking of? What kinds of fruits/vegetables do you eat more of? (GB) All three participants laughed at this one. One said that it makes it sound like you're part of a vegetable-eating competition. All three had trouble choosing a response. The notion of "other people I know" seemed kind of vague—one woman said, "Well, I certainly eat more than my husband and kids, and I know them." Another one said that he knows a few vegetarians at work and can't come close to competing with them. I could have pushed to get a number (1–5) from each person, but what seems most compelling was that all three participants initially had difficulty answering, as they seemed unsure about what the appropriate reference group should be. One comment was: "It depends on who the "other people" are.." So this seems too vague for the numerical response to mean much.					

(continued)

Table 7.1 (continued)

	STRONGLY DISAGREE				STRONGLY AGREE
c. I never hesitate to go out of my way to help someone in trouble. Probes: Tell me more about that. What kind of help do you think this is asking about? (GB) This produced blank looks and silence, for all three. The transition between fruits-veggies and this "good Samaritan" question seemed abrupt and downright strange. When I probed by asking why he choose a 3, one participant said that it's extreme to say that you "never hesitate"—that he doesn't stop every single time he sees a broken-down vehicle. Overall this was just strange: I definitely would not intersperse these questions in-between the diet ones (see below for more on this).	1	2	3	4	5
d. Generally, I like sweet foods. Probes: What kinds of foods? What does "sweet foods" bring to mind? (GB) All three said yes, and gave answers of 4 or 5. They were talking about different specific types of foods—one really likes sugary candy, another was thinking of chocolate, and the third said, "Anything with sugar, even though it's bad for my teeth." I probed to see whether they all seemed to be talking about foods that contain sugar, and it appeared that they did.	1	2	3	4	5

		STRONGLY DISAGREE				STRONGLY AGREE
Interestingly, one person said that he likes all sweet foods, whether they contain natural or artificial sweeteners. So this brings up the fact that not all "sweet" foods necessarily contain sugar, so if the inclusion of sugar in the food is a key element, then we might need to say that, like "foods that contain sugar and taste sweet."						
e. I eat enough fruits and vegetables to keep me healthy. Probes: Why do you say that? What does "to keep you healthy" mean, to you? (GB) This produced some interesting discussion about how much one should eat, how often, etc. But it seemed easy enough to answer, for all three; they answered with 5, 4, and 4, and these answers seemed coherent, and consistent with further probing (they think they should eat more F/V than they currently do). Again, notions of being "healthy," as for the first item, consisted of avoiding disease and longevity.		1	2	3	4	5

f. I have never intensely disliked anyone.
Probes: Why do you say X?
  What does it mean to "intensely dislike" someone?
  Are you thinking about feeling that way for a short time, or for a really long time?
		1	2	3	4	5

(continued)

Table 7.1 (continued)

	STRONGLY DISAGREE				STRONGLY AGREE
(GB) Again, this looks like a "lie scale" item that doesn't belong here. All three answered it easily enough—they have ALL intensely disliked someone (5) and could describe those feelings at length (generally it was a persistent feeling, rather than just being angry temporarily). But the major point is that the flow of the questions is awful. One participant laughed and said, "If you're asking about food, this one only makes sense for a cannibal."					
g. I enjoy trying new foods. Probes: What types of foods? What kinds of "new foods" have you tried lately? (GB) All three S's answered this easily enough (all three = 5). However, one said that he likes to try new ethnic varieties of food, like Thai, Ethiopian, and so on, but that he won't try new vegetables because he knows he hates most of them. So, if the intent is to include new manners of preparation of food (e.g., Indian-style rice rather than American-style rice), this may be ok. If the intent is literally to ask about new food items that one hasn't eaten before (not just prepared differently), we may not be getting that. I'm not sure it's clear what we mean by "new foods."	1	2	3	4	5

interviewer's general approach and specific performance. In fact, it is virtually impossible to avoid doing so. There are several reactions that the reader-analyst could have to the results presented in Table 7.1, and I will discuss each in turn.

1. The interviewer didn't clearly discuss each probe question, so we don't have specific information that addresses every probe, and this makes it difficult to analyze each element probed

This objection is fair enough—except that in the real world of interviewing, it is doubtful that the interviewer even asked every probe and recorded answers to them systematically, or that she should endeavor to do this. In practice, strict adherence to asking each probe, and getting an answer to each, can be an unrealistic approach, for several reasons. I cover this more fully elsewhere (Willis 2005), but in brief, the conversational nature of probing makes it unnatural to ask each probe in turn, as if these are survey questions. Often the participant may have already answered them spontaneously, by thinking aloud. Or it may turn out that the scripted probes are not the most interesting questions to ask, so the interviewer may have decided to substitute other probes—or to just listen to what the person had to say. In any event, the analyst is faced with information that is more free-form, and less strictly related to the probes, than might appear from a review of the cognitive interviewing guide. As such, we must carefully read each comment and disentangle the various points and arguments, as the written data are not necessarily in a form most convenient to the analyst.

2. The interviewer injected some opinions about question design, rather than sticking to what was said by the participants

This is best evidenced by the inclusion of several "expert review opinions" (e.g., "So overall this item produced no obvious problems, though I wonder whether it's so 'easy' that we'll get near total agreement (i.e., if we find that 98% of every demographic group agrees, is that useful information?)." Is this an example of inappropriate behavior? If our objective is to obtain information that is useful in guiding questionnaire design, the issue of whether obtaining 98% responses in one category, though hypothetical, is certainly worth considering by the design team, and might lead to a decision to either modify or eliminate the item. These are the types of issues that designers grapple with constantly and are a very useful product of the process of cognitive interviewing. Note that the interviewer did clearly demarcate this comment as her own opinion, as opposed to reporting it as an empirically-based conclusion (i.e., she didn't say that "it is clear that almost all survey respondents will choose 5"). Such generalizations are almost always dangerous with small samples—but that does not mean that the results are not suggestive, in leading to hypotheses about question function (IF the question behaves in this way, THEN it may not be useful). For this reason, informed discussions about the questions—opinions, even—can be very useful to the analyst, as long as they are not presented as empirical observations (see Chapter 5).

3. The whole focus of the investigation was flawed—instead of picking out problems, it would be better to fully understand what each question provided, and then to let the designers decide whether these are problems

This might be the reaction of a practitioner whose focus was radically of the Descriptive (reverse engineering) type: Rather than attempting to be Reparative, cognitive interviewing should simply determine what each item captures: that is, all the types of "health" that eating fruits and vegetables promotes; all the types of fruits and vegetables that are thought of by each participant, and so on. In response, however, many investigators would defend the current approach for the following reasons:

(a) It is what clients tend to want. Most simply, they often ask for identification of problems with the existing version and recommendations for modifications. I find this to be a compelling argument.
(b) Simply describing what the question "captures" is sometimes insufficient. We may capture the fact that the item about whether I have ever intensely disliked anyone includes the possibility of cannibalism, but the key implication of that participant's comment was arguably that the placement of the item is a problem—and implies interpretations that are obviously not the intended ones. This is something that needs to be repaired, and it is worthy of being described as such.

(c) Finally, it is often the case that the cognitive interviewer is in a very good position to identify and attempt to repair problems—more so than the intended consumer of the findings (i.e., client, collaborator, designer). A good cognitive interviewer is also a proficient questionnaire designer and may be able to see problems, as well as solutions, that would never occur to subject matter experts who are not similarly engaged on a regular basis in this aspect of the science.

So, what did the interviewer find?

With those points out of the way, consider the specific interviewer comments associated with each sample evaluated question and whether these signify problems. Because this can be difficult to judge, I create three categories in which to place our conclusions:

1. Based on participant behavior and understanding of the measurement objectives, a *clear problem* has been observed.
2. A *potential problem* has been observed that requires further discussion by the design team—this would be a subtle or on-the-fence type of observation, or one that requires more information concerning the objectives of either the item or of the overall investigation.
3. *No problem* was observed, relative to the measurement objectives of the survey.

Taking each of the tested questions in turn, I will now review the notes taken by this interviewer and suggest which of the three aforementioned outcomes appears to apply, using annotation that interprets the interviewer's comment.

a. Eating fruits and vegetables will help me live a healthy life

All three of my participants referred to the show card. Without that, I doubt that the response categories would have worked at all. Note that there's research (Alwin & Krosnick,1991) indicating that ALL scale categories should have verbal labels—and NOT just the endpoints, so I would consider doing that (e.g., somewhat agree...).

All three participants strongly agreed (5) and said that of course eating fruits and vegetables makes one healthy. They mentioned hearing this through the media and from doctors. By "healthy life" they were thinking of both avoiding disease and living a long time. When I asked what types of fruits and vegetables they were thinking about, one started mentioning a string of both fruit and vegetable types, which I interpreted as being prompted by the probe as opposed to necessarily what she had said initially, and the other two just said they weren't thinking of any type in particular.

So overall this item produced no obvious problems, though I wonder whether it's so "easy" that we'll get near total agreement (i.e., if we find that 98% of every demographic group agrees, is that useful information?).

Judgment of Analyst: (3) No Clear Problem Was Observed. The interviewer does a creditable job of indicating both how the question was answered, and also the basis for the answers, by including a description of what key components of the question "healthy life" and "fruits and vegetables" were referring to. There is little evidence of any particular problem based on the interviewer's understanding of the intent of the item, but rather than stopping at saying "there were no problems," she has provided at least some information on what the question captures in the Descriptive sense. The comment at the end, as stated earlier, is an opinion; to the degree that the item produces nondifferentiated responses, this is a classical indication of an analysis challenge (i.e., a ceiling effect).

I would expect that most analysts working in an inspect-and-repair mode would conclude, strictly on the basis of the observed behavior of the participants, that *no clear problem* was observed. However, this may not be the end of the story. Given the question the interviewer raises about the utility of the item as a measure (i.e., her opinion), it would seem advisable to consider this as potentially being a problem and to note this as something for further discussion (that is, although a problem was not literally observed, a potential one was suggested). It is possible that the client or principal investigator may say that it is extremely useful to find, for example, that virtually 100% believe fruits and vegetables are important for health, although their responses to other items may indicate a more nuanced perception, or a disconnect between belief and behavior.

b. I eat more fruits and vegetables than other people I know

All three participants laughed at this one. One said that it makes it sound like you're part of a vegetable-eating competition.

All three had trouble choosing a response. The notion of "other people I know" seemed kind of vague—one woman said, "Well, I certainly eat more than my husband and kids, and I know them." Another one said that he knows a few vegetarians at work and can't come close to competing with them.

I could have pushed to get a number (1–5) from each person, but what seems most compelling was that all three participants initially had difficulty answering, as they seemed unsure about what the appropriate reference group should be: One comment was: "It depends on who the 'other people' are." So this seems too vague for the numerical response to mean much.

Judgment of Analyst: (1) A Clear Problem Was Observed. The fact that it is reported that all three had difficulty answering is telling, and immediately indicates evidence of a *clear problem* with the item. The comment that the key term "other people I know" is vague also seems like a defect, especially given that a participant spontaneously stated that "it depends on who the other people are"—note that this illustrates the value, to the analyst, of quotes, as these lend credibility to the conclusion. Overall, there is little question that this item would be flagged as requiring rehabilitation—at least based on these three interviews.

c. I never hesitate to go out of my way to help someone in trouble

This produced blank looks and silence, for all three. The transition between fruits-veggies and this "good Samaritan" question seemed abrupt, and downright strange.

When I probed by asking why he choose a 3, one participant said that it's extreme to say that you "never hesitate"—that he doesn't stop every single time he sees a broken-down vehicle.

Overall this was just strange: I definitely would not intersperse these questions in-between the diet ones (see below for more on this).

Judgment of Analyst: (1) A Clear Problem Was Observed. Nonverbal behavior, such as a blank look, can be compelling, is good for interviewers to document, and is something for the analyst to pay attention to. Certainly this in itself indicates a *clear problem*. Further, the comment that the abrupt transition in topic seemed strange—whether to the participants, the interviewer, or both (note that this is unfortunately not indicated), is difficult to ignore and would seem exceedingly salient. I would argue that at this point the analyst, or other decision makers in the design team, would be inclined to use their judgment to come to a similar conclusion, rather than demanding the conduct of additional interviews to verify this result!

d. Generally, I like sweet foods

All three said yes, and they gave answers of 4 or 5. They were talking about different specific types of foods—one really likes sugary candy, another was thinking of chocolate, and the third said, "Anything with sugar, even though it's bad for my teeth." I probed to see whether they all seemed to be talking about foods that contain sugar, and it appeared that they did.

Interestingly, one person said that he likes all sweet foods, whether they contain natural or artificial sweeteners. So this brings up the fact that not all "sweet" foods necessarily contain sugar, so if the inclusion of sugar in the food is a key element, then we might need to say that, like "foods that contain sugar and taste sweet."

Judgment of Analyst: (2) A Potential Problem Has Been Identified. A simple sounding question elicits some interesting observations. It may not be clear to respondents whether "sweet" means that it contains sugar, versus artificial sweetener—and it is not clear to the interviewer either, as she doesn't know what is intended to be included or excluded. The resolution to these issues may be unclear to the analyst as well, who may conclude that a *potential problem* exists, but that it not possible to tell without further discussions with the designers.

e. I eat enough fruits and vegetables to keep me healthy

This produced some interesting discussion about how much one should eat, how often, etc. But it seemed easy enough to answer, for all three; they answered with 5 (Strongly Agree), 4, and 4, and these answers seemed coherent and consistent with further probing (they think they should eat more F/V than they currently do). Again, notions of being "healthy," as for the first item, consisted of avoiding disease and longevity.

Judgment of Analyst: (3) No Clear Problem Has Been Observed. Critically, the interviewer notes that the answer given by each of the three participants (5, 4, 4) is consistent with their further elaboration, based on probing. This finding well represents what I have considered (Willis, 2005) to be a major approach to cognitive interviewing: determining whether the answer to the evaluated item matches the description that is based on the results of elaborative probing (and note that this also describes the logic underlying Pattern Coding). Based on this finding, the analyst may note *no clear problem*. Further, an analyst having a strong Descriptive rather than Reparative perspective might key on the finding that "healthy" was identified as (a) avoiding disease and (b) longevity, and to consider those two theme codes, perhaps to be followed up via further interviews.

f. I have never intensely disliked anyone

Again, this looks like a "lie scale" item that doesn't belong here. All three answered it easily enough—they have ALL intensely disliked someone (5) and could describe those feelings at length (generally it was a persistent feeling, rather than just being angry temporarily). But the major point is that the flow of the questions is awful. One participant laughed and said, "If you're asking about food, this one only makes sense for a cannibal."

Judgment of Analyst: (1) A Clear Problem Has Been Observed. The interviewer is somewhat remiss in not clearly identifying fact from opinion ("this looks like a lie scale item that doesn't belong here". However, there is additional empirical evidence (one participant laughing and making a wry comment) that the item's placement is problematic, and this would certainly be supported by making reference to functioning of the other "lie scale" item (c). As the analyst, I would be inclined to apply some judgment and conclude that there is a *clear problem* with the item based on the reactions of these three participants, the reaction/opinion of the interviewer, the evidence derived from other items—as well as my own belief that the general rule of questionnaire design to avoid abrupt transitions between items is violated here. As such, this may be a good example of a case where a variety of sources of information must be considered and interwoven, rather than strictly parsing and narrowly considering only the literal "data" from the interviewer's notes.

g. I enjoy trying new foods

All three S's answered this easily enough (all three strongly agreed = 5). However, one said that he likes to try new ethnic varieties of food, like Thai, Ethiopian, and so on, but that he won't try new vegetables because he knows he hates most of them.

So, if the intent is to include new manners of preparation of food (e.g., Indian-style rice rather than American-style rice), this may be ok. If the intent is literally to ask about new food items that one hasn't eaten before (not just prepared differently), we may not be getting that. I'm not sure it's clear what we mean by "new foods."

Judgment of Analyst: (2) A Potential Problem Has Been Identified. Interestingly, the interviewer identifies two interpretations of the item, with "new foods" being either (a) new preparations of already-experienced foods versus (b) food items not previously consumed. There may be other interpretations of "new foods" that are yet unidentified, and a Descriptive analysis would likely call for more interviews in order to more fully flesh out this concept (as saturation has very likely not been achieved!). The Reparative investigator would be inclined to conclude that there is a *potential problem* with the item—there are multiple interpretations, but it is unclear in the absence of more information concerning the views, data needs, and objectives of the designers whether this is in fact a problem. This type of finding is an excellent basis for further discussion, which could result either in a decision that this *is* a defect (a particular interpretation is desired) or that it is *not* (any interpretation of "new foods" may be considered in scope).

Overall Conclusion, Concerning Case Study 1. The interpretation of cognitive interviewing results is hard. Especially for Reparative studies, the interviewers' comments are useful—in fact, they are our main source of information—but they are not in themselves conclusive. It is for this reason that I have emphasized the need to match investigator requirements with the empirical results, to make the difficult decisions concerning "whether the question works" or not. Clearly, making such decisions requires the analyst to have a clear vision of the measurement objectives of the item and of the questionnaire more broadly as a measurement instrument. The most useful conclusion from cognitive testing is often that these objectives are *not* clear enough that the survey questions can be meaningfully critiqued, let alone repaired. For this reason, one common outcome of an initial round of cognitive interviewing is *the provision of guidance that the analyst needs in order to conduct what is, in effect, a cognitive interview of the designer or client.* Even if only three interviews are conducted, this may be an opportune time to clarify question objectives, and perhaps to make appropriate modifications prior to further testing. If we can use what we have discovered—even in just a few interviews—to ask probing questions related to the investigator's own interpretations, that puts us one step closer to being in a position to make conclusions about how well participants' interpretations are in concert with those.

7.3. Case Study 2. Mixing Analysis Models Within a Single Dataset

To my knowledge, the differing analysis models identified in Figure 4.1 have not been described, let alone applied in any systematic way. Therefore, an example that includes the selection of several of these within the same study could be enlightening and point toward the best uses of each. In the absence of "real" data to address this, I have developed a workable simulation of how the results of testing of a particular project might look, based on the application of several of my five defined coding approaches, and that specifically includes (a) *text summaries*; (b) a top-down, *cognitive coding* approach; and (c) a bottom-up, *theme coding* approach. My intent is to show that differing analysis approaches can be applied within the same investigation, in a way that does not create conflict. Further, this exercise provides an opportunity to showcase a software tool—the Q-Notes online system for the analysis of cognitive interviews (described in Chapter 5)—that can be applied in a way that hopefully makes the analyst's life easier and the overall task more systematic and rigorous.

Questionnaire items evaluated. I have chosen select findings from an archival cognitive testing dataset—hopefully an interesting one—that resulted from 20 cognitive interviews used to evaluate a questionnaire designed to assess self-reported racial and ethnic discrimination (see Shariff-Marco et al., 2009). The questions I have chosen for purposes of illustration are listed in Table 7.2.

Table 7.2
Racial-Ethnic Discrimination instrument: Examples of items cognitively tested

Question	Item Wording as Tested
1	The first question is about your overall health. Would you say that in general your health is excellent, very good, good, fair, or poor?
2-1	The next questions are about your background. First, do you consider yourself to be either Hispanic or Latino?
2-2	Which of the following do you consider to be your race: White, Black or African American, Asian, Native American, or something else?
2-3	In this country, how do other people usually think of you? Would you say White, Black or African American, Hispanic or Latino, Asian, native Hawaiian or Other Pacific Islander, American Indian or Alaska Native, OR some other group?
2-4	The next questions are about your experiences concerning how you may have been treated by others. We are asking these questions to see if they may be related to a person's health. In your day-to-day life, have any of the following things ever happened to you?: [Yes or No for each] You have been treated with less courtesy or respect than other people You have been treated unfairly by people on the street or in a public setting You have been treated unfairly by neighbors You have received poorer service than other people at restaurants or stores You have been treated unfairly by fellow students, teachers, and professors You have been treated unfairly by your coworkers, employers, or bosses People have made fun of your accent or the way you speak People act as if they think you are not smart People act as if they are afraid of you People act as if they think you are dishonest People act as if they're better than you are You have been called names or insulted You have been threatened or harassed You have been treated unfairly when getting medical care You have been treated unfairly by the police or the courts

(continued)

Table 7.2 (continued)	
Question	Item Wording as Tested
2-5	Over your entire lifetime, how often would you say this(these) experience(s) has(have) happened to you—Almost every day, At least once a week, A few times a month, A few times a year, OR Less than once a year?
2-6	In the past 12 months, how often (has this/have these) experiences happened to you—Almost every day, At least once a week, A few times a month, OR A few times during the year?
2-7	Overall, how stressful have you found (this/these) experience(s) Would you say Not at all stressful, A little stressful, Somewhat stressful, OR Extremely stressful?
2-8	Have you ever been treated unfairly by other [FILL WITH RESPONDENT'S RACE/ETHNICITY]?

Entering items and notes into a qualitative analysis program (Q-Notes). For this project, the original data consisted of interviewer notes. These were originally written by hand and were later entered into the Q-Notes system along with the items tested and the participant's response to the question. Most of the work involved consists of entering this information. Once entered, there are a variety of ways to access and view the data. Most simply, the analyst can view, for a particular interview, the target item, the response given, and the interviewer notes for that item, within that interview (see Figure 7.1).

Between-interview level analysis. Beyond viewing the results for a particular interview, the next logical level of analysis involves viewing the results for a particular item across all interviews. First, for the general health item: *Would you say that in general your health is excellent, very good, good, fair, or poor?*, the distribution of the 20 responses (as calculated by Q-Notes) is illustrated in Table 7.3.

However, we are also interested in the qualitative information that is "behind the numbers." The Q-Notes analysis program provides a listing of the responses and comments in tabular form, and that can be sorted in a number of ways (these results are depicted in Table 7.4).

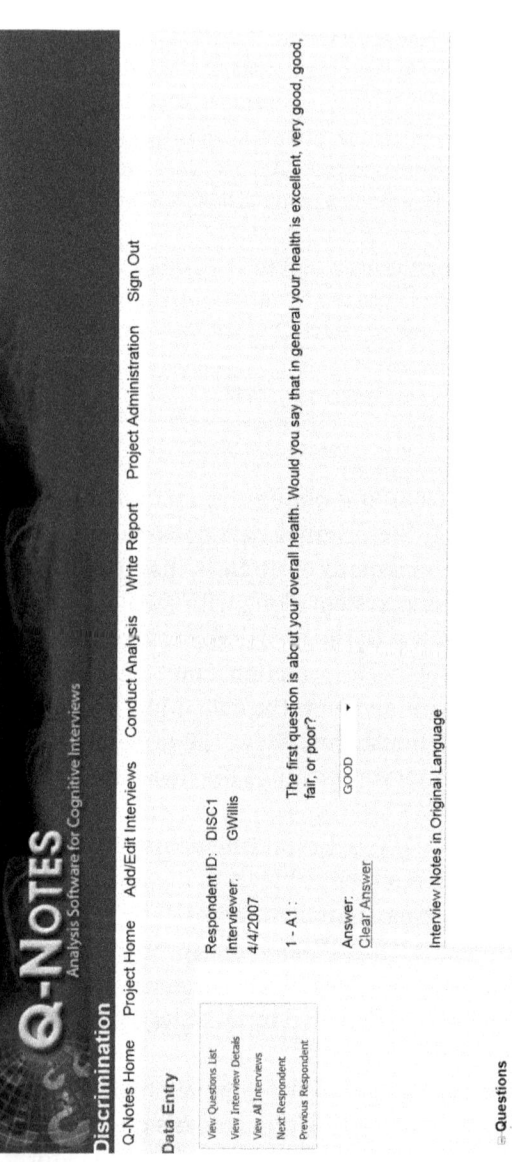

Figure 7.1. Illustration of Q-Notes data entry screen for Interviewer Notes.

Table 7.3
Distribution of responses to general health question, from Q-Notes database

Response Selected	n
Excellent	2
Very good	6
Good	11
Fair	1
Poor	0
Total	**20**

Analysis Option: Text Summary Analysis

To begin conducting a qualitative analysis, the listing of notes provides a way to do a quick review of the variation in responses to probe questions and other interviewer notes and observations. The common *Text Summary* approach would rely on a mental "crunching" of the data in such a way that the analysis can attempt to data-reduce the information into a reasonably brief summary. An attempt at this, for the item on general health status, would produce a summary like the following:

> *There was no indication of misunderstanding or difficulty with the item. It appeared that the responses given (Excellent—Fair) corresponded fairly well with the supporting explanations given by the participants: Although we did not obtain a wide range, and the majority were Good, it did seem that there was a tendency for people to report less than Excellent health for a variety of reasons, including (a) having risk factors for disease such as needing to lose weight or inactivity, (b) both short- and long-term health conditions (being sick, having diabetes), and even (c) not knowing whether one has a hidden medical condition. Finally, the great majority of responses involved somatic health, so the interpretation of the item seemed to be in terms of physical health, as opposed to mental, emotional, or other forms.*

Table 7.4

Q-Notes listing of interviewer notes from 20 cognitive interviews of the item: *Would you say that in general your health is excellent, very good, good, fair, or poor?*

ID	Answer	Interview Notes	Age	Gender
12	EXCELLENT	PROBE: Why do you say excellent? He said he eats right, works out at least 1 hour daily, enjoys outdoor sports, is health conscious, gets sunlight	24	Male
13	EXCELLENT	PROBE: Why do you say excellent? Has had only 1 cold per year and no broken bones. Recovered fine from a stabbing and can still run very fast.	26	Male
18	VERY GOOD	NO NOTES RECORDED	26	Male
8	VERY GOOD	PROBE: Why do you say very good? Right now thinks he's very good, but not tip-top because she has some extra weight on her.	52	Female
10	VERY GOOD	PROBE: Why do you say very good? I run, walk, try to eat right (went from regular foods to organic foods because they are more natural)	45	Male
17	VERY GOOD	NO NOTES RECORDED	45	Male
15	VERY GOOD	PROBE: Why do you say very good? Since arriving here nearly 5 years ago, she said she has lived in sanitary health conditions and her foot is doing better. Analyst: New theme—"sanitary conditions" = health physical environment	25	Female
16	VERY GOOD	NO NOTES RECORDED	26	Male

(continued)

Table 7.4 (continued)				
11	GOOD	PROBE: Why do you say good? Goes to the gym for workouts and keeps himself fit. Chose good and not a higher rating because there could be something wrong with him that he doesn't know about.	45	Male
19	GOOD	Have had some health problems—bad cough that was hard to diagnose.	26	Male
4	GOOD	PROBE: Why do you say good? Feels fine but does not know what is going on inside his body where he cannot see.	36	Male
2	GOOD	PROBE: Why do you say good? Overweight—so health isn't excellent—and her triglycerides aren't great.	27	Female
5	GOOD	PROBE: Why do you say good? He chose that answer because he is diabetic, 63 years old, and a little overweight.	45	Male
6	GOOD	PROBE: Why do you say good? Has seasonal allergies; gets few colds; currently on medication	52	Female
7	GOOD	Had a cyst removed; was hospitalized for a bacterial infection 1 year ago; occasionally smoke and drink	45	Male
3	GOOD	PROBE: Why do you say good? Smokes and is a little overweight—doesn't exercise—or eat healthy.	36	Male
20	GOOD	Because of mental health condition, she has to take a great deal of medication daily	42	Female

(continued)

Table 7.4 (continued)				
1	GOOD	Participant is routinely active—has four children—never gets sick—sleeps well—checks in with her doctor—she's been told recently by her doctor to lose some weight, otherwise she would have said excellent.	27	Female
14	GOOD	PROBE: Why do you say good? Not very health focused. Not too athletic, just normal. Analyst: Interesting that the P views "normal" health as Good—which supports the common practice of having this be the middle response category.	25	Female
9	FAIR	Diabetic and has to take tons of meds, so while he feels healthy, relative to others he considers his health fair.	45	Male

Analysis Option: Theme Coding Analysis

The Text Summary may be useful and interesting, but it is somewhat lengthy to read and does not do a very good job of listing the findings in an efficient manner. As an alternative, Q-Notes is set up especially well for a Grounded-Theory-based, theme coding analysis approach (what I referred to in Chapter 4, Figure 4.1 as Analysis Model 4). Given that it was of interest to determine from this project what the general health item captured, in the Descriptive sense, theme coding is especially efficient. The comments associated with this item across the 20 cognitive interviews would be reviewed and emergent themes entered for this item. For instance, from the interview notes listed in Table 7.1, the emphasis on losing weight as an element of self-perceived health could be coded as a "Risk Factor" theme. After all the unique implicit themes were in this way built up from the data, the Q-Notes analysis system would then display the totality of these codes—shown for this item in Figure 7.2. As the Text Summary, the themes depict a wide variety of conceptualizations—even from just 20 interviews—indicating that "general health" is a complex construct, associated with the respondent's thoughts about both acute and chronic medical conditions, current risks of developing health conditions, and even the fact that one's true health status may be unknown, as some latent problem may be lurking beneath the surface. Analysis has in this case managed to "reverse engineer" the item in a way that uncovers its components, rather than attempting to "fix" something that is broken. A comprehensive report would include both the Text Summary and the theme codes in Figure 7.2.

Analysis Option: Cognitive Coding

In departure from the case of the general health item, there are other items in this dataset for which a Reparative approach may be of more interest, and a fundamentally different analysis strategy might be instead chosen. The set of items in Table 7.2 pertaining to racial and ethnic discrimination (2-4 through 2-8) were novel and called not only for an assessment of item

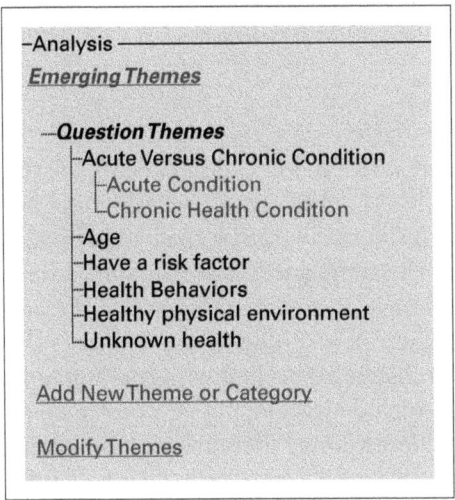

Figure 7.2. Table of Theme Codes for the survey item: "Would you say that in general your health is excellent, very good, good, fair, or poor?" – summarized by Q-Notes.

function but of whether this functioning was consistent with investigator requirements—especially that the items demonstrate a reasonable degree of cross-cultural comparability. As one example, the item: *Over your entire lifetime, how often would you say this(these) experience(s) has(have) happened to you? Almost every day, At least once a week, A few times a month, A few times a year, OR Less than once a year?* contains the reference period of one's entire lifetime. This could be problematic, given either memory challenges over that long a period or else the difficulty of summarizing these experiences over circumstances that vary over the course of the life period. Given that, the analyst could decide to guide the analysis by utilizing a cognitively based, top-down coding system that includes the following categories:

CO   Comprehension of the item (clarity)
RE   Recall/Memory difficulties due to length of the reference period
JE   Problems with Judgment or Estimation of the frequency
RC   Difficulties in selecting a Response Category
(NA) Not an applicable question for this person

This coding system is a close rendition of the original Tourangeau (1984) cognitive model; the Not Applicable code is consistent with the Logical-Structural code appended by Willis et al. (1991).

The Q-Notes system can be used to output the interviewer notes associated with each of the interviews for this target item (Table 7.5). In this case the cognitive codes have been applied at the level of each interview (rather than the alternative of higher level coding of the aggregated Text Summary level, as described in Chapter 4). I have edited the table to add the aforementioned codes to each interview. It does seem apparent that there were considerable problems associated with making judgments about what events to include (producing JE problems), and then with selecting a single response that summarizes these experiences (the RC code). This seems to have been a function of the sheer length of time to be accounted for in selecting a response, suggesting that a "lifetime" reference period is problematic. Although a Text Summary analysis may have produced the same effective conclusion, it can be useful to have this backed up quantitatively and summarized:

Of the 17 participants asked the question:

- 0 participants illustrated difficulties in understanding the item.
- 0 participants indicated that they had difficulty recalling the events asked about.
- 7 participants (41%) demonstrated problems related to determining a suitable response to the question; they could not summate or average the events to produce a single frequency (i.e., code JE, RC, or both were assigned).

Based on these results, the designers might think about whether to alter the reference period or about ways to otherwise repair the item. I am less sure that in this case, a Descriptive, Grounded Theory–based analysis describing item function would be particularly useful: The usual emphasis on "what the question captures" could of course be revealing, but that does not seem like the most compelling issue arising from testing of this item. It is of course possible that the codes that emerged might focus explicitly on problems encountered (e.g., the code "Difficulty in aggregating across diverse experiences" would seem reasonable). This would effectively imply the development of bottom-up codes, in a more Reparative vein—which may be a useful approach, in that it is clearly data driven as opposed to investigator imposed. However, I would not in this case expect the ultimate result to depart much from that of a cognitively based coding scheme.

Analysis Option: Pattern-Based Analysis Strategy

The final analysis approach that is identifiably different from those otherwise applied in this case study involves the use of a data display to illustrate patterns between items in the dataset or between items and critical probe questions. For the racial-ethnic discrimination instrument, one interesting research question giving rise to this form of analysis concerned the item: *How stressful did you find these (just reported unfair) experiences?* One way to study the functioning of this item is to assess, for each participant, the

Table 7.5

Cognitive-based coding of results of testing of item: "Over your entire lifetime, how often would you say these experiences have happened to you?"

ID	Answer	Interview Notes	Age	Gender	CODE
10	NONE	Could not answer: After hearing the question and responses, R asked, "For which one?" (indicating it is hard to average over disparate experiences). I repeated the responses, and P said it is hard to come up with an answer for his entire life—said it would be every day. During the ensuing discussion, he said that thinking only of now, he would probably say "once a month," but that it varies—depends on people's attitudes. PROBE: How easy or hard was it to choose that answer? NOTE. P said it was kind of hard to answer because most people try to push stuff like that (unfair experiences) back—they try to discard it. So you have to bring up memories you don't want to bring up.	45	Male	JE, RC
6	NONE	PROBLEM: P said it is hard to answer specifically for your entire life. Said her answer would be 25% of 100%. Said it has been bothering her to answer for "entire life"—to ask for specifics for that length of time is difficult. Said: "I'm not comfortable giving an answer." PROBE: How easy or hard was it to choose that answer? see previous comment	52	Female	JE, RC
7	A FEW TIMES A YEAR	PROBE: How did you decide to answer with [a few times a year]? The answer "just fit." P said you would not have known how to answer it this had been an open-ended question. PROBE: How easy or hard was it to choose that answer? Easy	45	Male	

9	A FEW TIMES A YEAR	PROBE: How did you decide to answer with [I]? I initially forgot to read the response categories and his response was first "it just occurred over a 3- or 4-year period." Then when I reread the question with the response categories he chose "a few times a year" but thinking about that 3- or 4-year period (when he was in college). However, these response categories will suggest that this happens throughout his life a few times a year, which is incorrect.	45	Male	RC
15	A FEW TIMES A YEAR	PROBE: How did you decide to answer with [a few times a year]? P said she was not sure how to answer this probe.	25	Female	
3	A FEW TIMES A YEAR	PROBE: How did you decide to answer with [I]? Happens more frequently than once a year, but not a real regular occurrence	36	Male	
20	A FEW TIMES A YEAR	PROBE: How did you decide to answer with [I]? Her response reflected her more recent adult life than her early adult years or her childhood. She chose her answer because she has taken great pains to insulate herself, making it unlikely these types of situations could occur now. Without putting boundaries on the time period, it seemed she thought the question would be difficult to answer because they don't occur at a constant frequency. There is variability by age, location, etc.	42	Female	JE
14	A FEW TIMES A YEAR	NO NOTES RECORDED	25	Female	

(continued)

Table 7.5 (continued)

ID	Answer	Interview Notes	Age	Gender	CODE
18	A FEW TIMES A YEAR	How did you decide to answer with [a few times a year]? P said that it is the same everywhere. It can happen to him if he goes back to Peru on vacation. P reported things from his US experience only.	26	Male	JE
8	ALMOST EVERY DAY	PROBE: How did you decide to answer with [ ]? P lumped together all the experiences she reported and pictured what she actually experienced even just last week.	52	Female	
12	AT LEAST ONCE A WEEK	PROBE: How did you decide to answer with [at least once a week]? P was thinking about starting high school—at first he was thinking about answering almost every day but then decided it really was not as bad as every day. PROBE: How easy or hard was it to choose that answer? Not too easy but also not hard at all—he was reanalyzing all his memories—trying to choose between the first two response options—He said again that up to this moment it seems like every day but it wasn't really that bad.	24	Male	
13	LESS THAN ONCE A YEAR	PROBE: How did you decide to answer with [less than once a year]? As soon as I asked this question, he said, "Ah, now we get to clarify" (how general or specific our experiences have been). P said although he said yes to a lot of items, it wasn't a general experience. PROBE: How easy or hard was it to choose that answer? Easy—he has been thinking about this throughout the whole interview.	26	Male	

2	LESS THAN ONCE A YEAR	PROBE: How did you decide to answer with [I]? Re: issues at work—that happens once a year or so now, and the same with making fun of how she speaks/her accent—but, when she was in school, that happened all the time. PROBE: How easy or hard was it to choose that answer? Hard to answer across two different experiences, over entire lifetime.	27	Female	JE
5	LESS THAN ONCE A YEAR	PROBE: How did you decide to answer with [I]? "Because it hasn't happened a lot of times in my life…maybe once in 5 years or once in 10 years." PROBE: How easy or hard was it to choose that answer? "It wasn't hard."	45	Male	
11	LESS THAN ONCE A YEAR	PROBE: How did you decide to answer with [less than once a year]? "It doesn't happen on a regular basis."	45	Male	
19	LESS THAN ONCE A YEAR	How did you decide to answer with [less than once a year]? Based on age and what he has been doing the last 15 years. PROBE: How easy or hard was it to choose that answer? For the last 15 years, he has been in a professional, politically correct atmosphere. From ages 0 to 7, no. For the last 15 years, yes. Less than once a year. His work experience dominates.	26	Male	JE
1	LESS THAN ONCE A YEAR	PROBE: How did you decide to answer with [I]? Participant was thinking of the specific incident five years ago with the coworker at a food store where she worked.	27	Female	

relationship between the response given to this item (i.e., level of stress) and his or her response to the probe: "What kind of stress are you thinking of?" Presumably, degree of stress reported (e.g., a little, somewhat) should be consistent with the elaborated response to the follow-up probe. Table 7.6 contains the relevant data display, which is a simple form of what I refer to in Chapter 4 as a *chart*, under the pattern analysis model.

Interestingly, only 8 of the 14 participants who reported at least "a little stress" answered the probe "What kind of stress are you thinking of" in a way that specifically mentioned what can be regarded as psychological factors such as "mental distress" (these are marked with *) Other explanations did not directly define stress but mentioned issues such as (a) ways to avoid unfair treatment in the first place (avoidance) and (b) the *effects* of stress. Note that these individuals were able to provide answers to the original question, however (e.g., "a little," "somewhat"), perhaps indicating that they were responding to some other, self-defined conceptualization (that became evident only once the probe was administered).

There are several possible conclusions: To be fair, one may be that the cognitive probe was insufficient in assessing what participants were thinking (although as probes go, this is a fairly straightforward one). Alternatively, the investigators may need to consider the possibility that "stress" is not a sufficient description of the feelings produced by perceptions of unfair treatment. Interestingly, one individual provided a telling suggestion:... *it would have been easier to answer something like: "What kinds of feelings do you have when you experience unfair treatment? Then it would be easier to come up with word—anxiety, resentment, etc."* Based on this insight, the question designers might consider revising the question to instead consist of a checklist of items to ascertain how the respondents felt after such episodes—with "feeling stressed" one of several options—rather than assuming stress to be the dominant (or only) reaction.

Note how the pattern-based analysis approach differs from an alternative such as theme coding. When developing themes by only attending to the narrative responses contained in the notes, the analyst will of course be concerned with chronicling interpretations such as psychological stress, versus other reactions, and it can be expected that these themes will emerge. However,

Table 7.6
Pattern-based analysis of evaluated item: How stressful did you find these (just reported unfair) experiences?; Q-Notes data report

ID	(a) Answer	(b) "What Kind of Stress Are You Thinking of?" *Note: Pattern = Relationship between (a) and (b)*
15	NOT AT ALL STRESSFUL	No definition: Said she always tries to improve her knowledge, to keep on learning.
8	NOT AT ALL STRESSFUL	Effects of stress: It can give you low self-esteem and affect your eating and exercise habits negatively. She also attributed "stress injuries," cancer, ulcers, and excess body weight to stress.
11	A LITTLE STRESSFUL	Psychological stress*
19	A LITTLE STRESSFUL	Avoidance: Avoiding situations that bring out likelihood of unfair treatment by others (he declines to talk about American Indian issues with just anybody)
13	A LITTLE STRESSFUL	NO definition: Just say he doesn't hold onto his stress
16	A LITTLE STRESSFUL	Mental stress, not physical*
2	SOMEWHAT STRESSFUL	Effects of stress: Makes it hard to go to work and express herself—has to make a bigger conscious effort to keep her emotions in check.
5	SOMEWHAT STRESSFUL	When it happens, he immediately feels "bothered and sensitive to it"; he goes home to think about it or discusses it with a family member or friend. Is also in your subconscious. Consciously you know it happened and it's also in your subconscious*
6	SOMEWHAT STRESSFUL	Feeling anxious; array of moods—angry, sad, and mad moods.*

(continued)

Table 7.6 (*continued*)		
7	SOMEWHAT STRESSFUL	Frustration when treated unfairly*
9	SOMEWHAT STRESSFUL	Momentary reaction involving increased attention: He feels very self-conscious in reaction to any comment about his accent, but if no one says anything to him, he doesn't worry about whether his accent is noticeable or not.
14	SOMEWHAT STRESSFUL	Life difficulty: How hard it is at work to gain the respect of coworkers.
18	SOMEWHAT STRESSFUL	Fear (experience with the police); Anxiety, frustration for trying to understand or control things that are outside of your control* *For him, it would have been easier to answer something like: "What kinds of feelings do you have when you experience unfair treatment? Then it would be easier to come up with a word—anxiety, resentment, etc.*
12	SOMEWHAT STRESSFUL	Mental distress—things that make you go over and over them again—may blame yourself or feel guilt.*
1	EXTREMELY STRESSFUL	Avoidance: Quit job to avoid further incident with threatening coworker
10	EXTREMELY STRESSFUL	Anxiety attacks, nervousness, being fearful*

the themes tend to stand alone, apart from the context of the individuals who produced them (e.g., a set of five themes may emerge from the data, whether the study has 20 or 200 participants). Analysis of patterns, on the other hands, forces a consideration *at the individual participant level* of the correspondence between the response given to the question and the interpretation of that item. This leads naturally to a consideration of whether there is sufficient overlap between these that the investigators can conclude that the item "works," given their objectives and expectations.

Back to the Beginning: Text Summaries

One more example target question within this case study reiterates, once again, that there is sometimes no need to make use of coding schemes, theory building, or any other complex form of analysis: There is a lot to be said for scanning through a list of interviewer notes and being struck by an insight concerning question function. To illustrate: The final question in Table 7.2 is *"Have you ever been treated unfairly by other [FILL WITH RESPONDENT'S RACE/ETHNICITY]?"* The filled-in part of this survey question is based on a previous question asking how the respondents think of themselves: for example, Black, White, Asian, Hispanic, or something more specific like Vietnamese, Cuban, Sioux, etc.

The comments made by interviewers for this question in Table 7.7 were based on responses to the probes "Tell me more about that"; "What type of unfair treatment does it sound like we're talking about?"; and "Earlier when I asked you about unfair treatment, were you thinking of how other {FILL SELF-REPORTED RACE/ETHNICITY} have treated you?" These interviewer notes reveal a varied assortment of stories and experiences. However, just by reviewing the major findings, two appear to emerge most strongly:

1. The question has different meanings depending on how "other [FILL]" is actually filled. One of the interviewers notes this specifically with respect to Asians (Participant 14): If the question posed is "Have you ever been treated unfairly by other Asians" because the individual has previously self-identified as Asian, then the "other Asians" in this question could be members of a completely different group (e.g., I am Vietnamese, and the question then refers to non-Vietnamese Asian groups like Chinese, Korean, and so on). On the other hand, for a respondent who had self-identified more specifically as Vietnamese earlier, the question only asks about "other Vietnamese." Hence, the question does not provide a consistent measure of either in-group or out-group interactions, as this depends on the level of specificity of the self-reported fill that serves as the label defining group membership. A researcher with a Reparative orientation might consider this a defect to be addressed—given the variability in implied meanings.

Table 7.7

Interview summary notes concerning tested item: *"Have you ever been treated unfairly by other [FILL RACE/ETHNICITY]?"*

ID	Answer	Interview Notes
20	NONE	PROBE: Tell me more about that. She wasn't sure whether to say yes or no because she is estranged from her family, which is probably more a problematic family dynamic. Then she added that it is somewhat related with Native American because she thinks her parents believe that they are less worthy of equal treatment as Native Americans and think she has broken some unwritten social law by getting a PhD and making a life for herself. She then added that perception is fairly common in Native American culture.
1	No	PROBE: What kind of unfair treatment does it sound like we're asking about? Participant noted this could mean treating some people differently than others—not speaking to them, ignoring them even though they live in the neighborhood... She noted that other than the one instance, she's had no problems—America is pretty fair in general.
16	No	PROBE: What kind of unfair treatment does it sound like we're asking about? He said, "Like they look down on you, maybe."
11	No	PROBE: What kind of unfair treatment does it sound like we're asking about? Being insulted.
12	Yes	PROBE: Tell me more about that: "Same thing—ignorance level—sometimes if you are more intelligent, they will treat you unfairly. PROBE: Earlier when I asked you about unfair treatment, were you thinking of how other Hispanics have treated you?—Yes

(continued)

Table 7.7 (continued)

3	Yes	PROBE: Tell me more about that. Going out to dinner—less attention from waitress than a wealthier couple.
8	Yes	PROBE: Earlier when I asked you about unfair treatment, were you thinking of how other {FILL SELF-REPORTED RACE/ETHNICITY} have treated you? Yes.
10	Yes	PROBE: Tell me more about that. In her school years, they called her names As a teen: Oh yes. As an adult, also yes. Her looks have changed and now she is called prissy and cutie.
13	Yes	PROBE: Tell me more about that: When he joins a new Native American group, he has to prove himself over and over again. PROBE: Earlier when I asked you about unfair treatment, were you thinking of how other {FILL SELF-REPORTED RACE/ETHNICITY} have treated you? He said he was not thinking about other Native Americans when he answered the other items.
2	Yes	PROBE: Tell me more about that: Her friends—making fun of the way she speaks; and they cut her hair (which used to be very long), and lots of teasing.
5	Yes	PROBE: Tell me more about that: In Chicago he worked as a Clinical Director and found himself constantly having to discipline employees, many of whom were of the same race. His subordinates were upset because of this. PROBE: Earlier when I asked you about unfair treatment, were you thinking of how other {FILL SELF-REPORTED RACE/ETHNICITY} have treated you? –No

(continued)

Table 7.7 (continued)		
6	Yes	PROBE: Tell me more about that: She said that in professional situations, information has been given out but not to her because she was not as friendly. She felt discriminated against by others of the same race.
7	Yes	PROBE: Tell me more about that. Certain coworkers over the years did not treat him fairly—not because or race but because they didn't like him. PROBE: Earlier when I asked you about unfair treatment, were you thinking of how other (Whites) have treated you? Yes.
9	Yes	PROBE: Tell me more about that. He said this is really in relation to where he grew up. So he was thinking about "other people who did not grow up in the South"
14	Yes	PROBE: Tell me more about that. It's coworkers from other Asian groups. Interviewer note: *Note that this question functions differently for Asians than for other groups, if it is presented broadly as "Asians": Asians consist of multiple groups (Chinese, Vietnamese, Koreans, etc.), so this can refer to being treated unfairly by other Asian groups, rather than "others of your own group." This is not the same situation as being asked whether you are treated unfairly by other Whites, or by other Vietnamese, etc. So this seems most problematic for Asians, where there are clearly defined disparate groups. I would think that we want to ask this question at as specific a level as possible, and we really need to think through what this question is intended to capture, and the extent to which the interpretation may vary across groups.*

(continued)

Table 7.7 (continued)		
18	Yes	PROBE: Tell me more about that. Yes—He said that he has been treated unfairly by other immigrants who have been here a very long time.
		PROBE: Earlier when I asked you about unfair treatment, were you thinking of how other {FILL SELF-REPORTED RACE/ETHNICITY} have treated you? He said that he thought about the way other groups have treated him, not the way others of his own group.
19	Yes	Yes, because he is multiracial and doesn't always fit in.
		PROBE: Earlier when I asked you about unfair treatment, were you thinking of how other {FILL SELF-REPORTED RACE/ETHNICITY} have treated you? No, he was thinking about the White world.

2. As a second major result: The final probe—*Earlier when I asked you about unfair treatment, were you thinking of how other {FILL SELF-REPORTED RACE/ETHNICITY} have treated you?* pertains to an earlier target item asking about whether one has been treated unfairly—but which itself does not specify *by whom*? It appears that there are two camps among these participants: those who had been thinking of in-group relationships when they answered the initial question, and those who had not. This implies a perhaps untenable degree of variability in interpretation of that item. This too serves as food for thought, for both the analyst and designers.

Simply based on observing the observations of the cognitive interviewers, and choosing the most significant findings, the analyst would be in a position to bring these major themes back to the development team for discussion. As in this example, this could be done in the absence of any coding, and it requires little in the way of quantification or detailed analysis techniques.

In one sense, these are issues that—once identified—emerge as clear, inherent problems with the item that are to be grappled with. The implication is that, despite having access to a range of sophisticated analysis techniques, it is sometimes valuable to rely on simply reading and thinking. In other cases, it may be useful to rely on a quantitative compilation of participant responses to target items, of their interpretations of these, of explicit codes, or of salient response patterns. Again, our analysis procedures are complimentary tools, not competitors.

7.4. Case Study 3. Comparing Analysis Models When Applied to a Single Dataset

The final case study applies each of the five analysis models in Figure 4.1, in parallel, to a single set of cognitive testing results. To this end, I present a case study of a project that relies on the conduct of a single round of eight cognitive interviews. The topic of the questionnaire is the use of complementary and alternative medicine (the results are based on an existing cognitive interviewing report that has been edited for purpose of illustration).

Admittedly, this is a somewhat artificial exercise. As I have suggested throughout the book, the objectives of the cognitive testing tend to influence not only the analysis phase but also the way that information is collected in the first place. As such, it is not really the case that an identical set of results would end up being analyzed in these different ways, as the data produced initially would likely differ, based on analysis philosophy. An analysis with a strong Reparative emphasis will focus—sometimes laser-like—on detecting and documenting "things gone wrong," whereas a purely Descriptive analysis will probe to collect as much data as possible on the full functioning of the question, without attending so much on what is problematic about it. With that caveat, given the same basic set of results, it is still possible to show how the path between initial data collection, and the production of conclusions, may differ as a function of the analysis strategy adopted.

Complementary and Alternative Medicine: Screener Question. For the example I have selected, eight interviews were conducted by two interviewers, devoted to a single survey question intended for interviewer-administration to members of the general public within a population-based health survey: *In the past 12 months, have you received complementary or alternative medicine?* (There were other evaluated questions in the cognitive interviews, but I will not discuss those.) A cognitive interviewing procedure was selected in which the target item is read by the cognitive interviewer, and then the participant is probed, using a concurrent probing approach. The initial probe, "*What, to you is 'complementary or alternative medicine'?*" is scripted and proactive in nature (what I label an Anticipated probe, in Willis, 2005). Beyond that, the interviewer is left to rely on probes that are more reactive (i.e., to the behavior of the participant) and are unscripted (i.e., Emergent probes). The data from the cognitive interviews therefore consist of (a) the answer the participant gives to the target survey question (assuming that the individual is able to provide one; (b) the probe question(s) that the cognitive interviewer administers; and (c) the notes recorded by the cognitive interviewer, including any verbatim quotes produced by the participant, either via thinking aloud or in response to probing.

How does one analyze these interviews? Next, I list the results of each interview, and for each, indicated how analysis would proceed under each of the five models illustrated in Chapter 4, Figure 4.1:

1. Text Summary (of interviewer notes)
2. A Cognitive coding scheme, involving the four Tourangeau categories of Comprehension (C), Recall/Retrieval (RR), Decision/Judgment (D), and Response Mapping (RM)
3. A Question-Features-based system (the Question Appraisal System, or QAS)
4. Theme coding
5. Pattern coding

First, I indicate how analysis would be accomplished at the *individual* interview level—that is, prior to any attempts at aggregation of results. So I apply each of the five methods separately to all eight cognitive interview results. Following that, I tackle the task of aggregating these results over the eight interviews, again in a manner that invokes each of the five alternative analysis approaches.

Interview 1 (Interviewer AB)
Interviewer: In the past 12 months, have you received complementary or alternative medicine?
Participant: Uh, not really sure…Maybe.
Interviewer: (Probe) What, to you, is "complementary or alternative medicine"?
Participant: Complimentary sounds like something that's free—like complimentary tickets to a movie.
Interviewer: (Probe) What about "alternative" medicine?
Participant: Uh, I just know "alternative rock"…
Interviewer: (Probe) Why did you say "not sure" to the question?
Participant: Well…medical care isn't free, so No to that part. But I wasn't so sure about the alternative part.
Interviewer: (Probe) When I mention complementary or alternative medicine, is there anything else that makes you think of?
Participant: Not really, no…
Interviewer: (Probe) And what time period were you thinking about, when I asked the question?
Participant: It was a year—12 months.

Analysis

1. **Interviewer notes—for Text Summary** The participant interpreted "complementary" as "complimentary"—or free, which is a basic misinterpretation of the meaning of the item. He also didn't know what "alternative" was. So the key concepts appeared not to be well understood.
2. **Cognitive codes: C (Comprehension issue); RM (Response Mapping)** [note: RM is assigned because "not sure" fails to match the requirement of Yes/No]
3. **Question Feature (QAS) Codes: 3b—Technical term; 3c—Vague**
4. **Theme codes:**
    (a) "Complementary medicine" as medicine that is free
    (b) "Alternative medicine" unknown
    (c) 12-month reference period used
5. **Pattern-based chart** (Table 7.8). Note: Includes, in column at right, the answer to a previous target question: "In the past 12 months, did you receive *any* type of medical or health care?")

CASE STUDIES IN ANALYSIS : 211

Table 7.8
Pattern-Based Chart for Participant #1

CAM in Past 12 months?	Repeated Question?	Understood "Complementary" as Intended?	Understood "Alternative" as Intended?	Used Time Period (12 months)?	*Any* Care in Past 12 months?
Unsure	No	No	No	Yes	Yes

Interview 2 (Interviewer AB)
Interviewer: In the past 12 months, have you received complementary or alternative medicine?
Participant: Sure—I do yoga and take herbs and stuff like that.
Interviewer: (Probe) What, to you, is "complementary or alternative medicine"?
Participant: Stuff that's not mainstream. It's beyond going to the doctor for a check-up and getting prescriptions when you have a cold. It's like working with nature to stay healthy.
Interviewer: (Probe) You mentioned yoga and herbs, and also said "stuff like that." So what else would that stuff be?
Participant: I guess—vitamins, but the natural kind.
Interviewer: (Probe) Do you remember what time period the question was asking about?
Participant: (pause) What I do now, right? Like, in the past month or so.
Interviewer: (Probe) When I mention complementary or alternative medicine, is there anything else that makes you think of?
Participant: OK, I would say, uh, if you have a disease like cancer there are things like apricot pits or whatever that are supposed to be naturally healing, you know? But I'm not sure if those work 'cause you'd have to do research and draw your own conclusions. I mean some of it is natural—I guess most of it is, but that doesn't mean that it works. Just that people try it.

1. **Interviewer notes—for Text Summary**
   The participant interpreted complementary/alternative as "not in the mainstream, and working with nature." She appeared to distinguish between two elements: (a) prevention (keeping healthy) and (b) treatment (for a particular disease). It seems as though both elements are in scope,

relative to the data objectives (i.e., the "medical" definition that we are working from).

On the other hand, she didn't remember the time period, though it's difficult to know how much of a problem this is, given that she said Yes anyway (if she had said No, but was only thinking about the past month, then there's the possibility of a response error, given that she may have been missing things that occurred previously within the 12-month period—so problems with the time period are something to watch in other interviews).

2. **Cognitive Codes: C (Comprehension), RR (Recall/Retrieval)**
3. **Question Feature (QAS) Codes: 3d—Reference Period (not well specified)**
4. **Theme codes:**
    (a) **Working with nature**
    (b) **Not mainstream medicine**
    (b) **Subthemes: (1) Prevention: keeping healthy generally versus (2) treatment for disease**
    (c) **One-month reference period used**
5. **Pattern-based chart (Table 7.9)**

Interview 3 (Interviewer AB)
Interviewer: In the past 12 months, have you received complementary or alternative medicine?
Participant: (laughs) No. Not in the past 12 months. Not ever.
Interviewer: (Probe) What, to you, is "complementary or alternative medicine"?
Participant: Yeah... things that cost a lot but don't do anything. Like homeopathic medicine, where you dilute something so

Table 7.9
Pattern-Based Chart for Participant #2

CAM in Past 12 months?	Repeated Question?	Understood "Complementary" as Intended?	Understood "Alternative" as Intended?	Used Time Period (12 months)?	*Any* Care in Past 12 months?
Yes	No	Yes*	Yes*	No	Yes

*Analyst note: The interviewer didn't probe on "complementary" and "alternative," separately, so it is difficult to know how to fill these cells.

much that what you're left with is pretty much water. Only it costs a lot more. And then there's junk like "energy healing"—it's all a scam, far as I'm concerned.

Interviewer: (Probe) Can you tell me more about the types of medicine or treatment you *have* used in the past 12 months?

Participant: My doctor. Regular physical exam. Eye doctor...let's see. Oh, of course, yeah, well I got in a car accident years ago and it still causes some shooting back pain. I just went to my chiropractor for that. And acupuncture helps, too.

Interviewer: (Probe) So—when's the last time you went to the chiropractor?

Participant: Just last week.

Interviewer: (Probe) And what about acupuncture?

Participant: Same—last week. It helps. Feels better...for awhile, anyway.

Interviewer: (Probe) Tell me more about the chiropractor and acupuncture treatment.

Participant: Um. not sure what you're after. They do the manipulation, and then I get followed up by a needle treatment, which at first I thought like, wow I really do not like needles. But those needles are really thin and they just do not...do not...hurt, take it from me, because I'm a baby about needles. But I don't even get nervous anymore.

Interviewer: (Probe) So, do you think of the chiropractor and acupuncture as complementary and alternative medicine, or something else?

Participant: Those things are pretty standard anymore. I think of them like going to the doctor.

1. **Interviewer notes—for Text Summary**

    This person interpreted complementary/alternative as things that are outside of "normal" medical care, that are of suspect value, and that are in effect "scams." Interestingly, he *does* receive what we regard as CAM—both chiropractic and acupuncture, but we're not getting this by asking just about "complementary or alternative medicine."

    Given the vagueness of these terms, I propose that we revisit the approach we're taking here and use a checklist approach that asks about "Any of the following types of complementary or alternative medicine" and then gets a

yes/no for each major specific type, checklist style. This takes longer, but a more concrete approach will likely work better.
2. Cognitive codes analysis: C (Comprehension)
3. Question feature (QAS) codes: 3b—Technical Term; 3c—Vague
4. Theme codes:
   (a) CAM as "scam"
   (b) CAM excluded appropriate treatments (acupuncture, chiropractor)
   (c) CAM as outside of normal treatment
   (d) 12-month reference period used
5. **Pattern-based chart** (Table 7.10)

Interview 4 (Interviewer AB)
Interviewer: In the past 12 months, have you received complementary or alternative medicine?
Participant: Not in the past 12 months, no. Not me, personally. Like I said before, no doctors or medical stuff for me in the 12 months.
Interviewer: (Probe) What, to you, is complementary or alternative medicine?
Participant: OK, this is something I know a little about—I read up on it because my mom was sick and she was considering anything. As I recall ... complementary means not ... regular, un, non-standard-type medicine, that goes along with regular medicine from the doctor. So like the word says, they complement one another. Alternative is just what is sounds like—an alternative to regular established, accepted medicine.
Interviewer: (Probe) OK, thanks. So, what types of things are complementary medicine—can you give me some examples?

Table 7.10
Pattern-Based Chart for Participant #3

CAM in Past 12 months?	Repeated Question?	Understood "Complementary" as Intended?	Understood "Alternative" as Intended?	Used Time Period (12 months)?	*Any* Care in Past 12 months?
No	No	No	No	Yes	Yes

Participant: Wow, let's see. I think taking some kinds of natural vitamins, along with a medication might count. Oh, like if there is a medicine that upsets your stomach, you take some type of herb that helps offset that.

Interviewer: (Probe) And what about alternative medicine? Can you give me examples?

Participant: Yeah, stuff that you do instead of regular medicines. Like, Chinese medicines or Indian medicines or things that traditionally would have been used for what ails you. Stuff that you take.

Interviewer: (Probe) And how about other things you may do, rather than take—like yoga or meditation.

Participant: Hmm. No you asked about medicine, right?

Interviewer: OK, the question was: In the past 12 months, have you received complementary or alternative medicine.

Participant: Yeah, you said medicine, which is something you take—"Take your medicine like a good girl," right? So that's not yoga or things you do. Those aren't medicine.

1. **Interviewer notes—for Text Summary**
   Participant had a textbook understanding of both complementary and alternative medicine: "Complementary means not...regular, un, non-standard-type medicine that goes along with regular medicine from the doctor. So like the word says, they complement one another. Alternative is just what is sounds like—an alternative to regular established, accepted medicine." So, that is perfectly consistent with our objectives for the question.
   But she goes on to indicate that the use of "medicine" implies that this means "something you take"—which excludes yoga and other activities that we mean to include. This seems like a very good point: Does it really make sense to call this "medicine"? Maybe we should be using "medicine or treatment of any type"?
2. **Cognitive codes: C (Comprehension)**
3. **Question feature (QAS) Codes: 3b—Technical Term; 3c—Vague**
4. **Theme codes:**
   (a) **Complementary as additional to regular medicine**

(b) Complementary as vitamin, herb
(c) Alternative as substitute for regular medicine
(d) Alternative as Chinese medicine, Indian medicine
(e) "Medicine" excludes yoga and other activities that do not involve taking a medication
(f) 12-month reference period used
5. **Pattern-based chart** (Table 7.11)

Interview 5 (Interviewer CD)
Interviewer: In the past 12 months, have you received complementary or alternative medicine?
Participant: What's that again?
Interviewer: OK: In the past 12 months, have you received complementary or alternative medicine?
Participant: No...what do you mean?
Interviewer: (Probe) Well, when I say "complementary and alternative medicine," what does that make you think of?
Participant: No idea. That's why I asked you.
Interviewer: (Probe) Well, can you tell me what kind of medicine you have taken?
Participant: What kind of medicine I have taken? Like my prescriptions? Um, blood pressure medicine: Benicar, and Lipitor for my cholesterol, and sometimes I take Lorazepam.
Interviewer: (Probe) Um, OK—how about—what types of medical care have you had—in the past...12 months?
Participant: Like...seeing my doctor? Two doctors. No, three. My regular GP, my heart specialist, and a psychiatrist.
Interviewer: (Probe) OK... uh, anything else?

Table 7.11					
Pattern-Based Chart for Participant #4					
CAM in Past 12 months?	Repeated Question?	Understood "Complementary" as Intended?	Understood "Alternative" as Intended?	Used Time period (12 months)?	*Any* Care in Past 12 months?
No	No	Yes	Yes	Yes	No
Interviewer note: Although this person had a good grasp of the distinction between "complementary" and "alternative," the use of "medicine" was a problem. We do not have a place on the chart to indicate this.					

Participant: Nope. So what about what you were asking me in the first place? What was that?
Interviewer: About complementary and alternative medicine?
Participant: Yeah, what's that?
Interviewer: Well, we are trying to ask about getting treatment other than the regular doctor—like... natural herbs or acupuncture or... um, energy healing (laughs). I should know this, there's a whole list of them.
Participant: Oh, hell, that flaky stuff—no, none of that.

1. **Interviewer Notes—for Text Summary**
   The participant was an older man who had no idea what I was talking about—he kept asking me what CAM is, so I finally told him. But this is a case where it's OK for someone to not know something because they have never done it.
2. **Cognitive codes:** C (Comprehension)
3. **Question feature codes (QAS): 3b**—Technical Term
4. **Theme codes**
   (a) **"Complementary and Alternative Medicine" unknown**
   (b) CAM (when described) as "flaky stuff"
   (c) [MISSING reference period—unprobed]
5. **Pattern-based chart** (Table 7.12)

Interview 6 (Interviewer CD)
Interviewer: In the past 12 months, have you received complementary or alternative medicine?
Participant: Sure.
Interviewer: (Probe) Tell me more—what have you taken?
Participant: (pause). How confidential is this interview?

Table 7.12
Pattern-Based Chart for Participant #5

CAM in Past 12 months?	Repeated Question?	Understood "Complementary" as Intended?	Understood "Alternative" as Intended?	Used Time Period (12 months)?	*Any* Care in Past 12 months?
No	Yes	No	No	N/A	Yes

Interviewer: Completely. We will never connect your name to anything you say, and we destroy anything that will identify you in any way. I can turn off the tape recorder if you want.

Participant: No, that's OK. Marijuana.

Interviewer: (Probe) To you, is that complementary and alternative medicine?

Participant: Yeah, of course—that's why they call it "medical"—meaning medical marijuana. I heard it helps with glaucoma, and calming you down instead of taking anxiety medicine.

Interviewer: (Probe) So why did you... receive that form of complementary or alternative medicine?

Participant: Uh, I didn't really "receive it"—I smoked it. Why? To get high.

Interviewer: (Probe) Was that for any kind of health reason?

Participant: No, not really (laughs). Well, I was in a place where it's legal, and it is meant for medical use, but that's not really why, for me. But it was medical marijuana, and that's what it's supposed to be for, so when you asked, I said yeah, right, it's medicine.

Interviewer: (Probe) And how long ago are you talking about?

Participant: Maybe about six months. Not exactly sure. Somewhere around there... yeah. Say six months, give or take a month. About time to do another visit (laughs).

Interviewer: (Probe) OK, so what else do you consider complementary or alternative medicine?

Participant: Hmm. OK, any kind of drug that isn't, like, mainstream—like I read that you can use peyote on their skin to treat burns. It isn't just for getting high or acting all crazy. There are uses for some things that... are illegal, which I think is stupid because... it may do some good for somebody.

Interviewer: (Probe) OK, anything else you can think of? As far as complementary or alternative medicine?

Participant: Um, no, not really.

1. **Interviewer notes—for Text Summary**
    Three interesting points:
    (a) The individual used a type of CAM, but not necessarily for health reasons. This pertained to marijuana in the current case, but I could see this also applying for some other activities (e.g., yoga) that are defined as

"medicine" but that are also used for other purposes (enjoyment). So, are we interested in whether respondents have used these specifically in order to address health, or for *any* reason? If the former, does the question need to specify that "In the past 12 months, in order to remain healthy or to treat a health condition, have you used CAM?" Or we could consider asking whether they have used CAM, and then later adding a "why" question to distinguish those who are engaged in the activity as therapy, as opposed to other reasons.

(b) His interpretation of CAM seemed to be limited to therapies that are not only out of the mainstream but perhaps also in a sense illicit: He mentioned marijuana and peyote, but couldn't think of anything else. This again suggests that the term CAM is nebulous, and that perhaps a checklist approach asking Yes or No about a series of specific activities would be more effective.

(c) The use of the term "received" seemed strange to him: If this was a form of CAM that one actively engages in (e.g., smoking marijuana), that doesn't match with the passive notion of "receiving" something. Again, this is a wording issue to consider.

As an aside, this discussion was sensitive for the participant—he asked about confidentiality, given that he had to admit to illicit behavior (marijuana smoking) in order to discuss the questions. I am not sure that this is as much an issue for fielded interviews, however, as those are much less invasive than is a probed cognitive interview.

2. **Cognitive codes: C (Comprehension); D (Decision)**
3. **Question feature (QAS) Codes: 3a—Wording; 3b—Technical Term; 6a—Sensitive Content**
4. **Theme codes:**
    (a) Purpose of CAM: Subthemes = (1) CAM as medical therapy; (2) CAM for other reasons (enjoyment)
    (b) CAM as illicit substance
    (c) Delivery of CAM: Subthemes (a) Active (e.g., smoking) versus Passive (e.g., take pill)
    (d) 12-month reference period
5. **Pattern-based chart** (Table 7.13)

Table 7.13
Pattern-Based Chart for Participant #6

CAM in Past 12 months?	Repeated Question?	Understood "Complementary" as Intended?	Understood "Alternative" as Intended?	Used Time Period (12 months)?	*Any* Care in Past 12 Months?
Yes	No	No	No	Yes	Yes

Interview 7 (Interviewer CD)

Interviewer: In the past 12 months, have you received complementary or alternative medicine?

Participant: Received? Like getting a shipment?

Interviewer: (Probe) Hmm, no, I don't think we mean that. OK, let me try another way. In the past 12 months, have you... gotten... any type of complementary or alternative treatment or medicine?

Participant: Oh, sure. Now I get it.

Interviewer: (Probe) So, what have you...

Participant: (Interrupting) Yeah, I go to the natural store and they have vitamins and all kinds of herbs. I always ask, "What's good for this, what's good for that," and they give me whatever I need. I don't know if it really works, but taking it makes me feel better already. Maybe all in my head, but so what, right? In the past 12 months? I have probably gone a dozen times.

Interviewer: (Probe) And any other type of complementary or alternative treatment, or medicine?

Participant: No... just the vitamins and herbs.

Interviewer: (Probe) So, to you, what else does "complementary and alternative medicine" mean?

Participant: Well, you fill up your medicine cabinet with stuff that maybe people used in the olden days but isn't seen as regular medicine. Some of it probably works. Some of it probably is poison. Who knows. But if people have been taking it for hundreds of years it's probably safe enough.

Interviewer: OK, so—earlier, when I asked about any kind of medical treatment in the past 12 months, you said "No" but you said "Yes" here, about complementary and alternative medicine...

Participant: Oh, I wasn't thinking about the vitamin stuff, then.

1. **Interviewer notes—for Text Summary**

    She first interpreted "received" as getting a shipment, so this clearly is a misunderstanding of what we mean. She interpreted CAM only as herbal remedies and pills that one takes—but does see these as outside the mainstream of medical treatment, as intended.

    It does seem that use of "received" has caused problems in a couple of interviews and should be reworded.

    Also, she had actually reported no medical care for the previous, more general question, although she said Yes here. She had a helpful explanation—that the initial question about "any type of medical or health care" doesn't capture one's own use of CAM, so we shouldn't necessarily expect that a No to the former implies a No to the latter. This means that we can't use the more general question as a filter to avoid the CAM question, at least in current form.

2. **Cognitive codes: C (Comprehension)**
3. **Question feature (QAS) codes: 3a—Wording; 3b—Technical Term**
4. **Theme codes**
    (a) CAM as herbal remedies and pills that are taken
    (b) "Receiving" as getting a shipment
    (c) 12-month reference period
5. **Pattern-based chart** (Table 7.14)

Interview 8 (Interviewer CD)
Interviewer: In the past 12 months, have you received complementary or alternative medicine?
Participant: No.

Table 7.14
Pattern-Based Chart for Participant #7

CAM in Past 12 months?	Repeated Question?	Understood "Complementary" as Intended?	Understood "Alternative" as Intended?	Used Time Period (12 months)?	*Any* Care in Past 12 months?
Yes	Yes*	No	No	Yes	No

*Analyst note: Needed repeat due to misunderstanding, so interviewer changed wording and repeated.

Interviewer: (Probe) What, do you, is complementary or alternative medicine?

Participant: I have no idea.

Interviewer: (Probe) Well, what types of things have you done as far as treatments or taking care of your health.

Participant: I walk. I don't smoke. I don't eat crap food.

Interviewer: (Probe) Sorry, not what I meant to ask. What types of medical treatments or medicines have you taken in the past 12 months?

Participant: I haven't been sick in years. I don't go to a doctor. Waste of money if you're not sick. And I don't need to take twenty pills like other people my age. They take pills to take care of problems you get from other pills. It's crazy.

Interviewer: (Probe) OK…thanks. Let's see.. Do you remember the time period the question was asking about?

Participant: No.

Interviewer: (Probe) OK, let me ask the question again. We're asking: In the past 12 months, have you received complementary or alternative medicine? So, what about things that aren't pills. Have you done anything like—yoga or energy healing…?

Participant: No. I walk for exercise. I'm healthy. I don't do those things. I don't go to the dentist. I don't join an exercise group. I live as God intended and I do just fine.

1. **Interviewer notes—for Text Summary**

    The participant was an elderly woman who doesn't get much medical care of any type, either mainstream or CAM. She didn't know what we meant, but it's pretty clear that her No was a real No in this case, so that didn't seem to be a problem. The question just doesn't seem to make much sense to ask something like this, out of the blue. That is, it asks about a very specific type of medical treatment (CAM) but the more general question about *any* type of medical care or treatment in the past 12 months, which could provide appropriate context, is separated by a number of other questions on an unrelated topic. So the CAM question comes across as strange, and even seemed somewhat off-putting or even offensive to her. I'm not sure how many people there are like her, however.

2. **Cognitive codes: C (Comprehension); D (Decision/Judgment)** *[Note: This code is sometimes used to capture item sensitivity.]*

3. Question feature (QAS) Codes: 4a—Inappropriate Assumption; 6a—Sensitive Content
4. Theme codes
   a. CAM irrelevant if no interaction with the medical system
   b. Reference period not used to answer
5. Pattern-based chart (Table 7.15)

Summarizing Over Interviews

The differences between the alternative analysis approaches appear most stark when the eight interviews are combined, especially with respect to the difficulty of completing this aggregation.

1. Project-Level Analysis Based on Text Summary

Moving from the individual interview level to a summary can be done by using a Successive Aggregation approach (Chapter 5) in which each of the two interviewers independently "writes up" his or her own (four) interviewer notes, and these reports are then combined. Or the interviews can be pooled and analyzed according to a harmonized, collaborative analysis model, where the members of the team work together to assess each interview and produce a summary judgment. Either way, this involves more than simply block copying all of the text-based comments—as this would simply create an unguided summary of the type that Miles and Huberman (1984) objected to on the basis of its challenges to easy interpretation by the human analyst. Rather, someone must review and synthesize these rich descriptions into a data-reduced form that is shorter, and readable, but that still retains

Table 7.15
Pattern-Based Chart for Participant #8

CAM in Past 12 months?	Repeated Question?	Understood "Complementary" as Intended?	Understood "Alternative" as Intended?	Used Time Period (12 months)?	*Any* Care in Past 12 months?
No	No	No	No	No	No

Analyst note: Interviewer reread the question eventually, not in order to get the person's answer to the question, but in order to remind her of the question before further probing.

the essence of the meaning contained within the text summaries. My attempt at this aggregates all eight interviews, but includes a brief between-interviewer assessment, to assess commonality across the two cognitive testers.

Text Summary (Based on Eight Interviews)

Target item: In the past 12 months, have you received complementary or alternative medicine?

   (A) *Comprehension/clarity issues concerning CAM*:
   Results were very consistent: Both interviewers observed a number of interpretations of the key concept "complementary and alternative medicine" that indicated this to be a problematic concept within the evaluated question. Only one participant correctly defined *complementary* as a complement to standard medical treatment, and *alternative* as an alternative to such care; it is not clear that any of the eight tested individuals completely understood what we are after.

   Mainly, the overall concept was interpreted in varying ways and in ways that departed markedly from what the questionnaire designers are intending. Misinterpretations included the following:
   1. "Complementary" care meaning "free" care
   2. CAM consisting of "scam" care that isn't effective
   3. CAM consisting of therapies that are widely viewed as illicit (e.g., marijuana)
   4. CAM *not* including activities which are in scope (yoga, chiropractor)
   5. Not understanding at all what CAM is—Unlike the problems above, however, these cases were not problematic, given that the people who never heard of CAM had also (apparently) not made use of these.

   (B) *Other wording issues*:
   1. *Receiving*: Two participants had trouble with use of "receiving"—one stating that he doesn't passively "receive" marijuana treatment (but is rather more active in his use); the second thinking that we literally were talking about receiving a package of pills.

Recommendation: Reword to eliminate "receive" and select wording that is more active rather than only passive—even "use" might be better.

2. *Medicine*: Use of "medicine" as part of the CAM phrase was misleading: One participant interpreted this as "something you take"—which excludes yoga and other activities that we mean to include.

Recommendation: Maybe we should be using "medicine or treatment of any type"?

(C) Timeframe issues:

Participants were mixed with respect to keying on the 12-month reference period. Some ignored this or could not remember when probed—but this seemed to be most pronounced for individuals for whom the answer was clearly No anyway (e.g., those who *never* use CAM), so this did not seem to necessarily cause problems that led to errors. In at least one other case, the person could not remember the time period but said Yes because she is a frequent CAM user—again, this did not cause problems. What we really do not know from this testing is how the question operates at the boundary of 12 months—that is, whether there is telescoping in or out of the appropriate period that would produce recall bias. But it is unlikely we will be able to ascertain that from a test of eight people.

Recommendation: Overall, the timeframe issues seem swamped by problems with interpretation/comprehension, so we should mainly focus on those problems, rather than the timeframe.

(D) Other conceptual issues:

1. Interestingly, one person made a useful distinction between CAM as *prevention* (keeping healthy) and as *treatment* (for a particular disease). It seems as though both elements are in scope, relative to the data objectives, but we are not helping respondents to think about these elements, given our current question wording.

2. One participant's comments brought out a distinction between (a) general use of CAM for any reason, versus (b) use specifically in order to improve/maintain health. This makes the most difference for activities (e.g., yoga, marijuana) that are not only CAM but are

widely used for other reasons. Especially if we take the recommended approach of using a checklist of specific CAM modalities (see my comment E below), we may need to consider whether this element should be made more explicit (i.e., that we mean use of these for health reasons only); and, if so, whether it should be worked into the initial item or as a follow-up (why did you use this?) question.
3. Logically, asking about specific use of CAM may make little sense for some people—especially those who have not received medical care of *any* kind in the past 12 months (it is like asking someone, out of the blue, if he or she drives a sports car after finding out they do not drive at all). One approach may be to try to skip respondents past the CAM question if they say No to the past 12-month item on any care, but there was also an indication that this will not work, because the first item does not really make people think about CAM modalities.

Maybe one way to solve these problems would be to go to a checklist approach that just allows a quick No response to a number of specific items.

(E) Overall recommendations:

Quoting from one of the interviewers: "Given the vagueness of these terms, I propose that we revisit the approach we are taking here and use a checklist approach that asks about "Any of the following types of complementary or alternative medicine" and then gets a yes/no for each major specific type, checklist style. This takes longer, but a more concrete approach will likely work better." This may, in fact, be a good avenue—we have used checklists successfully in the past when faced with vague, complex concepts (e.g., instead of asking about "foot problems," we ask Yes/No for a list that includes bunions, poor circulation, and so on...).

2. Project-Level Analysis Based on Cognitive Coding

As a very different way to analyze the results, we could produce a simple summary table, based on the frequencies of each assigned cognitive code, across all of eight interviews (Participant 1: C, RM

Table 7.16
Aggregated Cognitive Codes over eight CAM interviews

Cognitive Coding Category	Comprehension (C)	Recall/ Retrieval (RR)	Decision (D)	Response Mapping (RM)	Total
Frequency	8	1	2	1	**12**
Percent of total	66.7%	8.3%	16.6%	8.3%	**100%**

2: C, RR; 3: C; 4: C: 5: C; 6: C, D; 7: C; 8: C, D). There were 12 total codes, as illustrated in Table 7.16.

From the aggregated codes, it appears that comprehension-related problems dominate.

3. Project-Level Analysis Based on Question Feature (QAS) Coding

As for cognitive coding, because we rely on discrete, quantifiable coding categories, it is possible to produce a similar summary table, containing somewhat more information, given the more finely grained nature of the codes. We now have 15 code assignments represented across the interviews, consisting of six separate coding categories, with somewhat more expressive category descriptions (Table 7.17).

The most pronounced result is the observation that the term "complementary and alternative" is too technical for use in a general population survey.

4. Project-Level Analysis Based on Theme Coding

The theme coding results could be summarized through use of a pie-chart model (see Figure 4.4) or a more complex hierarchical representation (see Figure 4.5). I selected the former, to partition the range of interpretations the CAM item captures. This can be complicated by the fact that the type of reverse engineering of the evaluated question, into its component parts, may not produce one clear pie. Rather, there may be different pies to be cut up—by analogy, one pie is a pizza, another an apple pie, each composed of different ingredients. Consider our pizza to be the range of interpretations the CAM item captures, with respect to its semantic content (Figure 7.3). Parenthetically, a second pie chart (our apple pie) could be developed in order to capture perceptions of

Table 7.17

Question Feature (QAS) codes applied to eight CAM interviews

QAS Coding Category	Frequency	Percent of Total
3a: **WORDING:** Question is lengthy, awkward, ungrammatical, or contains complicated syntax.	2	13.3%
3b: **TECHNICAL TERM(S)** are undefined, unclear, or complex.	6	40.0%
3c: **VAGUE:** There are multiple ways to interpret the question or to decide what is to be included or excluded.	3	20.0%
3d: **REFERENCE PERIODS** are missing, not well specified, or in conflict.	1	6.7%
4a: **INAPPROPRIATE ASSUMPTIONS** are made about the respondent or about his/her living situation.	1	6.7%
6a: **SENSITIVE CONTENT** (general): The question asks about a topic that is embarrassing, very private, or that involves illegal behavior.	2	13.3%
Total	**15**	**100%**

the reference period involved. Because this involves a different dimension, I would not include this within the pie chart. Rather, I was able to identify 16 different implicit themes that appeared to be included in conceptualizations of "complementary and alternative medicine"—these are all given a place in the chart.

5. Project-Level Analysis Based on Pattern Coding

Finally, we can produce a summary data display for the pattern-based approach simply by mechanically aggregating the individual tables from the eight interviews. Note that this analysis method was the only one to actively make use of a preceding question within the evaluated questionnaire (concerning receipt

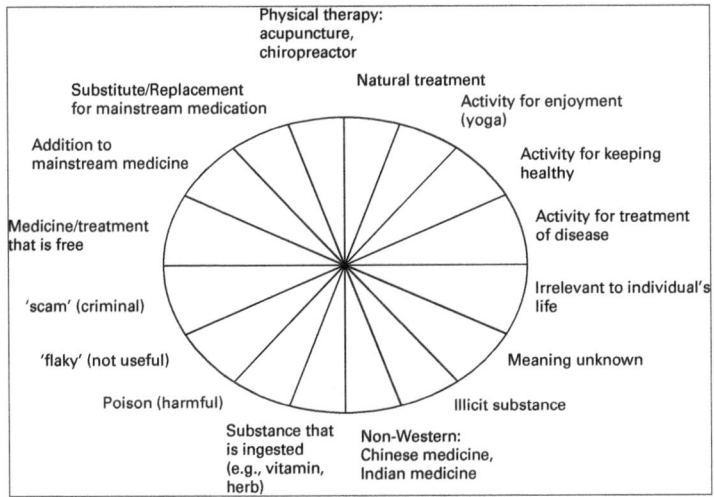

Figure 7.3. Theme codes representing interpretation of 'Complementary and Alternative Medicine'.

of any type of care in the past 12 months), as it is designed explicitly to clarify relationships between items (Table 7.18).

Patterns

(A) Comprehension of basic terms
   1. Understood *both* complementary and alternative: $n = 2$
   2. Understood *neither* of those: $n = 6$
   3. Understood one but not the other: $n = 0$
(B) Relationship between answer given to CAM question and understanding of key terms (complementary, alternative):
   1. Those saying "Yes" who understood CAM terms: $n = 1$
   2. Those saying "No" who understood CAM terms: $n = 1$

Interestingly, participants seemed to either understand *both* complementary and alternative (albeit rarely) or *neither*—in no case did someone understand one but not the other. There did not seem to be a strong relationship between answering the question *yes* or *no*, and understanding these terms. Although the sample is very small, the results suggest that we can have low confidence in any data arising from use of this item!

Table 7.18
Overall Pattern Coding analysis of eight CAM interviews

No.	CAM in Past 12 months?	Repeated Question?	Understood "Complementary" as Intended?	Understood "Alternative" as Intended?	Used Time Period (12 months)	Any Care in Past 12 months?
1	"Not sure"	No	No	No	Yes	Yes
2	"Yes"	No	Yes	Yes	No	Yes
3	"No"	No	No	No	Yes	Yes
4	"No"	No	Yes	Yes	Yes	No
5	"No"	Yes	No	No	N/A	Yes
6	"Yes"	No	No	No	Yes	Yes
7	"Yes"	Yes	No	No	Yes	No
8	"No"	No	No	No	No	No

Reflections on the Five Approaches

In Chapter 4, I discussed the relative strengths and drawbacks of each approach. However, relying on the admonition: "Don't tell me, show me"—I do hope that this fairly detailed demonstration does show more clearly the ways in which each approach deals with qualitative cognitive interviewing results, and where each may be the most appropriate. A few observations, specifically involving testing of the CAM question:

1. *Depending on the target audience, a combination of methods might be effective.* The varying methods have concomitantly varying strengths, which may make them useful in conjunction. A careful read of the Text Summary reveals a large amount of useful information, but this is difficult to capture at a glance, and the level of detail involved does seem to overwhelm and to perhaps obscure a bottom-line read on the major findings. Pairing this prose presentation with one of the summary tables, however—either from Cognitive coding or Question Feature coding—may make it evident from the start that miscomprehension was unacceptably (even staggeringly) high: The fact that 12 codes indicating cognitive problems were assigned across eight interviews (greater than one per interview) should itself raise eyebrows. A quick look at the code distribution shows that 67% of these problems involve comprehension—basically, a failure to communicate. The quick, bottom-line conclusion (clearly supported by the more extensive Text Summary) is that the question is simply not understood by human consumers.

2. *If we are in full Reparative mode, the Text Summary seems optimal.* I normally hedge on suggesting a "best" approach—but if I were meeting with the client in the morning and needed to make recommendations concerning what to do (anticipating the client will agree that there is something that needs to be done, questionnaire-design-wise), I would find the detailed Text Summary most useful, for two reasons. First, it is excruciatingly detailed concerning the exact nature of the problems identified, which then leads to rational notions concerning what, exactly, needs to be fixed (as I emphasized in Chapter 4, I do not believe that simply knowing that two thirds of

the problems involved "comprehension" is adequate for these purposes). Second, it is the nature of these reports to include ideas from the cognitive interviewers—especially recommendations that may constitute the "fixes" we are seeking. I am inclined to agree that asking a general question on "complementary and alternative medicine" is destined to be problematic, given the simultaneous technical and vague nature of this concept. As such, the suggestion to consider a checklist approach—asking the respondent to answer Yes or No to a series of specific exemplars of CAM—seems a much more suitable approach. This type of insight tends to come directly from the text summaries, more than from the other approaches.

3. *If I were doing a lot of cognitive interviews, I would not want to have to rely only on a Text Summary.* Imagine a situation where literally hundreds of cognitive interviews are conducted—as in one of the large, cross-cultural and multinational studies described by Miller et al. (2010). The idea of combining a huge number of text documents into a coherent report would be daunting. Instead, I would much prefer to have interviewers "preprocess" the analysis, perhaps through use of a pattern-based approach. Looking at that table, it is relatively easy to count up the number of instances in which the key concepts were not understood, and in this case, the table conveys the basic message (no, CAM terminology is not well understood). Further, the analysis of patterns between the columns may bring out interesting and useful information not otherwise in evidence. The use of the chart is in this case disadvantaged by the very small number of interviews, and key trends are difficult to elucidate. It does seem intriguing, however, that the small number of interviews done appears to illustrate that the participants tended to either understand *both* "complementary" and "alternative" as the researchers intended or else *neither* of these.

4. *A theme coding approach appears useful for doing what it is intended to do—efficiently showing "what the question captures."* Although one can possibly glean the same information from the text summaries, or the pattern table, the most attractive and easily digestible data display for illustrating

the variety of ways that CAM is thought about is perhaps the pie chart, flowchart, or similar data display. The act of coding themes systematically increases the likelihood that this depiction will be fully achieved—in the sense that it represents a comprehensive analysis, rather than one that is biased by only searching for problems. The theme approach does not necessarily lead to any quantitative summarization, but it is a reasonable approach to data reduction while retaining a high degree of richness.

5. *If I were going to publish the results, I would want to rely on tables of quantified codes.* Researchers are often interested not only in helping clients, and fixing up questionnaires, but also in producing articles that either illustrate how cognitive testing functions (as a Reparative tool); or how a particular concept is understood (e.g., fruits and vegetables, as by Thompson et al., 2011). In such cases, it is extremely useful to be able to include quantitative summary tables of the type that derive from cognitive, question-feature, or pattern-based coding.

6. *There is no single best method.* This has been my mantra throughout, and I also apply it to the example of complementary and aternative medicine items. The "best" practice surely depends on our testing objectives.

SUMMARY AND CONCLUSION

8.1. Chapter Overview

To close, I consider the initial questions posed and the way the information obtained from cognitive interviews will be made use of once a study has been conducted. I summarize the major points made in earlier chapters and then provide a final commentary on how the systematic analysis of cognitive testing produces several positive downstream effects. Finally, I pose the questions that researchers need to ask themselves, and answer, when they design and enact analyses.

8.2. Summary: Key Decisions for the Analyst

To condense and summarize much of the material in the preceding chapters, I review four major decisions the analyst needs to make in selecting an analysis approach. For each, I suggest the considerations that contribute to that decision.

8.2.1. Decision 1: Reparative Versus Descriptive Focus?

Finding and fixing problems—that is, employing a Reparative approach to "broken" survey questions—requires that we identify problems to fix. This orientation tends to lead toward the use of text summaries to describe our findings on a very detailed, question-by-question basis, as our detective work demands that, as Sherlock Holmes, we pay attention to the details. Reparative studies tend to focus, in a clinical sense, on the questionnaire at hand, analogous to diagnosis and treatment of a patient, sometimes without much explicit attention to the science of questionnaire design at a wider level (much as a physician treating a patient, who is typically is not attendant to research epidemiology). Reparative-oriented analysis tools tend to be selected in cases where the researcher is engrossed in a production environment, where "time is of the essence," and a client or collaborator is expecting the report as soon as possible.

Descriptive studies, on the other hand, tend to be less prescriptive about the need to identify problems within the questionnaire we have placed under our microscope, and they typically provide commentary or coding categories that are more general in nature, and that are consistent with the approach espoused by enthusiasts of classical qualitative methods such as Grounded Theory. The result of this process is presumably the understanding of how the item functions as a measurement device—knowing the range of interpretations it captures, and which it does not, should in turn allow questionnaire designers to determine fitness for use of this item in a particular context. *An implicit presumption is that items may not be universally good or bad*—so that whether problems exist depends on the way in which the item will be applied. Hence, a complete reporting of item function can serve as a source for multiple future investigations: Rather than simply treating the patient and then moving on to the next one, we strive to develop an accounting that has more permanence and that leads to a sophisticated level of understanding that facilitates future investigation.

In an ideal world, intensive and extensive Descriptive cognitive studies would be carried out on every survey question that we field. One way to move toward that ideal would be to increase the attention given generally to evaluation and pretesting of survey questionnaires. The survey methodology field has developed to the point where cognitive testing is viewed as a vital and accepted activity in the production of questionnaires, especially for federal surveys in the United States. However, this testing is often done according to a rushed, "just get it done" model, and where the accepted standard seems to be that it is enough to "do something." More attention and resources devoted to pretesting would serve to enhance the degree to which it can in fact serve as a rigorous science, as opposed to just one more activity on the assembly line that needs to be accomplished at some minimal level.

8.2.2. Decision 2: Should We Code Cognitive Interview Results?

As a related point, the tendency to assign codes, as opposed to relying only on text summaries, also depends on the nature of, and motivation for, the cognitive testing study. Many cognitive interviewing analyses make exclusive use of text summaries, without benefit (or the costs) of formal coding. I sense that this trend will continue, both for studies that are diagnostic of specific problems to be remediated and also for those for which a very detailed, down-in-the-trenches level of Descriptive analysis is desired. However, coding of results may be especially useful in several situations:

(a) When the researcher would like to establish a readable and easily reviewed representation of elements that the survey item captures—especially with a view toward future investigations that employ the items
(b) When the objectives include publication in a scientific journal or other report where systematic compilation and quantification of results is of benefit
(c) When the scope of the investigation is either large (e.g., many interviews) or complex (where cross-cultural comparability is assessed across multiple language or cultural groups)
(d) When the investigator is engaged in a methodological study to evaluate cognitive interviewing—for example, to determine whether the same types of issues and problems are identified across laboratories

Taking into account the interaction between the first two decisions: Overall, there does seem to be a strong relationship between whether a study is Reparative versus Descriptive, and whether coding of results is carried out: Reparative studies tend to eschew codes and rely on text summaries; Descriptive studies tend to include explicit coding. However, my view is that there is no conflict between the use of text summaries and codes—studies should use both where possible. Text summaries should be produced whenever feasible (rather than simply codes, which I believe are somewhat limited when they stand alone, unelaborated by rich description). The further application of a coding scheme, or development of emergent codes, should be thought through at the outset of the study. Rather than serving as an automatic or pro forma process, the investigator should determine what the codes will be used for, and whether those uses justify the time and effort necessary to produce them.

8.2.3. Decision 3: When Coding Is Done, Should It Be Top-Down, Bottom-Up, or Both?

Top-down coding may proceed from a particular model of the survey response process, such as the now-classic Tourangeau four-process model. Or it may extend the Reparative viewpoint by including a type of checklist of potential problems, such as the Question Appraisal System that focuses on the contribution of question features in producing problems. With the advent of a sociological and anthropological basis as the lens through which both questionnaire responses and cognitive interviews are viewed, top-down coding schemes have been expanded into a more extensive set that recognizes the contribution of cultural and linguistic elements (e.g., translation problems, cultural mismatch). These large-scale, deductive coding schemes can therefore become very detailed and even cumbersome—keeping control of these involves a good deal of training to apply the system selected.

As an alternative, inductive, bottom-up-based theme codes are attractive because they impose no particular a priori worldview to bias assessment of question function. These codes are also sometimes favored from a practical standpoint, as they do not require the learning of an up-front coding system. Codes that emerge from the data are, by definition, configured to fit the topic of study very well, although this feature does limit their generalizability to new questionnaires and environments. Further, bottom-up themes have the benefit of providing enhancement of our understanding at two levels: both the phenomenon or construct being studied (e.g., "disability") and how the survey questions designed to measure this phenomenon themselves function (literally "survey questions about disability").

I do believe that, at least in some cases, a compromise may be best, in which the investigator begins with several codes and then supplements and modifies these as data are collected. Consistent with a Constant Comparative Method in which data are continually compared with data already processed, it is possible, and in some ways optimal, to engage in both induction and deduction, to modify codes, and our overall understanding, continually over the course of the study. This is the approach that is most consistent with the Bayesian viewpoint that I have argued (in Chapter 3) underlies cognitive testing.

8.2.4. Decision 4: What Levels of Analysis Should Be Conducted?

This decision concerns the choice of analysis of the individual survey question, or of the relationships across survey questions, across interviewers, across subgroups, and so on. The capacity for attending to these multiple levels is not an attribute of any particular analysis approach. That is, both text summaries and coding systems can operate at multiple levels, as any method of summarization and data reduction can either collapse or parse in a way that distinguishes English and Spanish speakers, for example. However, there are particular approaches that facilitate analysis which explicitly accounts for multiple levels, and ways to cut the data.

Analysis procedures that are strongly grounded in the data, and that actively attend to the constant comparison method, lead the researcher to consider survey question functioning across multiple levels and to enable a complete analysis. Put more concretely, a theme coding approach endeavors to consistently ask whether the themes are convergent, or divergent, across cognitive interviewers, cognitive testing labs, subgroups, or languages. This practice naturally leads the analysts to consider where interpretation must account for the potential for variation across each of these, as opposed to overaggregating and producing simplistic conclusions concerning item function that may result from a less systematic approach. To combine several themes from prior chapters, I propose that one advantage of a systematic coding system is to provide a cognitive schema by which the analyst's own thought processes are targeted toward a number of critical considerations, in turn. This can be superior to attempting an unguided, global assessment of "Just what did we find?" from an unorganized complication of Text Summary notes.

8.3. A Broader View: Commonalities Across the Analysis Approaches

Figure 4.1 in Chapter 4 presented five identifiably distinguishable (and hopefully, by now familiar) coding approaches:

1. Text summaries
2. Cognitive coding
3. Question Feature coding
4. Theme coding
5. Pattern coding

Despite the inherent differences between these, I stress that another consistent theme is commonality of approach. In application, despite differences in background theoretical orientation, nomenclature and terminology, and in substantive analysis procedures, there seem to be fewer actual differences in the final product than one might expect. Put another way, once presented with the results of cognitive testing, differing analysis procedures tend to converge on common conclusions. Whether we endeavor to carry out a Descriptive or a Reparative study, the finding that a particular term is not well understood tends to lead to the conclusion that this term is problematic and must be replaced.

Similarly, assessment of what an item such as the general health question captures tends to be reported in terms of its range of interpretation, no matter which particular analysis approach is applied. In particular, many of the implications stemming from the problem codes used in cognitive coding bear resemblance to the parallel implications of findings from a theme coding study. Cognitive coding may indicate comprehension-interpretation difficulties due to an identified list of five separate interpretations of a concept, whereas a theme coding approach may identify the same five individual differences through a ground-up analytic strategy. The overused observation that "There's more than one way to skin a cat" may well apply to the analysis of cognitive interviews.

8.4. Conclusions

To close, I consider the benefits of careful, well-thought analysis procedures as they produce positive downstream effects for questionnaire design, and item testing, more generally. My overall message is that *careful analysis creates a body of knowledge concerning question/item function that is rich enough, and rigorous enough, to be relied on as a basis for informed decision-making concerning future use of the evaluated survey items.* These effects are, further, reciprocal: Better analysis makes us better questionnaire designers, which in turn leads us to use our accumulated knowledge to facilitative analysis. Of course, this process depends on whether we believe our own results, and can induce future consumers of our reports to believe them as well. Based on the data collection and analysis procedures we have used, how much confidence can we really have? Although this book is based mainly on analysis, I will repeat that we can only effectively analyze what we have collected, so threats to validity that we must consider need to involve both the collection, and the analysis, of cognitive testing data. Therefore, with regard to collecting and analyzing cognitive interview data, I end not with a set of recommendations or pronouncements but with questions that I believe the researcher must ponder, in deciding what to make of his or her results:

At the data collection point:

- Have we elicited the right information through our verbal reporting procedures? Was the probing biased?
- From the Reparative perspective: Did we invent problems that do not exist, or fail to locate those that do exist (i.e., by producing either false-positive or false-negative effects)?
- If interviews were done of the same individual, by two interviewers, would these interviewers likely elicit similar types of information from

the person? Or would one "make" the questions look problematic and the other not?

At the point of analysis:

- Once data are collected, does the process of analyzing them adequately produce the type of information we seek?
- Do the products of our analyses result in clear evidence concerning question function, without reference to guesswork or overly inferential interpretations?
- If two analysts took a look at our evidence, would they likely come to similar conclusions?

Concerning both conduct of testing and analysis:

- Have we provided an archival description of the methodology used, both for data collection and for analysis?
- Is the report specified to the extent that it allows future methodologists to fully understand the methodology we used?

Concerning the evaluation of our cognitive interviewing practices:

- Is our write-up comprehensive enough—and honest enough in its caveats—that future researchers can determine whether the procedures we have chosen have been effective in achieving the goals of better understanding survey questions?
- Do novel procedures, such as Web probing (Behr et al. 2014) lead to additional value and efficiency, as opposed to complication, with respect to both conduct and analysis of cognitive interviews?

As this book is meant as a beginning, rather than an ending, I look forward to the journey that cognitive interviewers take toward answering these questions.

REFERENCES

Adams, J., Khan, H. T., Raeside, R., & White, D. (2007). *Research methods for graduate business and social science students*. New Delhi, India: Sage.
Annechino, R., Antin, T. M. J., & Lee, J. P. (2010). Bridging the qualitative/quantitative software divide. *Field Methods, 22*(2), 115–124.
Bates, N., & DeMaio, T. (1989). Using cognitive research methods to improve the design of the decennial census form. *Proceedings of the US Bureau of the Census, Fifth Annual Research Conference*, 267–277.
Beatty, P. (2004). The dynamics of cognitive interviewing. In S. Presser, J. M. Rothgeb, M. P. Couper, J. T. Lessler, E. Martin, J. Martin, & E. Singer (Eds.), *Methods for testing and evaluating survey questionnaires* (pp. 45–66). Hoboken, NJ: Wiley.
Beatty, P. C., & Willis, G. B. (2007). Research synthesis: The practice of cognitive interviewing. *Public Opinion Quarterly, 71*(2), 287–311.
Behr, D., Braun, M., Kaczmirek, L., & Bandilla, W. (2013). Testing the validity of gender ideology items by implementing probing questions in Web surveys. *Field Methods, 25*(2), 124–141.
Behr, D., Braun, M., Kaczmirek, L., & Bandilla, W. (2014). Item comparability in cross-national surveys: Results from asking probing questions in cross-national surveys about attitudes towards civil disobedience. *Quality and Quantity, 48*, 127–148.
Belson, W. A. (1981). *The design and understanding of survey questions*. Aldershot, England: Gower.
Bernard, H. R. (1988). *Research methods in cultural anthropology*. Newbury Park, CA: Sage Publications.

Biemer, P. P. (2011). Total survey error: Design, implementation, and evaluation. *Public Opinion Quarterly, 74*(5), 817–848.

Birks, M., & Mills, J. (2011). *Grounded theory: A practical guide.* London, England: Sage.

Blair, E. A., & Burton, S. (1987). Cognitive processes used by survey respondents to answer behavioral frequency questions. *Journal of Consumer Research, 14,* 280–288.

Blair, J. (2011). Response 1 to Krosnick's chapter: Experiments for evaluating survey questions. In J. Madans, K. Miller, A. Maitland, & G. Willis (Eds.), *Question evaluation methods* (pp. 239–251). Hoboken, NJ: Wiley.

Blair, J., & Brick, P. D. (2010). Methods for the analysis of cognitive interviews. *Proceedings of the Section on Survey Research Methods, American Statistical Association,* 3739–3748.

Blair, J., & Conrad, F. G. (2011). Sample size for cognitive interview pretesting. *Public Opinion Quarterly, 75,* 636–658.

Blanden, A. R., & Rohr, R. E. (2009). Cognitive interview techniques reveal specific behaviors and issues that could affect patient satisfaction relative to hospitalists. *Journal of Hospital Medicine, 4*(9), E1–E6.

Boeije, H. (2002). A purposeful approach to the constant comparison method in the analysis of qualitative interviews. *Quality and Quantity, 36,* 391–409.

Boeije, H. R. (2010). *Analysis in qualitative research.* London, England: Sage.

Boeije, H., & Willis, G. (2013). The Cognitive Interviewing Reporting Framework (CIRF): Towards the harmonization of cognitive interviewing reports. *Methodology: European Journal of Research Methods for the Behavioral and Social Sciences, 9*(3), 87–95. doi: 10.1027/1614-2241/a000075.

Bolton, R. N., & Bronkhorst, T. M. (1996). Questionnaire pretesting: Computer assisted coding of concurrent protocols. In N. Schwarz & S. Sudman (Eds.), *Answering questions: Methodology for determining cognitive and communicative processes in survey research* (pp. 37–64). San Francisco, CA: Jossey-Bass.

Buers C., Triemstra, M., Bloemendal, E., Zwijnenberg, N. C., Hendriks, M., & Delnoij, D. M. J. (2013). The value of cognitive interviewing for optimizing a patient experience survey. *International Journal of Social Research Methodology, 17*(4), 325–340.

Cannell, C. F., Miller, P. V., & Oksenberg, L. (1981). Research on interviewing techniques. In S. Leinhardt (Ed.), *Sociological methodology* (pp. 389–437). San Francisco, CA: Jossey-Bass.

Cantril, H., & Fried, E. (1944). The meaning of questions. In H. Cantril (Ed.), *Gauging public opinion* (pp. 3–22). Princeton, NJ: Princeton University Press.

Carlin, B. P., & Louis, T. A. (2009). *Bayesian methods for data analysis.* Boca Raton, FL: Chapman and Hall/CRC.

Charmaz, K. (2006). *Constructing grounded theory: A practical guide through qualitative analysis.* Thousand Oaks, CA: Sage.

Chepp, V., & Gray, C. (2014). Foundations and new directions. In K. Miller, S. Willson, V. Chepp, & J. L. Padilla (Eds.), *Cognitive interviewing methodology* (pp. 7–14). New York, NY: Wiley.

Chi, M. (1997). Quantifying qualitative analyses of verbal data: A practical guide. *Journal of the Learning Sciences, 6*(3), 271–315.

Collins, D. (2003). Pretesting survey instruments: An overview of cognitive methods. *Quality of Life Research, 12,* 229–238.

Collins, D. (2015). *Cognitive interviewing practice.* London, England: Sage.

Conrad, F., & Blair, J. (1996). From impressions to data: Increasing the objectivity of cognitive interviews. *Proceedings of the Section on Survey Research Methods, American Statistical Association,* 1–9.

Conrad, F., & Blair, J. (2004). Data quality in cognitive interviews: The case for verbal reports. In S. Presser, J. M. Rothgeb, M. P. Couper, J. T. Lessler, E. Martin, J. Martin, & E. Singer (Eds.), *Methods for testing and evaluating survey questionnaires* (pp. 67–87). Hoboken, NJ: Wiley.

Conrad, F., & Blair, J. (2009) Sources of error in cognitive interviews. *Public Opinion Quarterly, 73*(1), 32–55.

Conrad, F., Blair, J., & Tracy, E. (2000). Verbal reports are data! A theoretical approach to cognitive interviews. *Office of Management and Budget: Proceedings of the 1999 Federal Committee on Statistical Methodology Research Conference,* pp. 317–326.

Converse, J. M., & Presser, S. (1986). *Survey questions: Handcrafting the standardized survey questionnaire.* Newbury Park, CA: Sage.

Daveson, B. A., Bechinger-English, D., Bausewein, C., Simon, S. T., Harding, R., Higginson, I. J., & Gomes, B. (2011). Constructing understandings of end-of-life care in Europe: A qualitative study involving cognitive interviewing with implications for cross-national surveys. *Journal of Palliative Medicine, 14*(3), 343–349.

DeMaio, T. J., & Rothgeb, J. M. (1996). Cognitive interviewing techniques: In the lab and in the field. In N. Schwarz & S. Sudman (Eds.), *Answering questions: Methodology for determining cognitive and communicative processes in survey research* (pp. 177–195). San Francisco, CA: Jossey-Bass.

Denzin, N. K., & Lincoln, Y. S. (1994). *Handbook of qualitative research.* Thousand Oaks, CA: Sage.

Dillman, D. A. (1978). *Mail and telephone surveys: The Total Design Method.* New York, NY: Wiley.

Drennan, J. (2003). Cognitive interviewing: Verbal data in the design and pretesting of questionnaires. *Journal of Advanced Nursing, 42*(1), 57–63.

Emmel, N. (2013). *Sampling and choosing cases in qualitative research: A realist approach.* London, England: Sage.

Ericsson, K. A., & Simon, H. A. (1980). Verbal reports as data. *Psychological Review, 87,* 215–251.

Ericsson, K. A., & Simon, H. A. (1984). *Protocol analysis: Verbal reports as data.* Cambridge: MIT Press.

Feinstein, A. R. (1987). The theory and evaluation of sensibility. In A. R. Feinstein (Ed.), *Clinimetrics* (pp. 141–166). New Haven, CT: Yale University Press.

Fisher, R. P., & Geiselman, R. E. (1992). *Memory-enhancing techniques for investigative interviewing: The cognitive interview.* Springfield, IL: Thomas.

Fitzgerald, R., Widdop, S., Gray, M., & Collins, D. (2011). Identifying sources of error in cross-national questionnaires: Application of an error source typology to cognitive interview data. *Journal of Official Statistics, 27*(4), 569–599.

Forsyth, B. H., & Lessler, J. T. (1991). Cognitive laboratory methods: A taxonomy. In P. P. Biemer, R. M. Groves, L. E. Lyberg, N. A. Mathiowetz, & S. Sudman (Eds.), *Measurement errors in surveys,* (pp. 393–418). New York, NY: Wiley.

Forsyth, B., Rothgeb, J., & Willis, G. (2004). Does pretesting make a difference? In S. Presser, J. M. Rothgeb, M. P. Couper, J. T. Lessler, E. Martin, J. Martin, & E. Singer (Eds.), *Methods for testing and evaluating survey questionnaires* (pp. 525–546). Hoboken, NJ: Wiley.

Fowler, F. J., & Cannell, C. F. (1996). Using behavioral coding to identify problems with survey questions. In N. Schwarz & S. Sudman (Eds.), *Answering questions: Methodology for determining cognitive and communicative processes in survey research* (pp. 15–36). San Francisco, CA: Jossey-Bass.

Fowler, F. J., Lloyd, S. J., Cosenza, C. A., & Wilson, I. B. (2013, April). *An approach to systematically analyzing cognitive testing results.* Paper presented at the QUEST Workshop, Washington, DC.

Gerber, E. R. (1999). The view from anthropology: Ethnography and the cognitive interview. In M. Sirken, D. Herrmann, S. Schechter, N. Schwarz, J. Tanur, & R. Tourangeau (Eds.), *Cognition and survey research* (pp. 217–234). New York, NY: Wiley.

Gerber, E. R., & Wellens, T. R. (1997). Perspectives on pretesting: "Cognition" in the cognitive interview? *Bulletin de Méthodologie Sociologique, 55,* 18–39.

Glaser, B. G., & Strauss, A. (1967). *The discovery of grounded theory: Strategies for qualitative research.* Chicago, IL: Aldine.

Goerman, P. (2006). *Adapting cognitive interview techniques for use in pretesting Spanish language survey instruments.* [Statistical Research Division Research Report Series, Survey Methodology #2006-3]. Washington, DC: US Census Bureau. Retrieved March 2014, from http://www.census.gov/srd/papers/pdf/rsm2006-03.pdf

Grice, P. (1989). *Studies in the way of words.* Cambridge, MA: Harvard University Press.

Groves, R. M. (1989). *Survey errors and survey costs.* New York, NY: Wiley.

Guest, G., Bunce, A., & Johnson, L. (2006). How many interviews are enough? An experiment with data saturation and variability, *Field Methods, 18,* 59–82.

Hak, T., van der Veer, K., & Ommundsen, R. (2006). An application of the Three-Step Test-Interview (TSTI): A validation study of the Dutch and Norwegian versions of the Illegal Aliens Scale. *International Journal of Social Research Methodology, 9*(3), 215–227.

Heesch, K. C., van Uffelen, J. G. Z., Hill, R. L., & Brown, W. J. (2010). What to IPAQ questions mean to older adults? Lessons from cognitive interviews. *International Journal of Behavioral Nutrition and Physical Activity, 7*(35). doi: 10.1186/1479-5868-7-35.

Helliwell, J., Layard, R., & Sachs, J. (2013). *World happiness report*. New York, NY: United Nations Sustainable Development Solutions Network. Retrieved August 2014, from http://unsdsn.org/resources/publications/world-happiness-report-2013/

Hicks, W., & Cantor, D. (2011). *Health Information National Trends Survey 4 (HINTS 4) cycle 1 cognitive interviewing report: May 31, 2011*. Bethesda, MD: National Cancer Institute.

Izumi, S., Vandermause, R., & Benavides-Vaello, S. (2013). Adapting cognitive interviewing for nursing research. *Research in Nursing and Health*. doi: 10.1002/nur.21567.

Jabine T., Straf, M., Tanur J., & Tourangeau, R. (Eds.). (1984). *Cognitive aspects of survey methodology: Building a bridge between the disciplines*. Washington, DC: National Academies Press.

Jobe, J. B., & Hermann, D. (1996). Implications of models of survey cognition for memory theory. In D. Herrmann, C. McEvoy, C. Hertzog, P. Hertel, & M. K. Johnson (Eds.), *Basic and applied memory research, Vol. 2. Practical application* (pp. 193–205). Mahwah, NJ: Erlbaum.

Jobe, J. B., & Mingay, D. J. (1991). Cognition and survey measurement: History and overview. *Applied Cognitive Psychology, 5*(3), 175–192.

Knafl, K., Deatrick, J., Gallo, A., Holcombe, G., Bakitas, M., Dixon, J., & Grey, M. (2007). The analysis and interpretation of cognitive interviews for instrument development. *Research in Nursing and Health, 30*, 224–234.

Krosnick, J. A. (1991). Response strategies for coping with the cognitive demands of attitude measures in surveys. *Applied Cognitive Psychology, 5*, 213–236.

Lee, J. (2014). Conducting cognitive interviews in cross-national settings. *Assessment, 21*(2), 227–240.

Lee, S., & Grant, D. (2009). The effect of question order on self-rated general health status in a Multilingual Survey Context. *American Journal of Epidemiology, 169*(12), 1525–1530.

Leech, N. L., & Onwuegbuzie, A. J. (2008). Debriefing. In L. Given (Ed.), *The SAGE Encyclopedia of qualitative research* (pp. 200–202). Thousand Oaks, CA: Sage.

Levine, R. E., Fowler F. J, & Brown, J. A. (2005). Role of cognitive testing in the development of the CAHPS® Hospital Survey. *Health Services Research, 40*(6), 2037–2056.

Lewis, R. B. (2004). NVivo 2.0 and ATLAS/ti 5.0: A comparative review of two popular qualitative data analysis programs. *Field Methods, 16* (4): 439–469.

Lincoln, Y. S., & Guba, E. G. (1985). *Naturalistic inquiry*. Newbury Park, CA: Sage.

Loftus, E. (1984). Protocol analysis of responses to survey recall questions. In T. B. Jabine, M. L. Straf, J. M. Tanur, & R. Tourangeau (Eds.), *Cognitive aspects of survey methodology: Building a bridge between disciplines* (pp. 61–64). Washington, DC: National Academies Press.

Marin, G., Gamba, R. J., & Marin, B. V. (1992). Extreme response style and acquiescence among Hispanics: The role of acculturation and education. *Journal of Cross-Cultural Psychology, 23*, 498–509.

Miles, M. B., & Huberman A. M. (1984). *Qualitative data analysis: A sourcebook of new methods*. Beverly Hills, CA: Sage.

Miles, M. B., & Huberman A. M. (1994). *Qualitative data analysis: An expanded sourcebook* (2nd ed). Thousand Oaks, CA: Sage.

Miles, M. B., Huberman, A. M., & Saldana, J. (2014). *Qualitative data analysis* (3rd ed.). Thousand Oaks, CA: Sage.

Miller, K. (2003). Conducting cognitive interviews to understand question-response limitations among poorer and less-educated respondents. *American Journal of Health Behavior, 27*(S3), 264–272.

Miller, K. (2011). Cognitive interviewing. In J. Madans, K. Miller, A. Maitland, & G. Willis (Eds.), *Question evaluation methods* (pp. 51–75). Hoboken, NJ: Wiley.

Miller, K., Fitzgerald, R., Padilla, J-L., Willson, S., Widdop, S., Caspar, R.,... Schoua-Glusberg, A. (2011). Design and analysis of cognitive interviews for comparative multinational testing. *Field Methods, 23*(4), 379–396.

Miller, K., Mont, D., Maitland, A., Altman, B., & Madans, J. (2010). Results of a cross-national structured cognitive interviewing protocol to test measures of disability. *Quality and Quantity*. doi:10.1007/s11135-010-9370-4.

Miller, K., Willis, G., Eason, C., Moses, L., & Canfield, B. (2005). Interpreting the results of cross-cultural cognitive interviews: A mixed-method approach. *ZUMA-Nachrichten Spezial, 10*, 79–92.

Miller, K., Willson, S., & Chepp, V. (2014). Analysis. In K. Miller, S. Willson, V. Chepp, & J. L. Padilla (Eds.), *Cognitive interviewing methodology*, (pp. 35–50). New York, NY: Wiley.

Miller, K., Willson, S., Chepp, V., & Padilla, J. L. (2014). *Cognitive Interviewing Methodology*. New York, NY: Wiley.

Miller, K., Willson, S., & Maitland, A. (2008, August). *Cognitive interviewing for questionnaire evaluation*. Paper presented at the 2008 NCHS Data Users Conference, Washington DC.

Mitchell, G. J., & Cody, W. K. (1993). The role of theory in qualitative research. *Nursing Science Quarterly, 6*(4), 170–178.

Morse, J. (1994). Designing funded qualitative research. In N. K. Denzin & Y. S. Lincoln (Eds.), *Handbook of qualitative research* (pp. 220–235). Thousand Oaks, CA: Sage.

Murphy, J., Edgar, J., & Keating, M. (2014, May). *Crowdsourcing in the cognitive interviewing process*. Paper presented at the Annual Meeting of the American Association for Public Opinion Research, Anaheim, CA.

Napoles-Springer, A. M., Santoyo-Olsson, J., O'Brien, H., & Stewart, A. L. (2006). Using cognitive interviews to develop surveys in diverse populations. *Medical Care, 44*(11), S21–S30.

O'Brien, K. K., Bereket, T., Swinton, M., & Solomon, P. (2013). Using qualitative methods to assess the measurement property of a new HIV disability questionnaire. *International Journal of Qualitative Methods, 12*, 1–19.

O'Muircheartaigh, C. (1999). CASM: Successes, failures, and potential. In M. Sirken, D. Herrmann, S. Schechter, N. Schwarz, J. Tanur, & R. Tourangeau (Eds.), *Cognition and survey research* (pp. 39–62). New York, NY: Wiley.

Oppenheim, A. N. (1966). *Questionnaire design and attitude measurement*. New York, NY: Basic Books.

Pan, Y., Landreth, A., Park, H., Hinsdale-Shouse, M., & Schoua-Glusberg, A. (2010). Cognitive interviewing in non-English languages. In J. A. Harkness, M. Braun, B. Edwards, T. P. Johnson, L. Lyberg, P. Mohler,...T. W. Smith (Eds.), *Survey methods in multinational, multiregional and multicultural contexts* (pp. 91-113). Hoboken, NJ: Wiley.

Pan, Y., Wake, V., Chan, G., & Willis, G. B. (2014, March). *A comparative study of English and Chinese cognitive interviews.* Paper presented at the Comparative Survey Design and Implementation Workshop, Bethesda, MD.

Payne, S. L. (1951). *The art of asking questions.* Princeton, NJ: Princeton University Press.

Piaget, J. (1952). *The origins of intelligence in children.* New York, NY: International Universities Press.

Presser S., & Blair, J. (1994). Survey pretesting: Do different methods produce different results? In P. Marsden (Ed.), *Sociological methodology* (pp. 73-104). San Francisco, CA: Jossey-Bass.

Presser, S., Couper, M. P., Lessler, J. T., Martin, E., Martin, J., Rothgeb, J. M., & Singer, E. (2004). Methods for testing and evaluating survey questions. *Public Opinion Quarterly, 68*(1), 109-130.

Reeve, B. B., Willis, G. B., Shariff-Marco, S. N., Breen, N., Williams, D. R., Gee, G. C., Alegria, M., et al. (2011). Comparing cognitive interviewing and psychometric methods to evaluate a racial/ethnic discrimination scale. *Field Methods, 23*(4), 397-419.

Ridolfo, H., & Schoua-Glusberg, A. (2011). Analyzing cognitive interview data using the constant comparative method of analysis to understand cross-cultural patterns in survey data. *Field Methods, 23*(4), 420-438.

Rothgeb, J., Forsyth, B., & Willis, G. (2007). Questionnaire pretesting methods: Do different techniques and different organizations produce similar results? *Bulletin de Methodologie Sociologique, 96*, 5-31.

Rubin, H. J., & Rubin, I. S. (2004). *Qualitative interviewing. The art of hearing data.* (2nd ed.). Thousand Oaks, CA: Sage.

Sandelowski, M., & Barroso, J. (2002). Reading qualitative studies. *International Journal of Qualitative Methods, 1*(1). Retrieved August 2014, from http://ejournals.library.ualberta.ca/index.php/IJQM/article/view/4615/3764

Sandelowski, M., & Barroso, J. (2003). Classifying the findings in qualitative studies. *Qualitative Health Research, 13*(7), 905-923.

Schuman, H. (1966). The random probe: A technique for evaluating the validity of closed questions. *American Sociological Review,* 31, 218-222.

Schwarz, N., & Sudman, S. (Eds.). (1996). *Answering questions: Methodology for determining cognitive and communicative processes in survey research.* San Francisco, CA: Jossey-Bass.

Seale, C. (1999). *The quality of qualitative research.* London, England: Sage.

Shariff-Marco, S., Gee, G. C., Breen, N., Willis, G., Reeve, B.B., Grant, D.,...Brown, E. R. (2009). A mixed-methods approach to developing a self-reported racial/ethnic discrimination measure for use in multiethnic health surveys. *Ethnicity and Disease, 19*(4), 447-453.

Silverman, D. (2001). *Interpreting qualitative data. Methods for analysing talk, text and interaction.* London, England: Sage.

Simon, H. A. (1956). Rational choice and the structure of the environment. *Psychological Review, 63*(2), 129–138.

Smith, J., & Firth J. (2011). Qualitative data analysis; The Framework Approach. *Nurse Researcher, 18*(2), 52–62.

Snijkers, G., Haraldsen, G., Jones, J., & Willimack, D. (2013). *Designing and conducting business surveys* (Vol. 568). Hoboken, NJ: Wiley.

Spencer, L., Ritchie, J., & O'Connor, W. (2003). Analysis: Practices, principles and processes. In J. Ritchie, & J. Lewis (Eds.), *Qualitative research practice* (pp. 199–218). London, England: Sage Publications.

Sudman, S. (1976). *Applied sampling.* New York, NY: Academic Press.

Tashakkori, A., & Teddlie, C. (2003). *Handbook of mixed methods in social and behavioural research.* Thousand Oak, CA: Sage.

Thompson, F. E., Willis, G. B., Thompson, O. M., & Yaroch, A. L. (2011). The meaning of "fruits" and "vegetables." *Public Health Nutrition, 14*(7), 1222–1228.

Tourangeau, R. (1984). Cognitive science and survey methods: A cognitive perspective. In T. Jabine, M. Straf, J. Tanur, & R. Tourangeau (Eds.), *Cognitive aspects of survey design: Building a bridge between disciplines* (pp. 73–100). Washington, DC: National Academies Press.

Tourangeau, R., Rips, L. J., & Rasinski, K. (2000). The psychology of survey response. Cambridge: Cambridge University Press.

Tulving, E. (1972). Episodic and semantic memory. In E. Tulving & W. Donaldson (Eds.), *Organization of memory* (pp. 381–402). New York, NY: Academic Press.

Watt, T., Rasmussen, A. K., Groenvold, M., Bjorner, J. B., Watt, S. H., Bonnema, S. J., ... Feldt-Rasmussen, U. (2008). Improving a newly developed patient-reported outcome for thyroid patients, using cognitive interviewing. *Quality of Life Research, 17*, 1009–1017.

Willis, G., Lawrence, D., Hartman, A., Kudela, M., Levin, K., & Forsyth, B. (2008). Translation of a tobacco survey into Spanish and Asian languages: The Tobacco Use Supplement to the Current Population Survey. *Nicotine and Tobacco Research, 10*(6), 1075–1084.

Willis, G. B. (1999). Cognitive interviewing: A how-to guide. Retrieved August 31, 2014, from http://appliedresearch.cancer.gov/archive/cognitive/interview.pdf.

Willis, G. B. (2005). *Cognitive interviewing: A tool for improving questionnaire design.* Thousand Oaks, CA: Sage.

Willis, G. B. (2009, September 18). *Analysis of cognitive interviews.* Short course presented at DC-AAPOR, Bureau of Labor Statistics, Washington, DC.

Willis, G. B., & Lessler, J. (1999). *The BRFSS-QAS: A guide for systematically evaluating survey question wording.* Durham, NC: Research Triangle Institute. Retrieved August 2014, from http://appliedresearch.cancer.gov/areas/cognitive/qas99.pdf

Willis G. B., & Miller, K. (2011). Cross-cultural cognitive interviewing: Seeking comparability and enhancing understanding. *Field Methods, 23*(4), 331–341.

Willis, G. B., & Miller, K. M. (2008, October 9). *Analyzing cognitive interviews.* Short Course presented at the meeting of the Southern Association for Public Opinion Research, Durham, NC.

Willis, G. B., Royston, P., & Bercini, D. (1991). The use of verbal report methods in the development and testing of survey questionnaires. *Applied Cognitive Psychology, 5,* 251–267.

Willis, G. B., Schechter, S., & Whitaker, K. (1999). A comparison of cognitive interviewing, expert review, and behavior coding: What do they tell us? *Proceedings of the Section on Survey Research Methods, American Statistical Association,* 28–37.

Willis, G., & Zahnd, E. (2007). Questionnaire design from a cross-cultural perspective: An empirical investigation of Koreans and non-Koreans. *Journal of Health Care for the Poor and Underserved, 18,* 197–217.

Wilson, B. F., Whitehead, N., & Whitaker, K. (2000). Cognitive testing proposed questions for PRAMS in the NCHS Questionnaire Design Research Laboratory. *Proceedings of the Section on Survey Research Methods, American Statistical Association,* 989–993.

INDEX

Page numbers followed by an f *or a* t *indicate figures and tables respectively.*

A

accommodation, defined, 8
across-laboratory analysis, 149
analysis. *See also*
　analysis models; data analysis
　across-laboratory, 149
　background expertise and, 150–54
　cognitive aspects of, 8, 58–60
　commonalities across approaches, 240–41
　complete, 146
　defined, 3, 56
　example of, 8–11
　between-group, 147–49
　within-interview, 146–47
　between-interview, 147
　between-interviewer, 149
　levels of, 145–150, 239–40
　pattern-based, 147
　qualitative approach to, 58–60
　self-imposed analyst interpretation, 150
　sequence of steps in, 56
analysis continuum, 56
analysis models
　bottom-up coding, 99
　pattern coding, 107–13
　question feature coding, 76–84
　selecting, approach to, 113–15, 122–24
　strengths and limitations of, 113–15
　successive aggregation, 126–135
　text summary, 60–69
　theme coding, 99–107
　top-down coding, 69–70, 88–92
analysis satisficing, 50
analyst, key decisions for, 235–40
The Appraisal System for Cross-National Surveys, 92, 93t–95t
artificial intelligence, 76
"Art of Asking Questions" (Payne), 76
assimilation, defined, 8
Assumptions (QAS), 79t–80t
Atlas.ti, 155, 156
attributes, 155

B

Barroso, J., 160
Bates, N., 44
Bayesian approach to data collection, 52

Beatty, P. C., 16, 19
Behavioral Risk Factor Surveillance System (CDC-BRFSS), 103
behavior coding, 75
Behr, D., 47
Benavides-Vaello, S., 61
Bereket, T., 49
between-group analysis, 147–49
between-interview analysis, 147, 187
between-interviewer analysis, 149
between-laboratory cognitive interviewing study, 130t, 131f
"bins," 9
Blair, J., 12, 48–49, 57, 73, 74, 117, 119
Boeije, H., 61, 143, 160, 167
Bolton, R. N., 75
bottom-up coding, 99, 238–39
Brick, P. D., 12, 119
Bronkhorst, T. M., 75
Brown, J. A., 87–88
Brown, W. J., 74
Bunce, A., 49

C

Cancer Risk Factor study, 139, 147
Cannell, C. F., 25
CAQDAS (computer aided/assisted qualitative data analysis software), 154
case studies
  cognitive interviewing to evaluate disability questions, 134
  Comparing Analysis Models When Applied to a Single Dataset, 208–30
  Mixing Analysis Models Within a Single Dataset, 185–208
  parallel cognitive interviews, 129–133
  Reviewing an Interviewer Text Summary, 170–185
CDC-BRFSS (Behavioral Risk Factor Surveillance System), 103
Centers for Disease Control and Prevention, 103
charting, 136–39, 137t
Chepp, V., 33, 61, 78, 105f, 150

CIRF (Cognitive Interviewing Reporting Framework), 160, 161t
Clarity (QAS), 79t
CNEST (Cross-National Error Source Typology), 90, 92t
coded analysis, 69–70
coding
  behavior, 75
  borrowing elements from different models, 106–7
  bottom-up, 99
  cognitive coding, 70–76, 116–17, 193–95, 237–38
  computer-based, 75
  cross-culturally oriented, 88–92
  deductive, 70
  examples of, 82t–83t
  Feinstein coding system, 84
  hybrid coding schemes, 84–88
  Levine coding system, 87–88, 87t
  linguistic/sociocultural categories, 97
  matrix, 107
  O'Brien coding system, 84
  pattern coding, 107–13, 120–22, 230–32
  pie-chart, 104, 105f
  question feature coding, 76–78, 118
  theme coding, 99–107, 118–20, 192–93, 227–28
Cody, W. K., 26
Cognitive Aspects of Survey Methodology (CASM), 23–24, 26
Cognitive Classification Scheme (CCS), 88, 89t–90t
cognitive coding, 70–76, 116–17, 193–95, 237–38
  case study, 193–95
  characteristics of, 71
  comparability across investigations, 117
  defined, 60f
  keyword-based automatic, 75–76
  loss of information through, 117
  one-size-fits-all approach to, 117
  problems detected with 72t
  reliance on theoretical underpinning, 117

results of testing case study, 196t–99t
strengths and limitations of, 116–17, 237–38
suitability for quantification, 116–17
cognitive interviewing-based study, 74
Cognitive Interviewing Reporting Framework (CIRF), 160, 161t
cognitive interview. *See also* descriptive cognitive interviewing; reparative cognitive interviewing
analysis models for, 60f (*See also* analysis models)
analysis of, example, 8–11
analysis programs for, 154–58
assembly-line process of, 140
cognitive testing vs., 54
cognitive theory and, 26–30
combining data across, 126
conducting, 3–4, 12–14, 13f, 46–53
conflicting information from participants, 109
context and explanation, 3–4
cross-cultural, 88–92, 129–133, 148–49, 162
defined, 16
to evaluate survey questions, 4–7
evaluation of, 242
example of, 36–37
field survey questionnaire, 5t–6t
natural language in, 2
note-taking procedures, 59t
objective of, 16–17
origins of, 16–17
probing (*see* probe questions)
problems with, 10–11
problem type codes assigned for, 72t
purpose of, 17–21
qualitative research and, 28–34
reports (*see* reports/reporting framework)
results analysis, 12–14
sample cross-tabulation, 9t
sample size, 47–51

software programs for, 154–58
translating to common language, 140
cognitive laboratories, 17, 26, 126
cognitive probes. *See also* probe questions, 37t, 110t, 132–33, 204t–7t
cognitive protocol, 40
cognitive testing, 5–7, 35–36, 54, 77t, 160
Cognitive Testing Report Containing Interviewer Text Summary (case study), 170–185
cognitive theory, 22, 26–30
collaborative analysis, 135–140
Collins, D., 90
communication
failures, 65–69
researcher, 140–43
Comparing Analysis Models When Applied to a Single Dataset (case study), 208–30
complete analysis, 146
comprehension codes, 117
computer aided/assisted qualitative data analysis software (CAQDAS), 154
computer-based coding, 75
concurrent probing, 41–44, 45t
Conrad, F., 48–49, 57, 74
constant comparison method (CCM), 52, 146, 239
conversational speech, 3
cross-cultural cognitive interviewing case study, 129–133
classification schemes, 162
conduct of, 148–49
between-group analysis, 148
top-down coding, 88–92
cross-cultural research, sample findings of, 68t–69t
Cross-National Error Source Typology (CNEST), 90, 92t

D

data
defined, 2
notes vs. quotes, 57–58

data analysis. *See also* analysis
  Bayesian approach to, 52
  frequentist approach to, 52
  qualitative, 7–11, 40–41
data collection, 241
data display, 107–8, 136
data reduction, 106, 139
data source, 40–41
debriefing. *see* retrospective probing
deductive codes, 70, 238
DeMaio, T., 44
descriptive cognitive interviewing
  example of, 21
  Q-Notes for, 157
  reparative cognitive interviewing vs., 20–21, 235–37
  reverse engineering in, 19–20
  sample size, 50
  survey response process, 24
  vague quantifiers, interpretation of, 18–19
documentation. *See also* reports/reporting
  framework, 123, 159–160
Drennan, J., 12

E

elaborative probing, 42
embedded probing, 47
Emmel, N., 48
Ericsson, K. A., 27
ethnographic field notes, 57
ethnography, 30–32, 31t
ethnoscience, 31t, 32
expansive probing, 42
expert review, 150–51

F

false-positive reports, 111–12
Feinstein coding system, 84, 85t
Fisher, R. P., 16
Fitzgerald, R., 90
Forsyth, B., 81
Fowler, F. J., 73, 87–88
Framework of Sensitivity, 84, 85t
frequentist approach to data collection, 52

G

Geiselman, R. E., 16
General Cross-Cultural Problem Classification, 90, 91t
Goerman, P., 148
Grant, D., 150
Gray, C., 33, 61, 78
Gray, M., 90
"gray literature," 162
Grounded Theory, 30, 31t, 33, 78, 99
Guest, G., 49

H

Health Information National Trends Survey (HINTS), 62t
Heesch, K. C., 74
hierarchical representations to organize concepts, 104
Hill, R. L., 74
Huberman, A. M., 52, 106, 107–8, 109, 135
hybrid coding schemes, 84–88

I

input error, 67
inspect-and-repair procedure. *See also* reparative cognitive interviewing, 18, 20, 64, 180
Instructions (QAS), 79t
intensive interviewing, 28
interaction analysis (IA), 61
internal cognitive mechanisms, 27
International Institute for Qualitative Methodology (IIQM), 155
Internet probing, 47
Interpretivist perspective, 33–34, 99
interviewer-administered questionnaire, 97–98
interviewer results, 153
interviewer
  behavior, 153
  interpreting, process of, 141
  multiple cognitive, 126
  notes, 9, 57, 126
interview rounds, 51
investigator, position of, 7

item functioning, unbiased analytic approach to, 102
iteration, 51–53
iterative nature of qualitative research, 51
Izumi, S., 61

J
Johnson, L., 49
joint analysis, 135

K
keyword-based coding, 75–76
Knafl, K., 13, 106
Knowledge/Memory (QAS), 80t
Koreans, 90
Krosnick, J. A., 25

L
Lee, J., 92, 97, 128
Lee, S., 150
Lessler, J., 78
levels of analysis, 145–150, 239–40
Levine, R. E., 87–88
Levine coding system, 87–88, 87t
Lewis, R. B., 156
linguistic theory and survey response process, 25–26
Logical-Structural code, 194

M
Maitland, A., 104
matrix coding, 107
MAXQDA, 155
memory, demands on, 43
method, 22
Methodology (journal), 160
Miles, M. B., 52, 106, 107–8, 109, 115–16, 135
Miller, K., 13, 33, 104, 105f, 108, 110–11, 119–120, 134, 136, 146, 150
Miller, P. V., 25
Mitchell, G. J., 26
Mixing Analysis Models Within a Single Dataset (case study), 185–208
Morse, J., 30, 31
motivation, 25

N
Nápoles-Springer, A. M., 61
narrative summary, 61
National Center for Health Statistics (NCHS), 71, 156
National Opinion Research Center (NORC), 71
natural language, 3
node, 155
notes
 case study, 204t–7t
 ethnographic field, 57
 interviewer, 9, 57
 note-taking procedures, 59t
 quotes vs., 57–58
NVivo, 155, 156

O
O'Brien, K. K., 49, 84, 122
O'Brien coding system, 84, 85t
O'Connor, W., 107
Oksenberg, L., 25
one-size-fits-all approach to cognitive coding, 117
Oppenheim, A. N., 19
outlier cases, 152–53
output error, 67

P
Padilla, J. L., 105f
Pan, Y., 148
participants, 5
pattern-based analysis, 147, 195–202
pattern coding, 107–13, 120–22, 230–32
 data displays to portray, 107–8
 defined, 60f, 107
 descriptive purposes of, 120
 examining for consistency, 112–13
 example of, 108–13
 false-positive reports, 111–12
 large investigations and, 121

pattern coding (*cont.*)
  providing structure to cognitive interview, 120–21
  reparative purposes of, 120
  strengths and limitations of, 120–22
  theme coding vs., 200–202
Payne, S. L., 76
phenomenology, 30, 31t
Piaget, J., 8
pie-chart coding, 104, 105f, 147
positivism, 33
Presser, S., 73, 117
probe questions. *See also* think-aloud probing; verbal probing
  analysis of, 46
  difficulties with, 148
  embedded, 47
  examples of, 37–39, 37t
  random, 47
  standardized, 46–47
  Web (Internet), 47
Problem Classification Coding Scheme (CCS), 89t–90t
processing error, 67

Q

QAS (Question Appraisal System), 78–81, 79t–81t, 96–97, 238
Q-Bank, 167–68
QDA Miner, 155, 156
Q-Notes system, 154, 156–58, 187, 188f, 189t, 190t–92t, 194–95
qualitative analysis
  cognitive aspects of, 8
  of data, 40–41
  defined, 2
  quantitative vs., 1–4, 12
  researcher's role in, 7
  software programs for, 155–56
qualitative ethology, 31t, 32
qualitative research
  categories of, 30–32
  cognitive interviewing and, 28–34
  iterative nature of, 51
  "quality" of, 160
qualitative testing, approach to, 48
quantitative analysis, 1–4, 12

quantitative approach to sampling, 49
Question Appraisal System (QAS), 78–81, 79t–81t, 96–97, 238, 76–78, 118
  categories, 82t–83t, 86–87
  defined, 60f, 76
  Feinstein coding system, 84
  Levine coding system, 87–88, 87t
  O'Brien coding system, 84
  problems/errors in assumptions, 77t
  Question Appraisal System (QAS), 78–81, 79t–81t
  strengths and limitations of, 118
  theory of sensibility, 84
questionnaire
  difficulties in, 5
  disjunction in questions, 10–11
  interviewer-administered, 97–98
  objective of, 170–71
  pretesting, 13
  self-administered, 44
  sociocultural contributions to, 68
quotes
  notes vs., 57–58
  verbatim, 57

R

random probes, 47
raw data, 60f
reactivity effects, 44
Reading (QAS), 79t
recruitment process, 163
reparative cognitive interviewing
  defined, 18
  descriptive cognitive interviewing vs., 20–21, 235–37
  example of, 21
  expert opinion to review, 151, 153–54
  Q-Notes for, 157
  sample size, 50
reports/reporting framework
  background literature, 162
  conclusions, 166–67
  data analysis, 165
  data collection, 164–65

discussion, 166–67
ethics, 163
findings, 166
format of, 167
insufficient documentation, 159–160
participant selection, 163–64
procedural detail, 160
Q-Bank, 167–68
repository of, 167–68
research design, 162–63
research objectives, 161–62
strengths and limitations of, 167
transparency, 160
researcher communication, 140–43
research objectives, 161–62
Response Categories (QAS), 80t–81t
response process. *See also*
survey response process, 23–24
retrieval problem, example of, 66
retrospective probing, 41–44, 45t
reverse engineering. *See also* descriptive cognitive interviewing, 19–20, 26, 101
Reviewing and Interviewer Text Summary (case study), 170–185
Ridolfo, H., 19, 102
Ritchie, J., 107
Rothgeb, J., 81

S

sample size, 47–51, 143–45
Sandelowski, M., 160
satisficing, 25, 50
saturation. *See also* sample size, 48–49, 144–45
Schechter, S., 71, 72t
Schoua-Glusberg, A., 19, 102
Schuman, H., 47
scientific method, 1–2
Seale, C., 160
self-administered questionnaires, 44, 73
self-imposed analyst interpretation, 150
Sensitivity/Bias (QAS), 80t
Simon, H. A., 25, 27, 50

sociocultural contributions to question function, 68
software programs for cognitive interviews, 154–58
Solomon, P., 49
Spencer, L., 107
successive aggregation
case study, 129–133
collaborative harmonized analysis vs., 139–140
data compilation procedure, 127–29
defined, 126–27
example of, 129–133
failure of, 134–35
summarizing across laboratories, 128
summarizing within-interviewer, 127–28
summarizing within-laboratory, 128
Sudman, S., 48
survey questions. *See also* verbal probing
cognitive interviews to evaluate, 4–7
problems/errors in assumptions, 77t
Question Appraisal System (QAS), 78–81, 79t–81t
survey response process
cognitive model of, 24t
cognitive theory and, 23–25
defined, 22
linguistic theory and, 25–26
sociocultural influences on, 25–26
Tourangeau model of, 26
survey responses, qualitative augmentation of, 4–5
surveys. *See also* survey questions
estimates for, 3–4
natural language in, 3
pretesting, 7, 13
product-testing, 5
qualitative vs. quantitative, 1–4
Swinton, M., 49

T

tag, 155
targeted procedures, 36
text summary
  analysis approach, 189
  approach to, 60–61
  case study, 170–185, 189, 203–8
  communication failures, 65–69
  cross-cultural research, 68
  defined, 60, 60f
  efficiency of, 115
  example of, 61–63
  failure of agreement in, 64
  identifying problems, 152
  incomplete analysis in, 116
  input error, 67
  from interview notes, 61
  lack of grounding framework, 116
  multiple cognitive processes, 66–67
  output error, 67
  processing error, 67
  researcher's point of view, 64
  retrieval problem, 66
  richness of data, 115
  strengths and limitations of, 115–16
  uncoded approach to, 114f
  Venn diagram, 63–64
  volume, 115–16
theme coding, 99–107, 118–20, 192–93, 227–28
  analysis approach, 192–93
  approach to, 101–5, 118
  case study, 192–93
  defined, 60f, 99–100
  descriptive research, 101
  example of, 100–101
  full question function of, 118–19
  generalizability, lack of, 119
  Grounded Theory, 99
  hierarchical representations to organize concepts, 104
  intent of, 102
  interpretive processes, 119–120
  loss of information through, 119–120
  mixed approach to using, 106–7
  pattern coding vs., 200–202
  pie-chart coding, 104
  Q-Notes for, 157
  within a Reparative study, 106
  strengths and limitations of, 118–120
  variants of, 104
theoretical sampling, 51
theory
  defined, 22–23
  role of, 26
theory of sensibility, 84
think-aloud interview, 27
think-aloud probing, 36, 38t, 39–40, 75–76
thinking aloud, 17, 36–37
Thompson, F. E., 21
Thompson, O. M., 21
top-down coding
  approach to, 69–70
  complexity, 95–96
  cross-culturally oriented, 88–92
  focus, 96–98
  linguistic/sociocultural categories, 97
  selecting, 92–98
  when to use, 238
top-row listing, 136
Tourangeau, R., 23
Tourangeau model of survey response theory, 23, 26, 71, 86, 96, 194, 238
Tracy, E., 57
transcription, 57–58

U

uncoded analysis, 69–70, 114f
United Kingdom, 90

V

vague quantifiers, 18–19
Vandermause, R., 61
van Uffelen, J. G. Z., 74
Venn diagram, 63–64, 102

verbalizations, 39–40
verbal probes, defined, 17
verbal probing
  concurrent vs. retrospective,
    41–44, 45t
  example of, 7, 37–39, 37t
  features of, 38t
  interpretive process and, 33
  procedures of, 41–45
  think-aloud probing vs., 27,
    36, 39
verbal protocol, 57
verbal reporting/reports, 17, 35–41
"Verbal Reports Are Data!"
  (article), 57
verbatim quotes, 57
verbatim record, 75

W

Web probing, 47
Whitaker, K., 71
Widdop, S., 90
Willis, G. B., 13, 16, 19, 21, 27, 71, 78,
  81, 86, 88–90, 91t, 117, 122, 160,
  162, 167
Willson, S., 104, 105f, 150
within-interview analysis, 146–47
World Happiness Report, 2
"writing up the notes," 61

Y

Yaroch, A. L., 21

Z

Zahnd, E., 88–90, 91t, 162